ENTRY BARRIERS
AND
MARKET ENTRY
DECISIONS

ENTRY BARRIERS AND MARKET ENTRY DECISIONS

A Guide for Marketing Executives

FAHRI KARAKAYA
and
MICHAEL J. STAHL

QUORUM BOOKS
New York • Westport, Connecticut • London

Library of Congress Cataloging-in-Publication Data

Karakaya, Fahri.
    Entry barriers and market entry decisions : a guide for marketing
executives / Fahri Karakaya and Michael J. Stahl.
      p.   cm.
    Includes bibliographical references (p.) and index.
    ISBN 0-89930-547-4 (alk. paper)
    1. Barriers to entry (Industrial organization)   I. Stahl, Michael
J. II. Title.
    HD2756.5.K37 1991
    658.8'02—dc20   91-22019

British Library Cataloguing in Publication Data is available.

Library of Congress Catalog Card Number: 91-22019
ISBN: 0-89930-547-4

First published in 1991

Quorum Books, One Madison Avenue, New York, NY 10010
An imprint of Greenwood Publishing Group, Inc.

Printed in the United States of America

The paper used in this book complies with the
Permanent Paper Standard issued by the National
Information Standards Organization (Z39.48-1984).

10 9 8 7 6 5 4 3 2 1

This book is dedicated to my wife Fera
for her continuous support and patience.
F.K.

In appreciation to my wife Barbara
for her understanding of the overtime
hours put into this book.
M.J.S.

Contents

Tables and Figures   ix

Preface   xiii

Chapter 1: Dynamics of Market Entry Barriers   1

Chapter 2: Barriers to Entry and Market Entry Decisions in
      Consumer and Industrial Markets   29

Chapter 3: Barriers to Entry in International Markets   53

Chapter 4: Product Life Cycle and Market Entry Barriers   75

Chapter 5: Barriers to Market Exit and Market Exit Decisions   97

Chapter 6: Managerial Consensus and Market Entry Strategy   125

Chapter 7: Profitability and Barriers to Entry   137

Chapter 8: Creating and Overcoming Barriers to Entry   149

Chapter 9: Conclusions   161

Appendix A: Market Entry Simulation Exercise   169

Appendix B: Market Entry Simulation Exercise for Entry into
      International Markets   189

Selected Bibliography   199

Index   205

Tables and Figures

TABLES

Table 1.1   Market Entry Barriers   4

Table 1.2   Importance of Barriers in Consumer Markets   8

Table 1.3   Percentage of Respondents Who Consider Market Entry
             Barriers Significant   10

Table 2.1   Duncan's Multiple Range Test for Early Market Entry
             Decisions into Consumer Goods Markets   38

Table 2.2   Duncan's Multiple Range Test for Early Market Entry
             Decision into Industrial Goods Markets   39

Table 2.3   Duncan's Multiple Range Test for Late Market Entry
             Decisions into Consumer Goods Markets   41

Table 2.4   Duncan's Multiple Range Test for Late Market Entry
             Decisions into Industrial Goods Markets   42

Table 2.5   Comparison of Market Entry Barrier Relative Weights
             for Early and Late Entry into Consumer Goods Markets   43

Table 2.6   Comparison of Market Entry Barrier Relative Weights
             for Early and Late Entry into Industrial Goods Markets   44

Table 2.7   Comparison of Market Entry Barrier Relative Weights
               for Early Entry into Consumer versus Industrial Goods
               Markets   45

Table 2.8   Comparison of Market Entry Barrier Relative Weights
               for Late Entry into Consumer versus Industrial Goods
               Markets   46

Table 3.1   Relative Importance of Market Entry Barriers   63

Table 3.2   Percentage of Respondents Who Consider Market Entry
               Barriers Significant   64

Table 4.1   Comparison of Barriers between Firms in Growth and
               Maturity Stages for Early Entry into Consumer
               Markets   86

Table 4.2   Comparison of Barriers between Firms in Growth and
               Maturity Stages for Late Entry into Consumer Markets   87

Table 4.3   Comparison of Barriers between Firms in Growth and
               Maturity Stages for Early Entry into Industrial Markets   87

Table 4.4   Comparison of Barriers between Firms in Growth and
               Maturity Stages for Late Entry into Industrial Markets   88

Table 4.5   Comparison of Barriers for Firms in Industries with
               Most Products in Growth and Maturity Stages for
               Early Entry into Consumer Markets   89

Table 4.6   Comparison of Barriers for Firms in Industries with
               Most Products in Growth and Maturity Stages for Late
               Entry into Consumer Markets   89

Table 4.7   Comparison of Barriers for Firms in Industries with
               Most Products in Growth and Maturity Stages for Early
               Entry into Industrial Markets   90

Table 4.8   Comparison of Barriers for Firms in Industries with
               Most Products in Growth and Maturity Stages for Late
               Entry into Industrial Markets   90

Table 5.1   Barriers to Exit   104

Table 5.2   Definition of the Variables   113

Table 5.3   Consideration of Barriers in the Exit Decision -
                 Declining Industry   114

Table 5.4   Consideration of Barriers in the Exit Decision -
                 Mature Industry   114

Table 5.5   Average Relative Weights - Declining Industry   115

Table 5.6   Average Relative Weights - Mature Industry   116

Table 6.1   Consensus Indices and Relationships with Company
                 Performance for Individual Barriers in Early
                 Entry into Consumer Markets   128

Table 6.2   Consensus Indices and Relationships with Company
                 Performance for Individual Barriers in Late
                 Entry into Consumer Markets   129

Table 6.3   Consensus Indices and Relationships with Company
                 Performance for Individual Barriers in Early
                 Entry into Industrial Markets   130

Table 6.4   Consensus Indices and Relationships with Company
                 Performance for Individual Barriers in Late
                 Entry into Industrial Markets   132

Table 6.5   Correlations of Return on Assets and Consensus
                 Using Single Index of Consensus   133

FIGURES

Figure 4.1   Classic Product Life Cycle Stages and Industry Sales
                 and profits   76

Figure 4.2   Two Pricing Strategies and Learning   80

Figure 5.1   An Example of Market Exit Simulation Exercise   112

Preface

Numerous firms enter markets each year in search of growth, but only a handful become successful. One of the major reasons for failure is underestimation of barriers and competitors' reactions to market entry. Barriers to entry are present in most markets, and they offer financial as well as psychological risks to marketing executives. However, risk taking is a part of life which also exists in the business world. A single risk taking can make or break an individual or an organization. Common sense would suggest that human beings reduce risk where possible. Thus, the objective of this book is to elicit the factors that can assist entrepreneurs or organizations to make astute market entry decisions.

Since all of us face a great number of barriers in our lives, the application of the barriers-to-entry concept is endless. While this book was written with marketing executives in mind, a spectrum of conceptual thoughts and empirical studies are integrated—making this work, for example, an ideal research tool for marketing strategy scholars.

ENTRY BARRIERS
AND
MARKET ENTRY
DECISIONS

Chapter 1

Dynamics of Market Entry Barriers

Ever-increasing competition in both domestic and international markets often forces firms to develop new products or find new markets for their existing products. Thus, many enter new or familiar markets through direct entry, acquisition, or diversification. However, entering any market is risky and sometimes difficult. Market entry barriers have been in existence for many years in many industries. Such barriers are likely to become even more important deterrents in multiple industries in the future as global competition continues to increase.

Day (1986) suggests that there are two major managerial decisions to make when considering market entry: (1) the timing of market entry (i.e., being a pioneer, being a fast follower or an early entrant, or being a late entrant), and (2) the mode of the market entry (e.g., internal development, acquisition, or joint venture). In addition to these two key decision areas, one must consider the type and magnitude of barriers to market entry and plan a strategy to deal with these barriers as well as to create barriers to entry for competition once in the market.

Bain (1956), and Caves and Porter (1977) claim that barriers to entry are often the source of excess profits for the firms already in the market. Therefore, incumbent firms find it important to create and maintain the magnitude of entry barriers. Similarly, potential entrants find it equally important to search for ways to overcome entry barriers so that they can be competitive once they manage to enter markets.

Porter (1980a, 125) defines entry barriers as "features of an industry that give incumbents inherent advantages over potential entrants." Similarly, Shepherd (1979) describes barriers to entry as anything that decreases the likelihood, scope, or speed of the potential competitors coming into the market . Barriers include all manner of specific devices, such as patents, mineral rights and franchises, as well as more general economic barriers. They also vary according to the characteristics of the market structure. According to Shepherd (1979), market entry conditions range from high to low entry barriers in pure monopoly, dominant firm, and tight oligopoly conditions, whereas free entry exists in monopolistic and pure competition markets.

Extensive economic theory on barriers to entry postulates how various elements of industry structure can impose disadvantages on entrants relative to incumbents. Barriers to entry result in fewer entries and therefore allow incumbents to enjoy above average profitability (Yip 1982a). Mann (1966) and Shepherd (1979) also support this view that barriers to entry influence profit rates.

The study of barriers to entry was pioneered by Bain (1956). According to Bain, the following characteristics of established firms serve as barriers to entry: (1) economies of scale, (2) product differentiation, and (3) absolute cost advantages.

Yip (1982a) modified Bain's original theory in three ways, by (1) including existing firms as potential and actual entrants, (2) using strategic groups to redefine a market into a fringe and a core and to distinguish between fringe entry and core entry; and (3) recognizing some acquisitions as an entry mode. Each of these weakened the effect of entry barriers.

Porter (1980b) has written extensively on barriers to entry. He has proposed six major sources of barriers to entry, some of which have been mentioned above. In addition to cost advantage and product differentiation, Porter suggests that capital requirements, customer switching costs, access to distribution channels, and government policy also serve as barriers to market entry.

To these barriers, Scherer (1970) added absolute cost advantages associated with the control (e.g., through patent or secrecy) of a superior production process or the possession of strategic raw materials and increasing delivered costs in the global markets, which result from high tariffs and transportation charges. Most of these preceding factors are identified as sources of market entry barriers in the theoretical work of Weizsacker (1980).

Through an extensive literature review, we identified 25 market entry barriers, which can be further classified into two categories: (1) competitor-activated or controllable barriers to entry and (2) environmental or uncontrollable barriers to entry. The competitor-activated barriers are usually generated by the firms already in the market. These barriers do not always deter the entry of other firms into markets, but they do influence the potential entrants' marketing strategies. Furthermore, they often force the potential entrants to take strong competitive measures in marketing their products. This situation sometimes permits the new market entrants to gain a good portion of the market. The environmental or uncontrollable barriers are usually generated by the nature of the market or by government agencies. In the short run, potential entrants can do very little to overcome this second category of barriers. The two groups of barriers are listed on the next page.

COMPETITOR-ACTIVATED OR CONTROLLABLE BARRIERS TO ENTRY

1. incumbents' cost advantages due to economies of scale
2. incumbents' cost advantages due to experience or learning curves
3. incumbents' absolute cost advantages
4. incumbents' superior production processes
5. product differentiation and customer loyalty
6. customer switching costs
7. access to distribution channels
8. heavy advertising by incumbent firms
9. research and development
10. price
11. trade secrets held by competitors
12. selling expenses
13. incumbents' proprietary product technology

ENVIRONMENTAL OR UNCONTROLLABLE BARRIERS TO ENTRY

1. capital requirements to enter markets
2. capital intensity of the market
3. government licensing requirements
4. incumbents' government subsidies
5. number of competitors
6. technology and technological change
7. high profit rates earned by incumbents
8. seller concentration and the magnitude of market shares held by incumbents
9. sunk costs
10. incumbents' expected reaction to market entry
11. incumbents' relatively easy access to raw materials
12. possession of strategic raw materials

The 25 barriers identified in the literature are listed with their references and summary implications in Table 1.1. These barriers are discussed individually in this chapter. However, the discussion is rather general in nature since we elaborate on these barriers in the later chapters.

Table 1.1
Market Entry Barriers[a]

BARRIERS	SOURCE	IMPLICATIONS
Incumbents' Cost Advantages Due to Economies of Scale	Perrakis and Warskett 1986; Porter 1980a; Schmalensee 1981; Yao 1988; Yelle 1979; Yip 1982a	Firms with economies of scale emerge as industry price leaders. It forces new entrants to enter markets in large scale and it is related to profitability and market share.
Incumbents' Cost Advantages Due to Experience or Learning Curves	Day 1984; Henderson 1984; Hofer and Schendel 1978; Lieberman 1987; Porter 1980	This reflects the accumulated output of all activities that add value to a product. Learning curve effects result in higher market share, higher accumulated volume, lower cost, and higher profitability in some industries. Usually, it cannot be kept proprietary. Thus, it is not a high barrier to entry.
Incumbents' Absolute Cost Advantages	Bain 1956; Porter 1980a; Scherer 1970, 1980; Weizsacker 1980	A very important barrier to entry, it is generally associated with technological change, proprietary product technology, favorable access to raw materials, favorable locations, patents of secrecy, and government subsidies.
Incumbents' Superior Production Processes	Bain 1956; Scherer 1970; Weizsacker 1980	This barrier results from having technical know-how, and it serves as an entry barrier mostly in high technology industries. It can be a major source of cost advantage.
Product Differentiation and Customer Loyalty	Bain 1956, 1962; Bass et al. 1978; Comanor and Wilson 1967; Hofer and Schendel 1978; Krouse 1984; May 1987; Porter 1980a; Reekie and Bhoyrub 1981; Schmalensee 1982; Smiley 1988; Yao 1988	Established firms have brand identification and customer loyalties due to advertising, being first in a market, customer service, or product differences.

4

Table 1.1 (continued)

BARRIERS	SOURCE	IMPLICATIONS
Customer Switching Costs	May 1987; McFarlan 1984; Porter 1980a	Switching costs prevent the buyer from changing suppliers, and technological changes can often raise or lower these costs.
Access to Distribution Channels	May 1987; Porter 1980a; 1985; Shimaguchi and Lazer 1979	First or early market entrants use intensive distribution strategies to limit the access to distributors for the potential market entrants.
Heavy Advertising by Incumbents	Brozen 1971; Comanor and Wilson 1967; Demsetz 1982; Harrigan 1981; Kardasz 1984; Kessides 1986; Lustgarten and Thomadakis 1987; Netter 1983; Reed 1975; Reekie and Bhoyrub 1981; Spence 1980; Watersen 1984	Heavy advertising by firms already in the market increases the cost of entry for potential entrants, and affects brand loyalty, and the extent of economies of scale by causing cost per dollar revenues to decline by increasing the sales volume.
Research and Development	Harrigan 1981; Lustgarten and Thomadakis 1987; Schmalensee 1983	This barrier is usually short-lived. Incumbent firms may prevent the entry of new firms into markets by investing in R&D. This increases technological scale economies and forces the ongoing industry context to evolve in a manner which would make subsequent attempts to entry even more ineffectual.
Price	Arnst 1977; Bain 1956; Horowitz 1984; Needham 1976; Smiley and Ravid 1983	Price warfare can act as a significant deterrent to new entry, particularly in industries where firms are more likely to lower their prices to fill the underutilized plants.
Trade Secrets Held by Competitors	Scherer 1970	Trade secrets held by incumbent firms often influence or cause cost advantages.

Table 1.1 (continued)

BARRIERS	SOURCE	IMPLICATIONS
Selling Expenses	Williamson 1963	Shifts in demand functions can result from selling efforts making market entry endogenous.
Incumbents' Proprietary Product Technology	Porter 1980b	This barrier results from having unique or advanced production techniques and gives firms advantages in terms of product quality or cost of production.
Capital Requirements to Enter Markets	Bain 1956; Eaton and Lipsey 1980; Harrigan 1981; May 1987; Porter 1980a	The need to invest large financial resources in order to compete or enter a market constitutes a barrier to entry. This barrier is higher in capital-intensive industries.
Capital Intensity of the Market	Harrigan 1981	Capital intensity discourages market entry, other factors being equal.
Government Licensing Requirements	Beaty et al. 1985; Berlew 1984; Harrigan 1985; Levinson 1988; Lott 1987; Moore 1978; Porter 1980a; Pustay 1985.	In addition to limiting the number of firms in a market, it also affects the types of firms active in a market. It is a common barrier in both domestic and foreign markets.
Incumbents' Government Subsidies	Bass et al. 1978; Dixit and Kyle 1985; Porter 1980a	Preferential government subsidies may give established firms long-lasting advantages in some industries. It is a very common barrier for firms attempting to enter foreign markets.
Number of Competitors	Harrigan 1981	Market entry is expected to be more likely to occur during periods of increasing incorporations and less likely after a lag, during which high numbers of business failures occur.

Table 1.1 (continued)

BARRIERS	SOURCE	IMPLICATIONS
Technology and Technological Change	Arrow 1962a; Ghadar 1982; Porter 1980a, 1985; Reinganum 1983	This barrier is usually present in high technology industries and can actually raise or lower economies of scale which is one of the major sources of cost advantages.
High Profit Rates Earned by Incumbents	Harrigan 1981	Evidence of successful performance by ongoing firms attracts new firms to enter markets. Therefore, low profit rates may act as barriers to entry.
Seller Concentration and the Magnitude of Market Shares Held by Incumbents	Bain 1956, 1968; Crawford 1975; Day 1977; King and Thompson 1982; Mann 1966	Entry is unlikely to be as easy in highly concentrated markets as in lesser concentrated markets. The higher the degree of concentration, the greater the effect of barriers on profits. Conversely, the lower the degree of concentration, the lower the effect of barriers on profit rates.
Sunk Costs	Baumol and Willig 1981; Kessides 1986; Yao 1988	Sunk costs contribute to entry barriers which can also give rise to monopoly profits, resource misallocation, and inefficiencies.
Incumbents' Expected Reaction to Market Entry	Needham 1976; Yip 1982b	Market entry may be deterred only if the incumbent firms are able to influence the potential entrant's expectation about the post-entry reaction of the incumbents.
Incumbents' Relatively Easy Access to Raw Materials	Porter 1980a	Established firms may have contracts with the most favorable suppliers of raw materials. Thus, this acts as a barrier to entry for potential market entrants, as well as a

Table 1.1 (continued)

BARRIERS	SOURCE	IMPLICATIONS
		cost advantage to the incumbent firms.
Possession of Strategic Raw Materials	Scherer 1970	Access to strategic raw materials contributes to firms' absolute cost advantages.

a. Adapted from Karakaya and Stahl (1989)

BARRIERS IN CONSUMER MARKETS STUDY

Importance of Barriers

A survey of 151 marketing executives who rated the 25 barriers listed in Table 1.1 indicates that not all barriers are perceived as equally important in consumer markets. Table 1.2 shows the mean ratings of each barrier and the percentage of respondents who assigned ratings of 5 or 4, where 5 was "extremely important" and 1 was "least important."

Table 1.2
Importance of Barriers in Consumer Markets

MARKET ENTRY BARRIER	Mean	% of Respondents[a]
Brand identification advantage held by incumbents	4.02	76.0
Incumbents with absolute cost advantages	3.90	68.0
Consumer loyalty advantage held by incumbents	3.87	69.5
Accessibility of the distribution channels	3.87	73.5
Capital requirements to enter a market	3.85	64.9
Incumbents with cost advantages due to economies of scale	3.84	70.8
Incumbents with proprietary product technology	3.83	65.8
Incumbents with superior production processes	3.75	64.0

Table 1.2 (continued)

MARKET ENTRY BARRIER	Mean	% of Respondents[a]
Capital intensity of the market	3.72	63.6
Magnitude of market shares held by incumbents	3.65	56.9
Heavy advertising by firms already in the market	3.63	61.6
The amount of sunk costs involved in entering a market	3.59	55.1
Research and development expense involved in entering a market	3.49	52.3
Low prices charged by incumbents	3.44	49.7
The amount of selling expense involved in marketing a product	3.44	49.0
Incumbents possessing strategic raw materials	3.36	48.6
Incumbents with cost advantages due to learning curves	3.30	42.4
Expected post-entry reaction of incumbents	3.29	43.7
Trade secrets held by competitors	3.15	39.0
Number of firms present in the market	3.11	34.2
Incumbents with government subsidies	3.01	37.8
Customers' costs associated with switching from one supplier to another	2.93	32.7
Government licensing requirements	2.88	28.8
Incumbents with relatively easy access to raw materials	2.79	28.7
High profit rates earned by incumbents	2.75	28.0

a. Percent of respondents who rated the importance of barriers 5 or 4 on a five point scale where 5 is "extremely important."

As shown in Table 1.2, executives rated the brand identification barrier the highest in terms of importance in deterring market entry (mean rating = 4.02), followed by the incumbents with absolute cost advantages barrier (mean rating = 3.90). These two barriers were rated as 5 or 4 on a 5 point scale by 76 and 68 percent of the respondents, respectively. The consumer loyalty advantage barrier has the third highest mean rating (3.87). However, 73.5 percent of the respondents rated it as 5 or 4. Therefore, one may conclude that marketing executives perceive this to be the second most important market entry deterrent. Furthermore, customer loyalty and product differentiation of incumbents are very similar in nature, and many firms have product differentiation advantages resulting from customer loyalties.

Importance of Porter's Six Barriers to Entry

An earlier study conducted by Karakaya (1987) tested six major market entry barriers: cost advantages of incumbents, product differentiation of incumbents, capital requirements, customer switching costs, access to distribution channels, and government policy. These six barriers first singled out by Porter (1980a), were tested for early and late market entry into consumer and industrial goods markets. The sample consisted of 139 marketing executives from 49 major U.S. corporations. The percentage breakdown of respondents who considered the market entry barriers to be significant is shown in Table 1.3.

Table 1.3
Percentage of Respondents
Who Consider Market Entry Barriers Significant

Barriers[a]	Consumer Market		Industrial Market	
	Early Entry	Late Entry	Early Entry	Late Entry
CAI	91	83	89	83
PDI	77	70	75	62
CR	80	78	84	76
CSC	73	70	75	69
ADC	77	56	60	55
GP	59	45	59	47
	n=139	n=139	n=137	n=137

a.   CAI = Cost Advantages of Incumbents
  PDI = Product Differentiation of Incumbents
  CR = Capital Requirements
  CSC = Customer Switching Costs
  ADC = Access to Distribution Channels
  GP = Government Policy

As shown in Table 1.3, the cost advantages of incumbents barrier appears to be the most important in any market entry situation, and the government policy barrier seems to be the least important in every market entry condition. The other barriers vary depending on the type of market entry. Therefore, in two different studies, the primary importance of cost advantages of incumbents was noted. Similarly, the lesser role played by government policy barriers was noted in both studies. The importance of entry barriers will be discussed further in the later chapters.

COMPETITOR-ACTIVATED BARRIERS TO ENTRY

Incumbents' Cost Advantages Due to Economies of Scale

Incumbent firms create barriers to entry by producing and marketing products in such large volumes that potential market entrants are discouraged from entering the market. However, this situation is true only in the absence of government interference (Yao 1988). Porter (1980b, 7) has stressed that a potential entrant will face barriers to entry as characterized by economies of scale, which he defines as "declines in unit costs of a product (or operation or function that goes into producing a product) as the absolute volume produced per period increases."

Scherer (1970) claims that the firm most likely to emerge as an industry price leader is the firm with the lowest cost and with learning accompanying production. According to Bain (1956), the economies of a large plant or firm are reflected in a decline of the production cost and the distribution cost per unit of output as the plant or firm increases planned capacity.

To act as a barrier to entry, economies of scale must reduce costs and give the incumbent firms a price advantage over the potential market entrants. Henderson (1984) states that economies of scale may not be a source of cost reduction unless they are required for growth. A cost reduction that is not accompanied by an increase in total output must be paid for by a reduction in operating cost. Furthermore, the cost of the capital involved must be offset by the reduction in operating cost. Otherwise, there is no cost reduction.

Hofer and Schendel (1978) pointed out that economies of scale are derived from one or more of the following: (1) the development of specialized knowledge or skills in the area, (2) the ability to take advantage of indivisibilities in existing technology, (3) the ability to take advantage of mass reserves, (4) the ability to spread fixed cost over larger volumes, and (5) learning curve effects. Schmalensee (1981) investigated economies of scale to determine their existence as a barrier to market entry. Schmalensee's findings support Bain's (1956) conclusion that economies of scale in production and distribution do not create large barriers to entry.   However, a recent study (Perrakis and Warskett 1986) that tests economies of scale as an entry barrier concludes that, contrary to Bain's

(1962) and Schmalensee's (1981) research, this barrier's entry deterrence is important. Further, Perrakis and Warskett suggest that economies of scale are not equally important in deterring market entry in every U.S. industry such as aircraft, refrigerators and freezers, computers, passenger cars and trucks, electric motors, turbogenerators, diesel engines, breweries, and cigarettes.

In assessing the importance of economies of scale, Bain introduced the limit pricing model of entry deterrence, in which established firms act as a perfect cartel and potential entrants expect these firms to maintain their pre-entry levels of output even after entry. However, this model has received much criticism, largely because it may not be profitable for established firms to keep output constant (see Scherer 1980).

Economies of scale deter the entry of competitors into markets by forcing the entrants either to attempt to enter markets on a large scale and risk strong reaction from the existing firms or to accept cost disadvantage (Porter 1980b). However, Needham (1976) argues that this depends on the ability of the established firms to influence potential entrants' expectations regarding the post-entry behavior of the established firms.

Yip (1982a) states that economies of scale are probably the most common entry barrier in that they exist in almost every industry. Furthermore, he suggests that they can exist at both the production plant and the firm levels. Plant-level scale economies result from using the most efficient machines in terms of per unit cost and from having warehousing and maintenance services. Firm level economies of scale are related to the accumulated output.

While many researchers argue the importance of economies of scale as a market entry barrier, some indicate doubts. Stigler (1968) has challenged the basic idea that economies of scale can actually create a meaningful market entry barrier. Similarly, only a substantial economy of scale can act as an entry barrier since the new entrants would also have to enter on a large scale to avoid losses (Scherer 1973) and compete effectively with the firms already in the market.

Incumbents' Cost Advantages Due to Experience or Learning Curves

According to the findings of the Boston Consulting Group (1970), the total variable cost, in constant dollars, declines by a constant percentage with each doubling of accumulated units of output or experience. Therefore, economies of scale are related to profitability as well as market share. Firms that produce in large volumes have an advantage over their competitors because of the low overhead cost per unit of product produced. As a result of this cost advantage, they often get large market shares. Studies indicate that there is a relationship between market share and profitability (Anderson and Zeithaml 1984; Buzzell et al. 1975; Buzzell and Wiersema 1981; Dalrymple and Parsons 1980; Gale 1972; Hax and Majluf 1982; MacMillan et al. 1982; Schoeffler et al. 1974; Shepherd 1972; Wakerly 1984). Therefore, economies of scale often create a profitable environment for firms.

According to Porter (1979), the experience or learning curve refers to the decline in unit cost that occurs in many industries with experience. It usually results from the efficiency achieved over a period of time by workers through much repetition. Often the experience curve serves as a barrier to entry, but sometimes it can be a shaky entry barrier on which to build a strategy. For example, if costs go down because of technical advances known generally in the industry or because of the development of improved equipment that can be copied or purchased from equipment suppliers, the experience curve is no entry barrier at all; in fact, new or less experienced competitors may actually enjoy a cost advantage over the leaders (Porter 1979) by benefiting from the experiences of incumbent firms.

Similarly, Smiley and Ravid (1983) suggest that the experience curve or the learning curve results from a learning process in which the average cost declines with increases in cumulative production. The general concept of learning by doing includes both firm-specific or proprietary learning, as used by Rosen (1972), and industrywide learning, where all the firms in an industry share the benefits of learning (Arrow 1962b). Lieberman (1984) has used a dynamic model of industry equilibrium to study how the rate of learning and information diffusion affects entry barriers and profits. His results show that market entry barriers are quite high when learning remains proprietary, but are substantially reduced when learning diffuses across firms.

The study conducted by Smiley and Ravid (1983) shows that a firm that is experiencing learning is in a better position to make credible (nonprice) threats of post-entry destructive conflict to potential entrants. Thus, the concept of learning can be used as an important strategic weapon to deter the entry of competitors into markets. This barrier is often important in high technology industries where high research and development costs are inevitable. For example, aircraft firms have extremely high research and development costs, and the aircraft that are produced early cost much more than the prices charged. With the anticipation that cost per aircraft will go down as more and more aircraft are produced, firms initially charge prices below their costs.

A well-publicized application of the experience curve in strategy formulation occurred in 1966. The Boston Consulting Group applied this concept to the General Instrument Corporation's future MIS technology cost behavior (Boston Consulting Group 1973). Similarly, the strategic implications of the experience curve were analyzed by Hax and Majluf (1982) and by Hadley (1976). According to the findings of these researchers, experience curve effects result in higher market share, higher accumulated volume, lower cost, and higher profitability. According to Porter (1985), technological change is the basis for the experience curve since the experience curve results from improvements in such factors as layout, yields, and machine speeds, all of which are types of technological change. Furthermore, technological change can lead to other absolute cost advantages such as low-cost product design.

Day (1984) states that experience is not restricted to production and technology factors, but reflects the accumulated output and all activities that add value to a product. For example, the costs of marketing, distribution, and service often depend on experience and present a combination of scale and knowledge factors.

Although many firms have benefited from the application of the experience curve, an innovator and/or a dominant firm may not always realize the benefits of the experience curve. This might be possible because of the temptation to charge high prices during the introduction and growth stages of the product life cycle. As suggested by Day (1975), this condition presents an incentive to higher-cost competitors to enter the market and attempt to increase their market shares. Hannan (1983) has also determined that in reaching an entry decision, the potential entrants are influenced by pre-entry prices. However, in his early theoretical work, Bain (1956) had argued that a monopolist in a market with high barriers to entry would have a "limit price" to deter entry, rather than charging a high price.

As noted above, the experience curve is not always fully utilized. In using an experience curve as a strategic tool (i.e., in pricing), the users must also be very cautious. Porter (1980b) states that the experience curve is not as strong an entry barrier as the economies of scale barrier because experience curve effects cannot be kept proprietary.

Henderson (1984) claims that the experience curve has been both applied and misapplied in the past. Although the experience curve can be a conceptual framework for long-range strategy development, it must be applied carefully. Effective application requires analysis of
the cost components and the products and markets. Analyses of the substitution effect, shared experience with competitors, relative growth rates of components, and correct definitions of competitive boundaries of comparative advantage must also be conducted. Furthermore, Henderson stresses that economies of scale, adaptation, and investment are the principal causes of the experience curve effect.

Incumbents' Absolute Cost Advantages

The cost advantages that result from anything other than economies of scale or learning curves are considered to be absolute cost advantages. For example, the geographical location of a firm may create advantages in the transportation costs of raw materials or products (due to proximity to suppliers or markets). In this category, Scherer (1970) includes cost advantages associated with the control (e.g., through patent or secrecy) of a superior production process or the possession of strategic raw materials, tariffs, and transportation charges for potential foreign competitors.

Incumbents' Superior Production Processes

This market entry barrier benefits incumbent firms in two ways: (1) by producing better-quality products and (2) by producing products at lower costs. Usually, firms obtain this advantage through utilizing up-to-date production technology and employing highly skilled or trained personnel. Therefore, firms find it very important to keep up to date on technological advances and employee training in order to acquire and keep this advantage as a barrier to market entry. For example, one of the reasons why U.S. auto manufacturers were behind the Japanese auto manufacturers in 1989 was a lag in production technology.

Product Differentiation and Customer Loyalty

According to Porter (1980b), established firms have brand identification and customer loyalties, which stem from past advertising, customer service, product differences, or simply being first into the industry. This barrier has received much attention in the marketing literature. It was first regarded as a market entry barrier by Bain (1956, 1962). In addition, Porter (1985) has pointed out that technology changes play an important role in the pattern of product differentiation.

Similarly, Schmalensee (1982) suggests that early market entrants often gain product differentiation advantages over later entrants because when customers become convinced that the first brand in any product class performs satisfactorily, that brand becomes the standard against which subsequent entrants are rationally judged. Therefore, it becomes harder for later entrants to convince consumers to invest in learning about their products than it was for those marketing the first brand.

Hofer and Schendel (1978, 37) present a different view of product differentiation. They claim that "product differentiation is aimed primarily at existing competitors, not at unknown potential entrants." If this is always true, then common sense dictates that product differentiation cannot act as a strong market entry barrier. However, one should note that although firms may not aim their product differentiation strategies at unknown potential entrants, they can still differentiate their products simply by being first into the market (Porter 1980b; Robinson and Fornell 1985). The reason for this is that buyers are already familiar with the brand on the market and they may not want to spend time in getting information about a new brand. Therefore, customers become brand loyal, which gives the original seller an advantage over its competition (Yao 1988). Furthermore, Yao (1988, 64) claims that "on the basis of positive information, customers will often prefer a higher-priced reputable product to an unknown product even if both products are of the same quality (because the customer does not know this)."

Customer Switching Costs

There are many sources of customer switching costs, but they usually result from investments that have already been made. The investments are often in the form of capital outlays, which are usually considered to be sunk costs, but sometimes they are in the form of personnel training and education. However, this situation is not true in all industries. For example, if a food distributor switches from one principal or broker to another few, if any, switching costs are involved.   In addition, switching costs are almost nonexistent for some products (as when, for example, a consumer switches from one brand of chewing gum to another).

According to Porter (1980b), switching costs lock the buyer to particular sellers, and usually technological changes can raise or lower these costs. Porter argues that there are six major sources of switching costs: (1) costs of modifying the product to match a new supplier's product, (2) costs of testing or certifying a new supplier's product to ensure substitutability, (3) investments in new accessory equipment that is necessary to use a new supplier's product, (4) investments in retraining employees, (5) costs of establishing new logistical arrangements, and (6) psychic costs of severing relationships with present suppliers.

McFarlan (1984) provides a good example of customer switching costs as a market entry barrier. He argues that while information technology has been used for support functions in most organizations, it can be used to achieve competitive advantage by building market entry barriers if cannot easily reproduce the service provided competitors. Further, he stresses that customers may be reluctant to switch to a competitor's service if the costs of switching are too high. Supporting this view, Wightman (1987) also claims that information technology is used to create barriers to entry. Such barriers are often sustainable over a long period of time, as in the case of the payments clearing system of the UK clearing banks.

Access to Distribution Channels

This market entry barrier has been neglected by researchers despite its importance. Unless firms can develop their own distribution channels or acquire other firms to act as their distributors (i.e., achieve vertical integration), access to distribution channels remains an important barrier to market entry. Oftentimes the first or early entrants use intensive distribution strategies to limit the access of potential market entrants to distributors .

Porter (1980b) suggests that a barrier to market entry can be created by the new entrant's need to secure distribution channels for its product. In addition, Porter (1985) determines that technological change can   influence access to distribution by allowing firms to bypass existing channels or, conversely, by increasing industry dependence on channels.

Heavy Advertising by Incumbent Firms

Numerous   researchers consider advertising a barrier to market entry. Kessides (1986) suggests that advertising creates barriers to entry because (1) it enhances consumer brand loyalty and therefore makes it more difficult for new entrants to induce brand switching, and (2) it makes small-scale entry inefficient, while large-scale entry would lower price and induce a retaliatory response from the incumbents. Strengthening this argument, Spence (1980) has found that advertising can contribute to market entry barriers; because it causes the cost per dollar of revenues to decline, advertising influences the extent of economies of scale.

Similarly, Vernon and Nourse (1973) hypothesized that there is a positive correlation between industry advertising intensity and industry profit rates. Their findings support this hypothesis, and they conclude that this relationship is due to the advertising entry barrier. In contrast, Needham (1976) disputes the conclusions of Vernon and Nourse and states that the issue remains unresolved based on their empirical research results.

More researchers believe that advertising creates brand loyalty, which results in raising entry barriers. This view is also supported by Comanor and Wilson (1967) and Reekie and Bhoyrub (1981).

Reed (1975) stresses that advertising techniques of product differentiation lead to high market entry barriers. Similarly, Demsetz (1982) claims that advertising expenditures–at least those incurred earlier by existing firms–may be a source of entry barriers. This view is also shared by Kessides (1986) in the sense that advertising constitutes a sunk cost barrier to entry.

An interesting case of an entry barrier dealing with advertising has been pointed out by Netter (1983). Netter claims that advertising has been used by incumbent politicians as an entry barrier. He argues that the uses of advertising in political and market competition are similar. Further, an incumbent has many characteristics of an established firm, while a political challenger resembles an entering firm. Thus, Netter stresses, it would be possible to draw inferences about the effect of advertising on the entry process in a product market by examining of the relationship between campaign advertising and election results. In his research, Netter presented empirical evidence that indicates advertising can be a barrier to entry.

Despite the conflicting findings, heavy advertising by incumbent firms remains as an important barrier. In Table 1.2, this barrier ranked eleventh in terms of its importance, based on the mean response rate. Also, approximately 62 percent of the respondents felt that it was a very important barrier in deterring market entry in consumer markets. The importance of this barrier might result from the fact that advertising often creates brand loyalty and requires potential market entrants to advertise as well. However, many firms are afraid to match incumbent firms' advertising budgets, or their financial conditions do not allow them to advertise heavily.

Research and Development

Incumbent firms may prevent the entry of new firms into markets by effectively investing in research and development (R&D) (Harrigan 198a). This situation increases technological scale economies and forces the ongoing industry context to evolve in a manner that would make subsequent attempts to enter even more ineffective.

By investing in R&D, firms try to keep ahead of competition. Oftentimes, high R&D expenditures give a firm competitive advantage by having superior products or by introducing new or improved products. However, this barrier is usually short-lived (Harrigan 1981) because competing firms learn about the new or improved products in the market and copy them or come up with their own products that are similar to those in the market. Firms that imitate the innovators sometimes may have an advantages over incumbent firms because they do not spend as much money in R&D, which causes the cost per unit to be lower. Thus, it is important for incumbent firms to continue their investments into R&D in order to develop better products or to improve the ones already in the market.

Price

Price warfare has been shown to be a significant deterrent to new entry (Harrigan 1981), particularly in industries where firms are more likely to lower their prices to fill underutilized plants, which would otherwise incur strong cost disadvantages. Price advantages of incumbents usually result from the cost advantages discussed earlier. Incumbents' ability to charge low prices often deters other firms from entering a market. If low prices do not deter market entry, then they usually give incumbent firms the competitive edge and help them use cost leadership as a strategy (Porter 1980b).

Needham (1976) stresses that it is always possible for established firms to deter entry by setting price and quantity at the entry-deterring level. Smiley and Ravid (1983) suggest that first movers can preempt the market through the use of a limit price and still make profits. However, a preemptive strategy that incumbents might prefer would be to limit market entry by some means other that price.

Trade Secrets Held by Competitors

Trade secrets held by incumbent firms often influence or cause cost advantages (Scherer 1970) and sometimes result in product differentiation because of the quality or some secret that goes into the product. For example, the "secret formula" held by Coca-Cola Company has kept the company a leader in the cola segment of the soft drink market. Similarly, a trade secret that results in cost advantages keeps the potential market entrant out of the market, as explained earlier.

Selling Expenses

Large amounts of money spent by incumbent firms to sell their products discourage potential market entrants (Williamson 1963). This is because the incumbent firms attempt to create selective demand for their products and the potential entrants may lack the necessary financial resources to do the same. However, this barrier may not always be a strong barrier since many firms attempting to enter markets may be willing to match the incumbent firms' selling expenses. Nevertheless, one should note that it is feasible for incumbent firms to reduce their costs as a result of achieving economies of scale in selling expenses and to enjoy cost advantages as well as high market shares.

Incumbents' Proprietary Product Technology

Firms with proprietary product technology sometimes have technology or technical know-how that they can use to produce their products at a lower cost and possibly to produce better-quality products than potential competitors can. This situation discourages firms from entering markets because the potential entrants know that they cannot be competitive.

ENVIRONMENTAL AND UNCONTROLLABLE BARRIERS TO ENTRY

Capital Requirements to Enter Markets and Capital Intensity of the Market

Capital requirements comprise a traditional form of economic market entry barrier which was first delineated by Bain (1956). Capital requirements act as an important barrier for various reasons. One of the most important reasons is the large sums of money required to enter a market, which is usually caused by the capital intensity of the business. Other reasons include the amount of sunk costs involved; a firm's inability to borrow funds, which is usually made worse by uncertain market conditions and credit histories; and the requirement to enter a market on a large scale so that the entering firm can be competitive in terms of price. In addition, access to production equipment can be a problem for many firms, especially if the products are produced outside the country (e.g., computers that the government would not allow to be sold to other countries to protect their national interests).

The need to invest a large amount of financial resources in order to enter or compete in a market creates a barrier to market entry, whether or not those resources must be raised in capital markets (Porter 1980b). Similarly, Yao (1988) suggests that despite the fact the capital requirements to enter a market might be extensive, borrowing funds might not pose a major problem. Thus, lower capital barriers to entry would result. The size of the borrowing firm and its past credit history will also be factors in reducing this barrier.

Harrigan (1981) argues that high capital intensity discourages entry, other factors being held constant, and expects higher labor intensity among firms in industries where capital requirements are relatively low. Furthermore, Harrigan claims that if the capital requirements for market entry are high, the likelihood of entry will be lower and the technological scale will be higher.

Eaton and Lipsey (1980) have studied the strategic use of capital by firms to create market entry barriers. These researchers' conclusions indicate that durability of capital acts as a barrier to market entry in certain markets.

Government Licensing Requirements

Government licensing requirements as well as other controls can easily limit the number of firms in a market (Porter 1980b). Although limiting the number of firms in an industry would decrease competition and constitute an unfair trade practice, such controls are often imposed to protect the public and the environment. Many studies in the past have shown the influence of this barrier on market entry. Some of these studies are discussed below.

Harrigan (1985) has considered the effect of issuing tradable government licenses on market equilibrium. Her findings indicate that licensing affects not only the number of active firms, but also the types of active firms in a market.

Regulatory reforms have had an important impact on the number of firms in industry and on the number of applications filed with the Interstate Commerce Commission to enter interstate motor carrier markets. Despite the numerical increases, Moore (1978) claims that because the operating authorities (permits) were so narrowly drawn, entry into the motor carrier industry was limited and competition hindered.

Pustay (1985) compares and contrasts empirically the impact of administrative and legislative reforms on entry into the motor carrier industry. His conclusions indicate that the effect of the Motor Carrier Act of 1980 was far broader, affecting entry into markets of all sizes, but especially the largest. The administrative reforms, however, had the effect of reducing some of the regulatory burdens placed on carriers.

The Drug Price Competition and Patent Term Restoration Act of 1984 has been termed the most important legislation for the pharmaceutical industry since the 1962 Kefauver Amendments. This 1984 act eliminated duplicative testing and provided market entry for generic drug competitors, while extending patent protection for future new products to 22 years. According to Grabowski and Vernon (1986), evidence indicates that the requirement that generic drugs duplicate the pioneer's safety and efficacy tests was a significant and growing barrier to entry in recent years. These researchers support their hypothesis with a study analyzing the 1983 data on the number of drugs among the top 200 pharmaceuticals with expired patents that also had no generic drug competitors. One could conclude from the above that the 1984 act has actually decreased the number of entry barriers in the pharmaceutical industry.

Incumbents' Government Subsidies

Preferential government subsidies may give established firms long-lasting advantages in some industries. This barrier is very common for firms attempting to enter foreign markets. While in the U.S. protection and subsidies are regarded

as unfair practices requiring countermeasures (Dixit and Kyle 1985), many foreign governments commonly protect high technology firms. The effort by the European Airbus consortium to compete with Boeing in the market for intermediate-range commercial jets is a well known-example.
Number of Competitors
    In the early stages of the product life cycle (PLC), relatively few firms are in the market, and this barrier is not very important. However, in the later stages of the PLC, many firms are usually competing for even small market shares. Thus, this barrier influences market entry decisions. Of course, the number of firms in a market depends on the type of market. Thus, every market is not saturated even in the maturity stage of the PLC.

Technology and Technological Changes

    This barrier is usually present in high technology industries and can actually raise or lower economies of scale which is a major source of cost advantages (Arrow 1962a; Ghadar 1982; Porter 1980a, 1985; Reinganum 1983). In addition, incumbents with new production technologies often deter market entry because the competitors do not always have the same technology or the financial resources to obtain the same or better technology so that they can be competitive.

High Profit Rates Earned by Incumbents

    Evidence of successful performance by ongoing firms attracts new firms to enter markets because these firms perceive market entry to be without risk. In contrast, however, low profit rates earned by the firms already in the market act as barriers to entry (Harrigan 1981).

Seller Concentration and the Magnitude of Market Shares Held by Incumbents

    Market entry is likely to be easier in less concentrated markets than in highly concentrated markets. In highly concentrated markets, the effect of barriers on entry is much greater than in less concentrated markets (Bain 1956, 1968; Crawford 1975; Day 1977; King and Thompson 1982; Mann 1966). Of course, the magnitude of market share is related to market concentration. In less concentrated markets, incumbent firms hold large market shares, and they are usually profitable firms. This condition influences potential entrants' market entry decisions and often deters market entry.
    According to Day (1977), the influence of market share is most evident with high-value-added products where significant barriers to entry exist and the competition consists of a few large, diversified corporations with large overheads. Firms with large market shares enjoy higher profits than do those with lower

market shares because they have lower per unit costs resulting from economies of scale in production and marketing.

Sunk Costs

Costs are sunk when they cannot be eliminated, even if the firm ends production (Yao 1988). Low sunk costs might lead to a high turnover rate (frequent market entry and exit), but low net entry (Kessides 1986). Advertising expenditures that cannot be recovered are usually sunk costs, and they have been empirically shown to create a sunk cost barrier to entry (Kessides 1986). The presence of sunk costs influences firms' market exit decisions. The opposite, however, encourages market entry, and the markets become contestable (Baumol, et al. 1982). Furthermore, these researchers argue that fixed costs act as barriers to entry in a market only to the extent that they are considered sunk upon entry.

Eaton and Lipsey (1980) suggest that sunk costs can take two forms: (1) when a firm leaves a market and only a fraction of the original fixed costs can be recovered and (2) if the capital invested cannot be removed immediately from the market. Similarly, Macleod (1987) suggests that costs that are sunk due to the existence of product-specific capital do not in general deter entry. Rather, entry deterrence is a necessary outcome only when costs are sunk due to the time it would take to leave the market.

Incumbents' Expected Reaction to Market Entry

The potential market entrants' expectations about the reaction of existing competitors influence their decision on whether or not to enter markets. However, this barrier may deter market entry only if the incumbent firms are able to influence a potential entrant's expectation about the post-entry reaction of the incumbents (Needham 1976; Yip 1982b). Interestingly, incumbent firms react differently to the market entry of new competition. Gatignon, Anderson, and Helsen (1989) have found that firms either react positively to entrants (retaliate or counterattack) with their weapons or they cut back (withdraw) their inelastic marketing mix variables.

Incumbents' Relatively Easy Access to Raw Materials

Oftentimes, the incumbent firms attempt to contract with the suppliers of raw materials on very good terms. This is especially true in the early stages of the product life cycle because the suppliers do not always know the value of their products and the demand for their products may not be very high. Thus, the contracts between suppliers of raw materials and incumbent firms limit the number of firms present in a market (Porter 1980b).

Possession of Strategic Raw Materials

Sometimes firms own or have control over certain raw materials that are scarce. This situation gives the incumbent businesses absolute cost advantages (Scherer 1970) because the other firms have to purchase these raw materials from other sources. Therefore, the cost advantage gained from the possession of raw materials or the scarcity of raw materials limits market entry to only a few firms.

CONCLUSIONS

Industrial economists and business and marketing strategy researchers have written extensively on barriers to entry. High barriers deter market entry and limit the number of firms in any given market. A considerable amount of research on this topic suggests that there are two major groups of barriers: (1) competitor-activated or controllable barriers to entry and (2) environmental or uncontrollable barriers to entry. Barriers in the second group are especially difficult to overcome since they usually exist, regardless of competition.

The importance of individual barriers varies depending on the timing of market entry (i.e., early entry versus late entry) and the type of market (i.e., consumer market versus industrial market). However, in general, six barriers proposed by Porter (1980b) appear to be the most important market entry deterrents. These six barriers are cost advantages of incumbent firms, product differentiation, capital requirements, customer switching costs, access to distribution channels, and government policy. To create these barriers or overcome them, however, certain conditions have to be met. Overall, economies of scale and learning curve effects determine the cost advantages barrier. Heavy advertising, proprietary product technology, and trade secrets make up the product differentiation barrier. The other four barriers may exist in most markets without any company present, although some of these barriers also can be created by competitors.

REFERENCES

Anderson, Carl R., and Carl P. Zeithaml. 1984. "Stage of the Product Life Cycle, Business Strategy, and Business Performance." *Academy of Management Journal* 27 (1): (March): 5-24.

Arnst, Catherine. 1977. "Witnesses Agree—IBM a Monopoly."*Computer World* 11 (September): 2.

Arrow, Kenneth. 1962a. "Economic Welfare and the Allocation of Resources to Innovation." In*The Rate and Direction of Inventive Activity*, R. Nelson. ed. Universities-National Bureau Conference Series, no. 14. New York: Arnold Press.

_____. 1962b. "The Economic Implications of Learning by Doing." *Review of Economic Studies* (June): 29.

Bain, J. S. 1956. *Barriers to New Competition*. Cambridge, Mass.: Harvard University Press.

_____. 1962. *Industrial Organization*. New York: John Wiley.

_____. 1968. *Industrial Organization*, 2d ed. New York: John Wiley.

Bass, Frank M. Phillippe Cattin, and Dick Wittink. 1978. "Firm Effects and Industry Effects in Analysis of Market Structure and Profitability." *Journal of Marketing Research* 15 (February): 3-10.

Baumol, William J., John C. Panzar, and Robert D. Willig. 1982. *Contestable Markets and the Theory of Industrial Structure*. New York: Harcourt Brace Jovanovich.

Baumol, William. J., and Robert D. Willig. 1981. "Fixed Costs, Sunk Costs, Entry Barriers and Sustainability of Monopoly." *Quarterly Journal of Economics* 96 (August): 405-31.

Beaty, Randolf P. John F. Reim, and Robert Schapperle. 1985. "The Effect of Entry on Bank Shareholder Wealth: Implications for Interstate Banking." *Journal of Banking Research* 16 (Spring): 8-15.

Berlew, Kingston F. 1984. "The Joint Venture–A Way into Foreign Markets." *Harvard Business Review* 62 (July - August): 48.

Boston Consulting Group. 1970. *Perspectives: The Experience Curve Reviewed*. Boston: Boston Consulting Group.

_____. 1973. "History of the Experience Curve."*Perspective* 125. Boston, Mass.

Brozen, Yale. 1971. "Bain's Concentration and Rates of Return Revisited." *Journal of Law and Economics* 14 (October): 351-69.

Buzzell, Robert D., B. T. Gale, and R. G. M. Sultan. 1975. "Market Share: A Key to Profitability." *Harvard Business Review* 53 (January- February): 97-106.

Buzzell, Robert D., and Frederick D. Wiersema. 1981. "Successful Share Building Strategy." *Harvard Business Review* 59 (January - February): 135-44.

Caves, R. E., and Michael E. Porter. 1977. "From Entry Barriers to Mobility Barriers." *Quarterly Journal of Economics* (May): 241-69.

Comanor, W. S., and T. S. Wilson. 1967. "Advertising, Market Structure and Performance." *Review of Economics and Statistics* 49: 423-40.

Crawford, Jean. 1975. "Seller Concentration, Entry Barriers, and Profit Margins: A Comment." *Industrial Organization Review* 3 (Fall): 176-78.

Dalrymple, Douglas J., and Leonard J. Parsons. 1980. *Marketing Management: Text and Cases*. 2d ed. New York: John Wiley.

Day, George S. 1975. "A Strategic Perspective in Product Planning." *Journal of Contemporary Business* 4 (Spring): 1-34.

_____. 1977. "Diagnosing the Product Portfolio." *Journal of Marketing* 41 (April): 29-38.

_____. 1984. *Strategic Market Planning: The Pursuit of Competitive Advantage*. St. Paul: West.

_____. 1986. *Analysis for Strategic Marketing Decisions*. St. Paul: West.

Demsetz, Harold. 1982. "Barriers to Entry." *American Economic Review* 72 (March): 47-57.

Dixit, Avinash, and Albert S. Kyle. 1985. "The Use of Protection and Subsidies for Entry Promotion and Deterrence." *American Economic Review* 75 (March): 139-52.

Eaton, Curtis B., and Richard G. Lipsey. 1980. "Exit Barriers and Entry Barriers: The Durability of Capitol as a Barrier to Entry." *Bell Journal of Economics* 11 (2): 721-29.

Gale, B. T. 1972. "Market Share and Return on Investment." *Review of Economics and Statistics* 54 (November): 412-23.

Gatignon, Hubert, Erin Anderson, and Kristiaan Helsen. 1989. "Competitive Reactions to Market Entry: Explaining Interfirm Differences." *Journal of Marketing Research* 26 (February): 44-55.

Ghadar, Fariborz. 1982. "Political Risk and Erosion of Control: The Case of Oil Industry." *Columbia Journal of World Business* 17 (Fall): 47-51.

Grabowski, Henry, and John Vernon. 1986. "Longer Patents for Lower Imitation Barriers: The 1984 Drug Act." *American Economic Review* 76 (May): 195-98.

Hadley, B. 1976. "A Fundamental Approach to Strategy Development." *Long Range Planning* 9 (December): 2-11.

Hannan, Timothy H. 1983. "Prices, Capacity, and the Entry Decision: A Conditional Logit Analysis. *Southern Economic Journal* 50 (October): 539-50.

Harrigan, Kathryn Rudie. 1981. "Barriers to Entry and Competitive Strategies." *Strategic Management Journal* 2 (4): 395-412.

_____. 1985. "An Application of Clustering for Strategic Group Analysis." *Strategic Management Journal* 6 (1): 55-73.

Hax, Arnold C., and Nicholas S. Majluf. 1982. "Competitive Cost Dynamics: The Experience Curve." *Interfaces* 12 (5): 25-34 (October).

Henderson, Bruce D. 1984. "The Application and Misapplication of the Experience Curve." *Journal of Business Strategy* 4 Winter: 3-9.

Hofer, Charles W., and Dan Schendel. 1978. *Strategy Formation: Analytical Concepts*. St. Paul: West.

Horowitz, Ira. 1984. "On the Use and Nonuse of Entry Deterrents." *Journal of Economics and Business* 36 (December): 371-89.

Karakaya, Fahri. 1987. "Modeling Market Entry Decisions: A Test of Porter's Market Entry Barriers." Ph.D., Clemson University.

Karakaya, Fahri, and Michael J. Stahl. 1989. "Barriers to Entry and Market Entry Decisions in Consumer and Industrial Goods Markets." *Journal of Marketing* 53 (April): 80-91.

Kardasz, S. W. 1984. "Simultaneous Equation Models of Profitability, Advertising and Concentration for Canadian Manufacturing Industries." *Quarterly Journal of Business and Economics* 23 (Winter): 51-64.

Kessides, Ionnis N. 1986. "Advertising, Sunk Costs, and Barriers to Entry." *Review of Economics and Statistics* (Netherlands) 68 (February): 85-95.

King, Ronald H., and Arthur A. Thompson, Jr. 1982. "Entry and Market Share Success of New Brands in Concentrated Markets." *Journal of Business Research* 10: 371-83.

Krouse, Clement G. 1984. "Brand Name as a Barrier to Entry: The ReaLemon Case." *Southern Economics Journal* 51 (October): 495-502.

Levinson, Marc. 1988. "Is Strategic Trade Fair Trade?" *Across the Board* 25 (June): 46-51.

Lieberman, Marvin B. 1984. *The Learning Curve and Competitive Strategy. Stanford GSB Research Paper Series*, no. 766. Palo Alto, Calif. Graduate School of Business, Stanford University: 1-25.

_____. 1987. "The Learning Curve, Diffusion, and Competitive Strategy." *Strategic Management Journal* 8 (September - October): 441-52.

Lott, John R. Jr. 1987. "Licensing and Nontransferable Rents." *American Economic Review* 77 (June): 453-55.

Lustgarten, Steven, and Stavros Thomadakis. 1987. "Mobility Barriers and Tobin's Q." *Journal of Business* 60 (October): 519-37.

McFarlan, Warren F. 1984. "Information Technology Changes the Way You Compete." *Harvard Business Review* 62 (May - June): 98-103.

Macleod, Bentley W. 1987. "Entry, Sunk Costs and Market Structure." *Canadian Journal of Economics* 20 (1): 140-51.

MacMillan, I. C., D. C. Hambrick, and D. L. Day. 1982. "The Product Portfolio and Profitability–A PIMS–Based Analysis of Industrial Product Businesses." *Academy of Management Journal* 25 (December): 733-55.

Mann, Michael H. 1966. "Seller Concentration, Barriers to Entry and Rates of Return in Thirty Industries, 1950-1960." *Review of Economics and Statistics* 48 (August): 296-307.

May, Thornton. 1987. "When Barriers are Irrelevant or Undefended: Non-Bank Banks Cash In." *Business Horizon* 30 (July - August): 51-55.

Moore, Thomas G. 1978. "The Beneficiaries of Trucking Regulation." *Journal of Law and Economics* 21 (2): 327-44.

Needham, Douglas. 1976. "Entry Barriers and Non-Price Aspects of Firms' Behavior." *Journal of Industrial Economics* 25 (September): 29-43.

Netter, Jeffrey M. 1983. "Political Competition and Advertising as ɒ Barrier to Entry." *Southern Economic Journal* 50 (October): 510-20.

Perrakis, Stylianos, and George Warskett. 1986. "Uncertainty, Economies of Scale, and Barriers to Entry." *Oxford   Economic   Papers* (UK) 38 (November): 58-74.

Porter, Michael. 1979. "How Competitive Forces Shape Strategy." *Harvard Business Review* 57 (March - April): 137-45.

_____. 1980a. "Industry Structure and Competitive Strategy: Keys to Profitability." In *Marketing Management and Administrative Action*, S. H. Britt, H. W. Boyd, Jr., R. T. Davis, and J. Larreche, ed. New York: McGraw-Hill.

_____. 1980b. *Competitive Strategy: Techniques for Analyzing Industries and Competitors*. New York: The Free Press.

_____. 1985. "Technology and Competitive Advantage." *Journal of Business Strategy* 5 (3): 60-78 (Winter).

Pustay, Michael W. 1985. "Reform of Entry into Motor Carrier Act of 1980 Necessary?" *Transportation Journal* 25: 11-24.

Reed, Omer L. 1975. "Psychological Impact Advertising and the Need for FTC Regulation." *American Business Law Journal* 13 (2): 99-107.

Reekie, Duncan W., and Pat Bhoyrub. 1981. "Profitability and Intangible Assets: Another Look at Advertising and Entry Barriers." *Applied Economics* 13 (4): 99-107.

Reinganum, Jenifer. 1983. "Uncertain Innovation and the Persistence of Monopoly." *American Economic Review* 73 (June): 741-48.

Robinson, William T., and Cleas Fornell. 1985. "Sources of Market Pioneering Advantages in Consumer Goods Industries." *Journal of Marketing Research* 7 (September): 219-42.

Rosen, Sherwin. 1972. "Learning Experiences as Joint Production." *Quarterly Journal of Economics* (August): 366-82.

Scherer, F. M. 1970. *Industrial Pricing: Theory and Evidence.* Chicago: Rand McNally.

_____. 1973. "The Determinants of Industrial Plant Sizes in Six Nations." *Review of Economics and Statistics* (May): 135-45.

_____. 1980. *Industrial Market Structure and Economic Performance.* 2d. ed. Chicago: Rand McNally.

Schmalensee, Richard. 1981. "Economies of Scale and Barriers to Entry." *Journal of Political Economy* 89 (6): 1228-38.

_____. 1982. "Product Differentiation Advantages of Pioneering Brands." *American Economic Review* 72 (3): 350-71.

_____. 1983. "Advertising and Entry Deterrence: An Exploratory Model." *Journal of Political Economics* 90 (August): 636-53.

Schoeffler, Sidney, Robert D. Buzzell, and Donald F. Heany. 1974. "Impact of Strategic Planning on Profit Performance." *Harvard Business Review* 52 (March - April): 137-45.

Shepherd, W. 1972. "The Elements of Market Structure." *Review of Economics and Statistics* (February): 25-37.

_____. 1979. *The Economics of Industrial Organization.* Englewood Cliffs, N.J.: Prentice-Hall.

Shimaguchi, Mitsuaki, and William Lazer. 1979. "Japanese Distribution Channels: Invisible Barriers to Market Entry." *MSU Business Topics* 27 (Winter): 49-62.

Smiley, Robert H. 1988. "Empirical Evidence on Strategic Entry Deterrence." *International Journal of Industrial Organizations* 6 (June): 167-180.

Smiley, Robert H. and Abraham S. Ravid. 1983. "The Importance of Being First: Learning Price and Strategy." *The Quarterly Journal of Economics* 98 (May): 353-62.

Spence, Michael A. 1980. "Notes on Advertising, Economies of Scale, and Entry Barriers." *Quarterly Journal of Economics* 95 (November): 493-507.

Stigler, George J. 1968. "Barriers to Entry, Economies of Scale, and Firm Size." In *The Organization of Industry.* Homewood, Ill.: Richard D. Irwin.

Vernon, J. M., and R. E. Nourse. 1973. "Profit Rates and Market Structure of Advertising Intensive Firms." *Journal of Industrial Economics* (September): 1-19.

Wakerly, R. G. 1984. "PIMS: A Tool for Developing Competitive Strategy." *Long Range Planning* 17 (June): 92-97.

Watersen, M. J. 1984. "Advertising Facts and Advertising Illusions." *International Journal of Advertising* 3 (3): 207-21.

Weizsacker, C. V. 1980. *Barriers to Entry: A Theoretical Treatment.* Heidelberg, Germany: Springer-Verlag Berlin.

Wightman, David W. L. 1987. "Competitive Advantage Through Information Technology." *Journal of General Management* 12 (Summer): 37-45.

Williamson, O. E. 1963. "Selling Expense as a Barrier to Entry." *Quarterly Journal of Economics* 77 (February): 112-28.

Yao, Dennis A. 1988. "Beyond the Reach of the Invisible Hand: Impediments to Economic Activity, Market Failures, and Profitability." *Strategic Management Journal* 9 (Summer): 59-71.

Yelle, Louis E. 1979. "The Learning Curve: Historical Review and Comprehensive Survey." *Decision Sciences* 77 (September): 302-28.

Yip, G. S. 1982a, *Barriers to Entry: A Corporate Strategy Perspective.* Lexington, Mass.: D. C. Heath.

_____. 1982b. "Gateways to Entry." *Harvard Business Review* 60 (September - October): 85-92.

Chapter 2

Barriers to Entry and Market Entry Decisions in Consumer and Industrial Markets

Decisions to enter consumer goods markets may indeed be different from those to enter industrial goods markets. Entry into industrial goods markets often requires a larger investment than does entry into consumer goods markets. This is mainly because of the nature of industrial products (i.e., capital goods) and the manner in which they are marketed (i.e., personal selling). Therefore, entry into industrial goods markets involves more financial risk than does entry into consumer goods markets, and requires decision makers to place more emphasis on market entry barriers.

Many of the market entry barriers in consumer goods markets differ from those in industrial goods markets. In fact, differences exist from industry to industry and even from company to company. However, the reasons for these differences can be categorized in terms of overall marketing strategy development, including the timing of market entry. Therefore, it is necessary to examine the differences in target markets and marketing mix variables as they relate to consumer and industrial products and barriers to entry. In addition, the timing of market entry influences the importance of barriers. Thus, this chapter reviews early and late market entry literature related to barriers.

DIFFERENCES IN MARKETING STRATEGY FOR CONSUMER AND INDUSTRIAL GOODS

Target Market

Most consumer goods are produced and marketed to consumers, while some are also purchased by profit and nonprofit organizations. Many firms marketing industrial goods have long lasting relationships with their customers. This situation influences customers to resist buying from new market entrants. The major differences between the target markets of consumer and industrial products lie in the buying process and the number of individuals involved in purchasing decisions.

Almost all industrial products are purchased by organizations where more than one individual usually has some sort of input into purchasing decisions. In addition, the various players have roles that change from product to product and from purchase to purchase. Many organizations have *buying centers*, an informal term used to describe the group of individuals involved in purchasing. Most buying centers include

- users
- influencers
- deciders
- approvers
- buyers
- gatekeepers

Some individuals often play more than one role-and sometimes all the roles. Thus, the structure of the target markets in industrial markets is much more complex than those in consumer markets and requires research by industrial marketers. The differences in the composition of the target markets for industrial and consumer products influence the magnitude and the type of market entry barriers.

Product

Industrial goods and consumer goods are different in nature because the functions of the two are not the same. Many of the products considered to be industrial goods are used to produce consumer goods that are aimed at the end users (consumers). The purpose and the importance of packaging, service, and warranties also vary between consumer and industrial goods. For example, many industrial products are packaged in corrugated boxes because product protection is the major goal when a package is designed. However, packaging is designed to protect as well as to promote most consumer products.

Service is very important for most industrial products, and it is often the key criterion used by purchasing departments. Service is also a dominant factor in the purchase of some consumer goods (i.e., major appliances and motor vehicles). Therefore, entry into markets where service is important can be difficult because the entrant must invest in service facilities.

Since product durability and quality are crucial for firms in industrial markets, most industrial products require and carry longer warranty periods than do consumer products. Providing warranties for longer periods requires production of high-quality products, which, of course, affects the cost of production, as well as the cost of capital outlay for production facilities. Thus, this condition creates the capital requirements barrier to market entry.

Distribution

While it is a common practice to distribute most consumer goods through one or more middlemen, only a handful of industrial goods are distributed this way. Usually, industrial goods manufacturers have their own distribution forces and ship directly from the manufacturing plants or warehouses. This practice necessitates greater financial investment to enter and remain in industrial markets.

The situation in consumer goods markets is different, but market entry still demands available distribution channels. Oftentimes, the firms already in a market have contracts with the existing distributors, thus creating the access to distribution channels barrier.

Promotion

Readily available directories of manufacturers and other organizations make identification of target markets easy in industrial markets. However, promoting and selling products to these target markets (i.e., personal selling) is difficult and costly. As mentioned earlier, most buyers of industrial goods rely on their personal relationships or past experiences when selecting vendors. This setting makes market entry risky for new entrants.

Oftentimes, promotion of industrial goods requires the utilization of highly skilled personnel (e.g., engineers, technicians). Employing the necessary personnel is expensive and competitive and translates into more financial investments for new market entrants-and sometimes into advantages for incumbent firms.

In both consumer and industrial goods markets, many incumbent firms experience advantages over potential entrants because they have differentiated their products. One of the ways most firms accomplish this is through heavy advertising. If the potential market entrants cannot match the incumbents' advertising efforts or advertise more than the incumbents to differentiate their products, market entry becomes difficult.

Price

Low prices charged by incumbent firms act as barriers to entry in both consumer and industrial goods markets. However, the importance of price as a barrier is not the same in the two markets. The professional buyers in industrial markets are concerned with what is often referred to as the *evaluated price*, which takes into consideration a variety of factors, such as "the amount of scrap or waste resulting from the use of material, the amount of work a machine will do, the power it consumes, loss or damage liability, and a host of other variables that generate or minimize costs" (Hill, Alexander, and Cross 1975, 59). However, in consumer markets, with the exception of some durable products (e.g., appliances, automobiles), most products are evaluated on the basis of their final cost to the consumer. In addition, unlike the ultimate consumer, the industrial buyer is motivated by profit goals, expense quotas, and cost-benefit guidelines (Hill, Alexander, and Cross 1975). This condition, coupled with the consideration of evaluated price, places extreme importance on price in industrial markets. As a result, low prices charged by incumbents become very important concerns to potential market entrants unless they can match them.

TIMING OF MARKET ENTRY

Whether a firm enters a market early or late influences that firm's success. However, the choice of early or late entry is not always up to businesses. Barriers to market entry govern whether companies enter markets early or late or never. If the market entry barriers are high, one would expect only a few firms to be in a market. Many firms would wait for market entry barriers to disappear, thus causing late market entry. However, if market entry barriers are low, one would expect many firms to enter markets early.

Advantages of Pioneering or Early Market Entry

Oftentimes, early market entry results in many advantages for early entrants or pioneers that cannot be overcome by potential entrants. These advantages vary in type and magnitude from industry to industry, but the majority develop into high barriers to market entry for potential competitors. Advertising is seen as an important market entry barrier in industries with high advertising to sales ratios because the later entrants have to create brand awareness as well as change the buying patterns of customers (i.e., overcome the barrier of customer switching costs) (Kerin, Varadarajan, and Peterson 1990). In one study, Fornell, Robinson, and Wernerfelt (1985) have determined that advertising and sales promotion expenditures were lower for pioneers than for later entrants.

Pioneering brands often become the standard against which the later entrants are judged (Howard 1989). Therefore, the later entrants usually have to spend more on promotion to induce customers to switch brands. According to Carpenter and Nakamoto (1990), consumers learn about brands and form preferences, which then translate into advantages for the pioneers or early entrants. This condition is true even in purchasing situations where the switching costs are very low. Schmalensee (1982) also indicates that when consumers try a pioneering brand, they are less likely to try trailing brands due to their unexplored quality. Thus, consumers perceive risks in trying new brands and costs in searching for new information about the new brand.

Interestingly, established companies are often not the first firms to enter new markets, even if they have obvious strengths. They frequently enter markets later. Established firms usually place a higher opportunity cost on capital, and they are often ill-prepared to take the technological and product risks necessary in the early phases of industry development (Porter 1980b). IBM's late entry into the microcomputer market is an example of an established firm's late entry into a market. However, because of IBM's favorable reputation, its late entry has been very successful.

In contrast to IBM's experience, the majority of studies indicate that to be first in the market with a product often provides definite advantages, such as higher market share, higher return on investment, lower production and marketing costs, and technological leadership. Along this same line of thinking, Schmalensee (1982) suggests that first-entrant advantages are greater for products with low unit costs and for "convenience goods" for which retailers do not provide much information. The advantages are often associated with the barriers created by the early market entrants. For example, first market entrants or pioneers have large market shares until new firms enter the market. Some market pioneers in consumer goods markets (e.g., Coca-Cola, Hallmark, and Kleenex) have been market leaders for a long time. Market share and some other advantages continue to exist, even after other firms enter the market (Abel and Hammond 1979; Bond and Lean 1977, 1979; Dalrymple and Parsons 1980; Porter 1980b; Robinson and Fornell 1985; Schmalensee 1982; Whitten 1979; Yelle 1979).

Porter (1980b) suggests that pioneering is most appropriate when

● image and reputation are important to the customer,
● experience effects are important and not easily copied,
● brand loyalty accrues to the pioneer, and
● cost advantages can be obtained by early commitment to suppliers and channels.

Dalrymple and Parsons (1980) suggest that a firm is probably better off to be first in pickles than third in soup, even though soup is a much bigger market. Similarly, Porter (1980a) states that being first or one of the early entrants can minimize entry costs and sometimes yields an advantage in product differentiation. Furthermore, simply being a pioneer can yield a favorable product image.

A recent study (Miller, Gartner, and Wilson 1989) that was aimed at examining the extent to which market entry order determines market share and other competitive factors, such as position and promotion, found pioneers have distinctive advantages. This study analyzed data on 119 new nonservice corporate ventures from the Profit Impact of Marketing Strategy (PIMS) research database. The results indicate that pioneers achieved larger market shares, higher quality, more differentiated products, and better service than did late entrants.

Most of Miller, Gartner, and Wilson's (1989) findings were replications of an earlier study conducted by Robinson and Fornell (1985), who examined the order-of-entry relationship to market share, cost advantages, consumer information advantages, and some relative marketing mix variables. The results of the study performed by Robinson and Fornell (1985) indicated that pioneers had larger market shares, lower sale prices, broader product lines, better-quality products, and distribution advantages. Furthermore, market pioneering yielded relative consumer information advantages by way of product experience or familiarity, which in turn provided pioneers with greater market shares in industries where purchase price and purchase frequency were low.

Lambkin (1988) also has examined the influence of order of market entry, using the same database as the above two studies. This researcher tested the belief that early entrants enjoy enduring competitive advantage over later entrants by comparing three entrant categories: (1) pioneers, (2) early entrants, and (3) late entrants. The results of the analysis support the hypothesis that pioneers enjoy a long-term profit advantage over their rivals. However, this high return is necessary to compensate for the large investment pioneers must make to develop new markets. Again, in this study, early entrants showed significant advantages over late entrants in both market share and profitability.

Using the PIMS database, Robinson (1988), studied 1,209 mature industrial goods businesses. Market pioneers had higher market shares than did later entrants. On average, market pioneers had a market share of 29 percent versus 21 percent for early followers and 15 percent for late entrants. Furthermore, pioneering firms tended to have higher product quality, broader product lines, and broader served markets.

In another study (Lambkin 1988) using the same database (PIMS), 129 start-up and 187 adolescent businesses were examined. Among startup businesses, on average, market pioneers had a market share of 24 percent, versus 10 percent for both early followers and late entrants. Among adolescent businesses, on average, market pioneers had a market share of 33 percent, versus 19 percent for early followers and 13 percent for late entrants.

Urban, Carter, and Mucha (1983) investigated the effects of order of entry on market share in 24 categories of frequently purchased brands of consumer goods. The results of this study indicate that although the pioneer's share decreases as each new firm enters, the pioneer holds a share differential. The innovator's share drops from 100 percent to 68.9 percent after the second brand enters, to 56.8 percent after the third entrant, and to 50.3 percent after the fourth brand enters. Furthermore, the market share decline is greater if the other brands can obtain a more advantageous positioning.

Two earlier studies performed by Bond and Lean (1977, 1979) also found that important long-lived advantages are enjoyed by pioneering brands of prescription drugs. Other studies also support the conclusion that pioneering brands have many advantages (Buzzell and Farris 1976; Urban et al. 1979; Whitten 1979).

Other first mover or early market entrant advantages identified by Porter (1985b) include the following:

- reputation
- preempting a positioning
- switching costs
- channel selection
- proprietary learning curve
- favorable access to facilities, inputs, or other resources
- definition of standards

- institutional barriers
- early profits

In addition, Porter stresses that first movers and early market entrants get the opportunity to define the competitive rules in a variety of areas.

Similarly, Smiley and Ravid (1983) suggest that the potential entrants are unlikely to have greater cumulative output than the incumbent or the early entrant since their attempts to gain market shares through cutting price can be matched immediately by the initial monopolist. Furthermore, the initial monopolist will lose less than the new entrant will in a price war due to the incumbent's first mover advantage.

The above advantages of being a pioneer or early market entrant can be summarized as follows:

- higher market share
- higher return on investment
- lower production and marketing costs
- product differentiation
- consumer information advantages, including favorable product image and company reputation
- favorable product quality
- ability to provide better product service
- favorable access to distribution channels
- technological leadership
- ability to create customer switching costs
- favorable access to resources (i.e., suppliers)
- ability to define product standards
- ability to define competitive rules
- higher long-term profits

In contrast to the above findings, Cooper (1979), who studied 100 new product failures and successes, has found that being first in a market offered no particular advantage. Similarly, Dillon, Calantore, and Worthing (1979) reached a parallel conclusion in their study of 109 firms that had introduced new products. These two studies also used the PIMS database, which has long been criticized for its sample. This is important to note because the majority of the firms sampled are large and usually successful companies.

First movers and early market entrants do have some disadvantages. As indicated by Porter (1985a), they face the following six disadvantages:

1. costs associated with being a marketing pioneer or early entrant including those necessary to
   a. gain regulatory approvals
   b. achieve code compliance
   c. educate buyers
   d. develop infrastructure in such areas as service and training
   e. develop complementary products

      f. absorb the high costs of early inputs because of scarce supplies and
         small-scale needs
2. demand uncertainty
3. changes in buyer needs
4. specificity of investments to early generation or factor costs
5. technological discontinuities
6. low-cost imitation.

As implied by Porter, the major disadvantage is that the first or early entrant must create primary demand for the product when none exists through a large investment in promotion. The competitors, however, find it convenient to piggyback since by the time they enter the market, the primary demand is already there (Jain 1981). This disadvantage, of course, translates into an advantage for followers and late entrants.

Schnaars (1986) classifies Nike as a successful pioneer entry in the running shoe mass market. However, Kerin, Varadarajan, and Peterson (1990) report that Nike, in a period of five years, lost a considerable amount of market share to a late entrant, Reebok. Nike's market share decreased from an estimated 35 percent in 1984 to 19 percent in 1988, whereas Reebok's share increased from 13.5 percent in 1985 to 32.2 percent in 1988.

The following is an interesting example of early market entry for an industrial product. Docutel Corporation was the first to introduce the automated teller machine (ATM) for banks in the late 1960s. The company had no competition until 1975, and in 1976 it had 60 percent of the market for ATMs. Its market share fell to 20 percent in 1977 and to 8 percent in 1978 (*Business Week*, 1978). Therefore, it is important to note that early entry does not always yield the long-term advantages claimed by several researchers.

Advantages of Late Market Entry

A recent study by Kerin, Varadarajan and Peterson (1990, 12) suggests that later entrants have eight advantages over market pioneers or early entrants.

1. *Demand uncertainty.* While the first mover may be required to make critical investment decisions such as plant capacity in the face of uncertainty over the level of future demand, later entrants can base their decisions on more current information.

2. *Product Differentiation.* Product differentiation is an option available to late entrants to offset the first mover's cost advantage. Offsetting factors permit a late entrant to charge a price premium and ensure long-term survival, while operating at a scale below the minimum efficient scale (MES-the smallest volume for which unit costs reach a minimum).

3. *Scope effects.* It might be possible for the late entrant to offset the scale-related and/or experience-related cost advantages of the first mover by exploiting its existing assets in manufacturing, marketing, and distribution.

4. *Cost of imitation relative to innovation*. The fact that imitation costs are lower than innovation costs in a number of industries may also enable the late mover to partially offset the scale-related and experience-related cost advantages of the first mover.

5. *Free-rider effects*. Late movers may be able to "free-ride" on the first mover's investments in R&D, buyer education, and infrastructure development.

6. *Shifts in technology and/or customer needs*.   Technological discontinuities and changes in customer needs constitute gateways for entry by late movers.

7. *Incumbent inertia*. The vulnerability of the first mover is often enhanced by incumbent inertia. Root causes of such inertia include being locked into a specific set of fixed assets, reluctance to cannibalize existing product lines, and organizational inflexibility. Rather than trying to gain a foothold in the second-generation technology, the first mover may attempt to counter the threat of a new technology by investing research funds in improving current technology.

8. *Learning from the pioneer's mistakes*. A late mover can achieve a competitive advantage by learning from the pioneer's mistakes in such areas as positioning, product features, and product characteristics and by doing things differently.

DIFFERENCES IN THE IMPORTANCE OF ENTRY BARRIERS IN EARLY AND LATE MARKET ENTRY CONDITIONS

A study conducted by Karakaya and Stahl (1989) found many differences in the importance of entry barriers in early market entry conditions for both consumer and industrial goods (the market entry simulation exercise used in this study is presented in Appendix A). The statistical differences were verified through the Analysis of Variance and Duncan Multiple Range Tests. In the study, 138 marketing executives' market entry decisions were modeled, using six market entry barriers as decision cues. Relative weights, which reflect the importance attached to each barrier, were also calculated so that comparisons could be made.

Early Market Entry

As Table 2.1 shows, three of the six barriers tested - cost advantages of incumbents, capital requirements to enter markets, and product differentiation - were perceived as significantly more important than the other three barriers when making early market entry decisions into consumer goods markets. It is also important to note that the differences in the importance of the two sets of barriers are rather large.

Table 2.1
Duncan's Multiple Range Test for Early Market Entry
Decisions into Consumer Goods Markets

MEAN RELATIVE WEIGHTS	Decision Cues[b]	RELATIVE WEIGHTS[a]					
		CAI	PDI	CR	CSC	ADC	GP
.208	CAI	-					
.196	PDI	NS	-				
.204	CR	NS	NS	-			
.130	CSC	S	S	S	-		
.141	ADC	S	S	S	NS	-	
.118	GP	S	S	S	NS	NS	-

a. S means the relative weights are significantly different, and NS means the relative weights are not significantly different at $\alpha=0.05$ level, using Duncan's Multiple Range Test.

b. CAI = Cost Advantages of Incumbents
   PDI = Product Differentiation of Incumbents
   CR = Capital Requirements
   CSC = Customer Switching Costs
   ADC = Access to Distribution Channels
   GP = Government Policy

n = 137

Table 2.2 shows that the cost advantages market entry barrier (mean relative weight = 0.237) differs significantly from all the other barriers, and it is clearly the most important market entry barrier when making decisions regarding early entry into industrial markets. The capital requirements barrier is significantly different from cost advantages, customer switching costs, access to distribution channels, and government policy, and it is the second most important barrier (mean relative weight = 0.193) in deterring firms from making an early entry into industrial markets. The product differentiation barrier differs significantly from the cost advantages and government policy barriers, and it is the third most important entry barrier (mean relative weight = 0.165).

Table 2.2
Duncan's Multiple Range Test for Early Market Entry
Decisions into Industrial Goods Markets

RELATIVE WEIGHTS[a]							
MEAN RELATIVE WEIGHTS	Decision Cues[b]	CAI	PDI	CR	CSC	ADC	GP
.237	CAI	-					
.165	PDI	S	-				
.193	CR	S	NS	-			
.149	CSC	S	NS	S	-		
.124	ADC	S	NS	S	NS	-	
.128	GP	S	S	S	NS	NS	-

a. S means the relative weights are significantly different, and NS means the relative weights are not significantly different at $\alpha=0.05$ level, using Duncan's Multiple Range Test.
b. Decision cues are defined in Table 2. 1.
n = 136

Late Market Entry

According to Schnaars (1986), late market entry strategies are usually designed to imitate firms that are forced, by default, to react to the moves of more insightful competitors. Late market entrants are often called "me too" entries, and they are unlikely to succeed, but a well-developed "second but better" entry backed by aggressive promotion may be able to surpass the pioneer's entry (Urban et al. 1986). However, in a recent study (Miller et al. 1989), followers or late entrants appear to enter with lower prices, but not with correspondingly lower costs. Therefore, the combination of low prices, no cost advantage, and low market share suggests that, as they mature, followers are likely to earn significantly lower profits than pioneers do.

Later entrants into an industry may tend to be firms with increased financial resources that can afford to wait until some of the uncertainties in the industry are resolved (as when IBM made a late entry into the microcomputer market). Firms with few resources, on the other hand, could have been compelled to enter early when the capital costs of entry were low (Porter 1980b).

Levitt (1965) favors a late market entry strategy for firms that can employ the so-called "used apple" policy. This policy implies that instead of bearing the burdens of pioneering in a market, the firm lets others enter the market first. If the market turns out to be attractive, the firm then enters the market. In a later article, Levitt (1966) argues that imitation is more plentiful than innovation and is a much more popular way to achieve business growth and profits. Similarly, Glazer (1985) states that later entrants choose to enter only successful markets that have reached an appreciable size.

Schmalensee (1982) suggests that when consumers become convinced that the first brand in any product class performs satisfactorily, that brand becomes the standard against which subsequent entrants' products are judged. Therefore, later entrants find it more difficult to convince consumers to try and adopt their products. This condition serves as a barrier to entry unless the new entrants have achieved brand preference with their other products in similar markets.

As studies mentioned earlier indicate, early market entrants or pioneers have cost advantages over later entrants. The cost advantages are usually due to experience curve effects or to economies of scale. In industries where experience effects are present, market pioneers benefit from early entry and offer a superior product for the same cost as competitors' lower-quality products (Abel and Hammond, 1979; Yelle, 1979). While the advantages gained by experience are difficult to overcome, later entrants could attain the same costs as the early entrants. Similarly, later entrants could match the product quality advantage held by early entrants.

According to Schnaars (1986), the products introduced by late entrants, often called "me too" products, are much more likely to fail. However, some marketers favor late entry for two major reasons: (1) the later entrants do not have to invest as heavily into promotional campaigns to educate the public about the new product as the pioneers do, and (2) later entrants do not have to take as much risk as the pioneers did because they have the opportunity to observe the performance of the pioneering brand.

Biggadike (1976) examined 40 late entries into new markets that were dominated by industrial manufacturing businesses. His results indicate that after four years, the average market share of these entrants was 15 percent and the market share of the largest existing competitor in each of the 40 businesses decreased from 47 percent to 28 percent after the new entrants came into the market. In general, late entrants faced long-lived problems in terms of market performance and had poor positions concerning product quality, price, costs, and distribution effectiveness.

Yip (1982) surveyed 69 late entrants into markets that were also dominated by industrial goods businesses. In this research, these late entrants also experienced long-lived problems in market performance and had poor positions in terms of product quality, price, costs, and distribution effectiveness. In addition, Yip hypothesized that the market share gains of entrants would be affected by (1) market structure and incumbent characteristics, (2) entrant characteristics, (3) entrant strategy, (4) incumbent reaction, and (5) time since entry. His analysis was, however, less successful in explaining entrants' market share gains than in explaining their entry modes.

Flaherty (1982) investigated the relationship between technological leadership and market share in ten semiconductor markets whose products were in the later stages of the product life cycle. In these markets, compared to late entrants, pioneers enjoyed considerable market share advantages.

In summary, based on the literature review, there are five major advantages of late market entry.

1. Late entry is not as risky as early entry.
2. Late entrants do not have to create primary demand; thus, their promotional expenditures are usually lower.
3. Late entrants may be able to enter markets with better products than the competitors' existing ones.
4. In late market entry situations, it becomes easier to identify target markets and define marketing mix variables.
5. Overall, market entry barriers are not as high as they are in early market entries.

Based on the study conducted by the authors of this book, many of the barriers vary in their importance in late market entry situations in both consumer and industrial markets. Table 2.3 illustrates differences in the importance of barriers for late entry into consumer goods markets. The cost advantages, product differentiation, and capital requirements barriers differ from the other three barriers. This is the same result as for the early entry decision. In addition, the customer switching costs barrier differs from the access to distribution channels barrier, and it is perceived as more important (mean relative weight = .148). This later finding is consistent with the literature review provided earlier, indicating that early entrants create the customer switching costs barrier.

Table 2.3
Duncan's Multiple Range Test for Late Market Entry
Decisions into Consumer Goods Markets

RELATIVE WEIGHTS[a]							
MEAN RELATIVE WEIGHTS	Decision Cues[b]	CAI	PDI	CR	CSC	ADC	GP
.217	CAI	-					
.193	PDI	NS	-				
.203	CR	NS	NS	-			
.148	CSC	S	S	S	-		
.128	ADC	S	S	S	S	-	
.107	GP	S	S	S	NS	NS	-

Table 2.3 (continued)
a. S means the relative weights are significantly different, and INS means the relative weights are not significantly different at $\alpha=0.05$ level, using Duncan's Multiple Range Test.
b. Decision cues are defined in Table 2 .1.
n = 137

In late entry into industrial markets, many of the barriers vary in importance, but the situation is a little different. Table 2.4 indicates that the cost advantages barrier significantly differs from all the other entry barriers, and it is perceived as the most important. This is the same as for the early market entry decision into industrial goods markets. However, the product differentiation and capital requirements barriers differ only from the cost advantages, access to distribution channels, and government policy barriers. Also, the customer switching costs barrier significantly differs from the access to distribution channels and government policy barriers.

In terms of the importance of market entry barriers, the cost advantages barrier is followed by the capital requirements, customer switching costs, product differentiation, access to distribution channels, and government policy barriers. Furthermore, this barrier is perceived as more important for entry into industrial goods markets than into consumer goods markets, based on the relative weights.

Table 2.4
Duncan's Multiple Range Test for Late Market Entry
Decisions into Industrial Goods Markets

RELATIVE WEIGHTS[a]							
MEAN RELATIVE WEIGHTS	**Decision Cues[b]**	**CAI**	**PDI**	**CR**	**CSC**	**ADC**	**GP**
.238	**CAI**	-					
.161	**PDI**	S	-				
.193	**CR**	S	NS	-			
.170	**CSC**	S	NS	NS	-		
.121	**ADC**	S	S	S	S	-	
.113	**GP**	S	S	S	S	NS	-

a. S means the relative weights are significantly different, and NS means the relative weights are not significantly different at $\alpha=0.05$ level, using Duncan's Multiple Range Test.
b. Decision cues are defined in Table 2 .1.
n = 136

DIFFERENCES IN THE IMPORTANCE OF BARRIERS BETWEEN EARLY AND LATE MARKET ENTRY CONDITIONS

The customer switching costs barrier, which appears to be a more important barrier in industrial goods markets, is the only barrier that differs in early versus late market entry conditions (Table 2.5). This barrier is perceived to be more important for late market entry decisions. This finding suggests that customers are unlikely to switch brands when the market is at either the growth or the maturity stage of the product life cycle because the possible benefits they may gain from switching brands may not offset the sunk costs they have.

Table 2.5
Comparison of Market Entry Barrier Relative Weights for Early and Late Entry into Consumer Goods Markets

DECISION[a]	AVERAGE RELATIVE WEIGHTS- EARLY ENTRY INTO CONSUMER MARKETS	AVERAGE RELATIVE WEIGHTS- LATE ENTRY INTO CONSUMER MARKETS	t-value
CAI	0.208	0.217	-0.80
PDI	0.196	0.193	0.26
CR	0.204	0.203	0.06
CSC	0.130	0.148	-2.49*
ADC	0.141	0.128	1.57
GP	0.118	0.107	1.33

a. Decision cues are defined in Table 2.1.
$n = 137$
* $p < 0.01$, two-tailed, paired sample t-test.

Statistical tests performed to determine which barriers differed in early and late market entry into industrial markets showed that only one was different (Table 2.6). The customer switching costs barrier was perceived as more important when making late market entry decisions. As indicated earlier, this finding is the same for consumer markets. Therefore, one may conclude that, regardless of the type of product involved, the customer switching costs barrier gains much importance in late entry situations for the reasons mentioned earlier.

Table 2.6
Comparison of Market Entry Barrier Relative Weights
for Early and Late Entry into Industrial Goods Markets

DECISION[a]	AVERAGE RELATIVE WEIGHTS- EARLY ENTRY INTO INDUSTRIAL MARKETS	AVERAGE RELATIVE WEIGHTS- LATE ENTRY INTO INDUSTRIAL MARKETS	t-value
CAI	0.237	0.238	-0.16
PDI	0.165	0.161	0.48
CR	0.193	0.193	-0.02
CSC	0.149	0.170	-2.54[*]
ADC	0.124	0.121	0.40
GP	0.128	0.113	-1.81

a. Decision cues are defined in Table 2.1.
n = 136
* $p < 0.01$, two-tailed, paired sample t-test.

As indicated earlier in this chapter, the importance of barriers to entry differs between consumer and industrial markets. Based on the study by the authors, these differences, however, are not always significant. Table 2.7 shows the barriers and the differences discovered. Statistical tests performed indicate that five of the six barriers tested were indeed different when making early market entry decisions in consumer versus industrial markets. Three of the barriers - cost advantages, customer switching costs, and government policy - were more important in early entry into industrial markets. These findings are consistent with other researchers' proposals (see Porter 1980b; Webster 1979). However, two of the barriers, product differentiation and access to distribution channels, were considered to be more important in early entry into consumer markets than into industrial markets. The capital requirements to enter markets is the only barrier that does not differ significantly.

Table 2.7
Comparison of Market Entry Barrier Relative Weights for Early Entry into Consumer versus Industrial Goods Markets

DECISION[a]	AVERAGE RELATIVE WEIGHTS- EARLY ENTRY INTO CONSUMER MARKETS	AVERAGE RELATIVE WEIGHTS- EARLY ENTRY INTO INDUSTRIAL MARKETS	t-value
CAI	0.208	0.237	-2.69[*]
PDI	0.196	0.165	2.60[*]
CR	0.205	0.193	1.74
CSC	0.130	0.149	-3.25[*]
ADC	0.141	0.124	2.59[*]
GP	0.117	0.128	-1.93[**]

a. Decision cues are defined in Table 2.1.
n = 136
* p<0.01, two-tailed, paired sample t-test.
**p<0.05, two-tailed, paired sample t-test.

When making late entry into consumer versus industrial goods markets, only the product differentiation and customer switching costs barriers differ in importance (Table 2.8). The product differentiation barrier is perceived as more important in consumer markets. This is possibly due to the fact that consumer products are heavily promoted through mass media in an attempt to create brand loyalty. Therefore, substantial marketing efforts and financial resources are required to overcome this barrier in consumer markets. In industrial markets, most products are sold through personal selling, and it is easier to persuade buyers to switch brands.

Customer switching costs also are more important when making late entry into industrial markets. Common sense dictates that customer switching costs are much higher in industrial goods markets than in consumer goods markets because of the size of the initial investment and the sunk costs accrued by potential customers. Therefore, market entry decision makers place more importance on customer switching costs when making entry decisions into industrial markets.

Table 2.8
Comparison of Market Entry Barrier Relative Weights
for Late Entry into Consumer versus Industrial Goods
Markets

DECISION[a]	AVERAGE RELATIVE WEIGHTS- LATE ENTRY INTO CONSUMER MARKETS	AVERAGE RELATIVE WEIGHTS- LATE ENTRY INTO INDUSTRIAL MARKETS	t-value
CAI	0.217	0.238	-1.80
PDI	0.194	0.161	2.85*
CR	0.201	0.193	0.87
CSC	0.149	0.170	-2.58*
ADC	0.128	0.121	0.94*
GP	0.107	0.113	-0.94**

a. Decision cues are defined in Table 2 .1.
n = 136
* p<0.01, two-tailed, paired sample t-test.

DIFFERENCES IN THE IMPORTANCE OF OTHER BARRIERS IN CONSUMER AND INDUSTRIAL MARKETS

The study conducted by the authors tested six entry barriers. However, as listed in Chapter 1, there are many other barriers, and some of these have important differences in consumer versus industrial markets. The differences in the importance of barriers that are thought to be significant are explained in the following pages.

Incumbents' Superior Production Processes

Since most industrial products are technical in nature, their production processes are complex and sophisticated. However, this is not to say that some consumer products do not involve complex production technologies. In addition to having patents, many industrial producers use secret production techniques that cannot not be copied by competitors (e.g., the production technology of the defense industry). This condition raises the barrier to market entry for competitors. Of course, the same argument can be made for some consumer goods, but this superior production processes barrier, should be more important for industrial producers in most cases.

Heavy Advertising by Incumbents

The amount and the type of advertising are both different in consumer and industrial markets. In consumer markets, producers often advertise heavily in an attempt to create brand loyalty, which translates into a barrier to market entry. In industrial markets, however, most producers do very little advertising. Personal selling is usually the most widely used promotional technique. In addition, the little advertising done is usually in trade magazines, and it oftentimes takes the form of publicity. Therefore, advertising as a barrier to entry is very weak in most industrial markets.

Research and Development

Although some consumer products often require very large investments in R&D, the amount of money invested in R&D for industrial products is usually higher due to their technical nature. The research and development barrier influences or governs the height of other entry barriers (e.g., cost advantages, superior production processes, product quality, trade secrets, proprietary product technology, capital requirements). This condition affects the importance of R&D as a barrier to entry more for industrial products than for consumer products.

Price

This barrier is, of course, related to the cost advantages barrier. However, many industrial buyers rate price as a much less important buying consideration than certainty of delivery, quality of the product, service, and technical assistance (Hass 1976). Nevertheless, this situation is not true in bidding situations where price determines sale. Therefore, the importance of this barrier depends on the purchasing situation. If bidding is not involved, then price is not a major barrier to entry in industrial markets.

The type of product is also a major concern when evaluating price for both industrial and consumer markets. For example, for most impulse items like chewing gum, magazines, and candy, price is not an important factor. However, for many major appliances in consumer markets and for raw materials in industrial markets, price becomes important. While it is feasible to differentiate consumer appliances through promotional efforts intended to justify higher prices, this is hardly the case in marketing raw materials. Therefore, the importance of this barrier varies with products and industries, as well as with competitive situations.

Trade Secrets Held by Competitors

This barrier influences the height of other barriers, including cost advantages, superior production processes, proprietary product technology, product differentiation, and product quality. Although one might think that this barrier is most prevalent in industrial markets due to the technical nature of most industrial products, it is equally dominant in consumer markets. Furthermore, it is equally important in both consumer and industrial markets since it does generate other entry barriers.

Selling Expenses

Selling expenses are usually higher for industrial products since most of them are sold through personal selling. A clarification needs to be made regarding this barrier. In the past, this barrier included promotional expenses devoted to advertising, sales promotion, publicity, and personal selling. However, today it is considered to be expenditures needed to personally sell products (e.g., salespersons' salaries and travel expenses). Thus, it includes the cost of personally selling products to industrial buyers and middlemen. With this in mind, selling expenses mostly apply to industrial products, some consumer products such as appliances and automobiles, and new consumer products that require selling to middlemen using a push strategy. In general, however, selling expenses are more important in industrial markets due to the high salaries of salespeople.

Incumbents' Proprietary Product Technology

This barrier is related to the superior production processes, and trade secrets barriers. It affects the height of several other barriers, such as product quality, price, and cost advantages. Unlike many other barriers, this barrier is equally important in both consumer and industrial markets because it presents a competitive edge to companies marketing either type of products.

Number of Competitors

The number of present competitors in any market has an impact on the entry decisions of potential market entrants. However, this situation is different in consumer versus industrial markets. Usually, in consumer markets, the number of firms is much greater than the number of firms in industrial markets. This is because of the large initial investments required to enter into most industrial markets. In addition, the failure rate for consumer products is much greater than for industrial products. For example, according to Department of Commerce statistics, the failure rate is 60 to 70 percent for consumer products versus 35 to 45 percent for industrial products. Thus, it is easier to compete in consumer markets than in industrial markets. This condition influences the number of firms in consumer and industrial markets. Overall, this barrier is more important in industrial markets than in consumer markets.

Technology and Technological Change

As it is with the other barriers, this barrier is also related to several other barriers, such as cost advantages, price, product differentiation, R&D, proprietary product technology, and sunk costs. Technological changes affect both industrial and consumer goods manufacturers, but this effect is more dominant among industrial producers because of the technical nature of most industrial products. Furthermore, most technological changes occur in industrial markets because of the large investments in R&D.

Sunk Costs

Sunk costs influence firms to remain in markets even when it is unprofitable to do so. However, sunk costs are often higher in industrial markets because of the nature of most industrial products. The amount of money invested in R&D, production technology, and skilled personnel creates an exit barrier for incumbent firms, while it becomes a barrier to entry for potential market entrants. Some consumer products also involve large sunk costs and keep potential entrants out of the market. However, sunk costs are not as high an entry barrier in consumer markets as in industrial markets.

Incumbents' Relatively Easy Access to Raw Materials

This barrier can influence both consumer and industrial firms equally. However, most industrial product manufacturers construct their plants near sources of raw materials to reduce transportation costs. Therefore, it is usually a more important barrier in industrial markets.

Possession of Strategic Raw Materials

Again, this barrier is equally important in both consumer and industrial markets, but it is more prevalent in industrial markets because of the nature of industrial goods. Firms possessing strategic raw materials usually achieve cost advantages over their competitors, which makes this barrier important.

CONCLUSIONS

As indicated in this chapter, the importance of many market entry barriers differs between consumer and industrial markets. In addition, many also differ between early and late market entry situations. Five of the six barriers tested by the authors differ significantly between consumer and industrial markets in early entry situations. The only one that does not vary is the capital requirements barrier. In the late market entry situation, however, only two of the barriers tested, product differentiation and customer switching costs, vary in importance. Product differentiation is more important in consumer markets, while customer switching costs have a greater effect in industrial markets. Interestingly, in consumer markets and industrial markets, a comparison of the six barriers for early and late entry conditions indicated that only one barrier is different. The customer switching costs barrier is more important in late entry situations for both consumer and industrial markets.

Of course, there are other barriers that vary in importance between consumer and industrial markets. However, these barriers have not been tested empirically. The assumed differences for these barriers are proposed in this chapter.

Many of the barriers tested also vary in importance within the same market entry situation. The cost advantages, product differentiation, and capital requirements barriers are more important in early entry into consumer markets than were the other three barriers tested (Karakaya and Stahl 1989). Similarly, the cost advantages, capital requirements, and product differentiation barriers are more important in early entry into industrial markets than were the other three barriers tested. In late market entry conditions, the situation was not much different in both consumer and industrial markets.

It is clear that there are some differences in the importance of entry barriers when making entry decisions into consumer versus industrial markets, as well as in early versus late entry situations. These differences usually result from the nature of the products and the target markets selected, as well as from the marketing mix variables. Therefore, when making market entry decisions, it is important to consider the type of market, the timing of entry, the kind of product being marketed, and the marketing mix variables.

REFERENCES

Abel, Derek, and John S. Hammond. 1979. *Strategic Market Planning.* Englewood Cliffs, N.J.: Prentice-Hall.

Biggadike, Ralph E. 1976. "Entry Strategy and Performance." Ph.D. diss., Harvard Business School.

Bond, R. S., and David F. Lean. 1977. "Sales Promotion, and Product Differentiation in Two Prescription Drug Markets." *Staff Report to the U.S. Federal Trade Commission.* Washington, D.C.

_____. 1979. "Consumer Preference, Advertising and Sales: On the Advantages from Early Entry," Working Paper 14, Bureau of Economics, U.S. Federal Trade Commision, Washington (October).

Business Week. 1978. "Docutel: Trying for Comeback by Dovetailing the New with the Old." October 30, 179-80.

Buzzell, Robert D., and P. W. Farris. 1976. *Marketing Costs in Consumer Goods Industries.* Report no. 76-111. Cambridge, Mass.: *Marketing Science Institute.*

Carpenter, Gregory S., and Kent Nakamoto. 1990. "Consumer Preference Formation and Pioneering Advantage." *Journal of Marketing Research* 26 (August): 285-98.

Cooper, R. G. 1979. "The Dimensions of New Product Success and Failure." *Journal of Marketing* 43 (Summer): 93-103.

Dalrymple, Douglas J., and Leonard J. Parsons. 1980. *Marketing Management: Text and Cases.* New York: John Wiley.

Dillon, William R. Roger Calantore, and Porter Worthing. 1979. "The New Product Problem: An Approach for Investigating Product Failures." *Management Science* 25 (December): 1184-96.

Flaherty, Theresa M. 1982. *Market Share Technology Leadership, and Competition in International Semiconducter Markets.* Working Paper no. 08. Cambridge, Mass.: Graduate School of Business Administration, Harvard University.

Fornell, Cleas, William T. Robinson, and Birger Wernerfelt. 1985. "Consumption Experience and Sales Promotion Expenditures." *Management Science* 31 (September): 1084-1105.

Glazer, A. 1985. "The Advantages of Being First." *The American Economic Review* 75 (June): 473-80.

Hass, Robert. 1976. *Industrial Marketing Management.* New York: Van Nostrand Reinhold.

Hill, Richard, Ralph Alexander, and James Cross. 1975. *Industrial Marketing.* Homewood, Ill.: Richard D. Irwin.

Howard, John A. 1989. *Consumer Behavior in Marketing Strategy.* Englewood Cliffs, N.J.: Prentice-Hall.

Jain, Subhash C. 1981. *Marketing Planning and Strategy.* Cincinnati: South-Western.

Karakaya, Fahri, and Michael J. Stahl. 1989. "Barriers to Entry and Market Entry Decisions in Consumer and Industrial Goods Markets." *Journal of Marketing* 53 April: 80-91.

Kerin, Roger A. P. Rajan Varadarajan, and Robert A. Peterson. 1990. *First Mover Advantages: A Synthesis and Critique. Working Paper.* Dallas: Southern Methodist University. 1-47.

Kotler, Philip. 1988. *Marketing Management: Analysis, Planning, Implementation and Control.* Englewood Cliffs, N.J.: Prentice- Hall.

Lambkin, Mary. 1988. "Order of Entry and Performance in New Markets." *Strategic Management Journal* 9 (Summer): 127-40.

Levitt, Theodore. 1965. "Exploit the Product Life Cycle." *Harvard Business Review* 43 (November-December): 81-94.

_____. 1966. "Innovative Imitation." *Harvard Business Review.* (September-October): 63.

Miller, Alex, William Gartner, and Robert Wilson. 1989. "Entry Order, Market Share and Competitive Advantage: A Study of Their Relationships in New Corporate Ventures." *Journal of Business Venturing* 4 (May): 197-209.

Porter, Michael. 1980a. "Industry Structure and Competitive Strategy: Keys to Profitability." *Financial Analysis Journal* 36 (July-August): 30-41.

_____. 1980b. *Competitive Strategy.* New York: Free Press.

_____. 1985a. *Competitive Advantage.* New York: Free Press.

_____. 1985b. "Technology and Competitive Advantage." *Journal of Business Strategy* 5 (3): 60-78 (Winter).

Robinson, William T. 1988. "Sources of Market Pioneer Advantages: The Case of Industrial Goods Industries." *Journal of Marketing Research* 25 (February): 87-94.

Robinson, William T., and Cleas Fornell. 1985. "Sources of Market Pioneering Advantages in Consumer Goods Industries." *Journal of Marketing Research* 7 (September): 219-42.

Schmalensee, Richard. 1982. "Product Differentiation Advantages of Pioneering Brands." *American Economic Review* 72 (3): 350-71.

Schnaars, Stephen P. 1986. "When Entering Growth Markets, Are Pioneers Better Than Poachers?" *Business Horizons* (March-April): 27-36.

Smiley, Robert H., and S. Abraham Ravid. 1983. "The Importance of Being First: Learning Price and Strategy." *Quarterly Journal of Economics* (May): 353-62.

Urban, Glen L. Theresa Carter, Steven Gaskin, and Zofia Mucha. 1986. "Market Share Rewards to Pioneering Brands: An Empirical Analysis and Strategic Implications." *Management Science* 32 (6): 645-59 (June).

Urban, Glen L., Theresa Carter, and Zofia Mucha. 1983. *Market Share Rewards to Pioneering Brands: An Empirical Analysis and Strategies Applications.* Working Paper no. 1454-83. Cambridge, Mass.: Sloan School of Management, Massachusetts Institute of Technology.

Urban, G. L., P. L. Johnson, and R. H. Brudnick. 1979. *Market Entry Strategy Formulation: A Hierachial Modeling and Consumer Measurement Approach.* Working Paper no. 1103-80. Cambridge, Mass.: Sloan School of Management, Massachusetts Institute of Technology.

Webster, Frederick. 1979. *Industrial Marketing Strategy.* New York: John Wiley.

Whitten, I. T. 1979. "Brand Performance in the Cigarette Industry and the Advantage to Early Entry, 1913-1974." In Urban, Glen L., Theresa Carter, and Zofia Mucha. 1983. *Market Share Rewards to Pioneering Brands: An Empirical Analysis and StrategiesApplications.* Working Paper no. 1454-83. Cambridge, Mass.: Sloan School of Management, Massachusetts Institute of Technology.

Yelle, Louis E. 1979. "The Learning Curve: Historical Review and Comprehensive Survey." *Decision Sciences* 10 (September): 302-28.

Yip, G. S. 1982. *Barriers to Entry: A Corporate Strategy Perspective.* Lexington, Mass.: D. C. Heath.

Chapter 3

Barriers to Entry
in International Markets

As a result of advances in communication and transportation among countries around the world, the exchange of goods and services has increased dramatically during the last decade. In some cases, many countries have become dependent on the products of other countries. Many U.S. companies have had difficulty entering international markets because of the existence of entry barriers. In addition, ever-increasing global competition, the threat of a single European market (the European Economic Community) in 1992, and a large U.S. deficit magnify the importance of entry barriers in international markets. Based on the authors' previous works in this field and a review of the current literature, it appears that very little research has been done concerning barriers in international markets.

According to a recent article in the *Wall Street Journal*, Hystler Company, a U.S. firm which has been producing and selling forklift trucks in Europe since 1952, has experienced difficulty meeting the regulations set by the European Economic Community (EEC). Hystler has struggled to make the required changes and has been relying on a West German parts supplier for parts that have to meet the new EEC standards. Hystler is probably one of the first U.S. firms to have difficulties. It is certain that many other U.S. firms will follow.

After an empirical study, Simon (1986) concludes that barriers to entry into Japanese markets are high. He also concludes that the intensity of competition and the recruitment of managers are considerably more important than institutional barriers (such as the behavior of public authorities/officials). The key success factors appear to be the endurance, patience, and commitment of the company. Short-term orientation and lack of flexibility are major causes of failures. Furthermore, Simon claims that the most successful entry mode into Japanese markets is the 100 percent-owned subsidiary. However, it also involves the highest risk.

Kotler (1986) suggests that barriers in international markets may include discriminatory legal requirements, political favoritism, cartel agreements, social and cultural biases, unfriendly distribution channels, and refusal to cooperate. In addition, many foreign governments require joint ownership, with the majority of shares being owned by domestic partners; require transfer of technological trade secrets to foreign countries; and have set limits on profits that can be taken out of the host country.

When barriers to entry are low, firms have little difficulty entering markets. For example, Fuji Corporation increased its market share in the United States considerably after sponsoring the 1984 Los Angles Summer Olympics. This was largely due to low customer switching costs, the absence of local economies of scale, and the fact that product differentiation was on a serious decline (Kim and Mauborgne 1988). However, most markets are different from the consumer photo film market, and they usually have some sort of barriers to entry.

CHOICES OF ENTRY MODES INTO INTERNATIONAL MARKETS

The barriers in international markets usually differ in magnitude and type from the barriers in domestic markets. Therefore, it is important that firms attempting to enter international markets understand these barriers in order to overcome them. One of the first decisions that a firm desiring to enter international markets must make relates to the mode of entry because different entry strategies face different barriers. In fact, a firm may need to change its entry mode depending on the barriers in various countries. Kotler (1988) lists five entry modes from which firms can choose: (1) indirect exporting, (2) direct exporting, (3) licensing, (4) joint ventures, and (5) direct investment.

Indirect exporting involves marketing a firm's products through middlemen. These middlemen work for commission or fee or sometimes buy the manufacturer's product and sell it in international markets. *Direct exporting* encompasses marketing a manufacturer's product directly to foreign markets by establishing foreign marketing divisions, employing traveling sales representatives, or using foreign-based distributors. *Licensing* requires an agreement with a foreign firm that wishes to purchase the manufacturing rights to a product. This strategy has been used successfully by Coca-Cola for many years. In a *joint venture*, a domestic firm enters into partnership with a firm located in a foreign country. *Direct investment* involves starting up production and marketing facilities or acquiring a local firm in a foreign country.

Each of these entry modes has its advantages and disadvantages. Selection of the entry strategy depends on many factors, but direct exporting is usually the most risky. With increasing global competition in international markets, many U.S. firms are now choosing market entry by way of licensing. For example, McDonald's and several other fast food companies have entered international markets during the last decade through franchising, which is not much different from licensing. Licensing poses very little or no risk to the licensor because it essentially sells the right to produce and market a product to a company in another country. The licensor can also control the quality and other important matters through the agreement.

Some business executives believe that the joint venture is probably the best way to enter international markets because the local partner shares the risk. In addition, most foreign governments are likely to cooperate because of the local company involvement. Berlew (1984) lists seven advantages of a joint venture in foreign markets: (1) participation in income and growth, (2) low cash requirements, (3) preferred treatment in developing countries, (4) more ready access to markets and to market information, (5) less drain on the company's managerial resources, (6) U.S. income tax deferral, and (7) creation of equity value for the parent.

The entry of Pepsi-Cola into India's huge consumer market by way of a joint venture is one example of making a successful entry and overcoming its major competitor, Coca-Cola. Pepsi-Cola formed a joint venture and offered to assist India in exporting its agro-based products and in bringing new food processing, packaging, and water treatment technology to India.

Kotler (1986) goes a step farther and relates megamarketing to joint venturing. He adds two more variables - power and public relations - to marketing strategy development in international markets where high entry barriers exist. Furthermore, Kotler terms this strategic thinking *megamarketing*, which is defined as the strategically coordinated application of economic, psychological, political, and public relations skills to gain the cooperation of a number of parties in order to enter and/or operate in a given market. The difficulties in joint venturing result from lack of knowledge about the potential partner in a foreign country. The International Trade Administration of the U.S. Department of Commerce, state export development agencies, and some international banks provide assistance in selecting sound partners in foreign countries.

According to Hout and Porter (1982), successful market entry and competition in international markets require the use of a "global strategy." This global strategy asks a company to think of the world as one market, instead of as a collection of national markets, and sometimes requires decisions as unconventional as accepting a project with a low return on investment because of its competitive payoff. Thus, an organization with such global view designs a strategy with the long-term objective in mind and engineers the strategies of local subsidiaries to achieve the overall corporate objective.

ENTRY BARRIERS UNIQUE TO INTERNATIONAL MARKETS

While many of the barriers discussed in Chapter 1 are also present in international markets, international marketing managers face some additional ones. Also, some of the barriers change in form and height in international markets. For example, a firm may find some barriers relatively easy to overcome in domestic markets, but almost impossible in international markets (e.g., access to distribution channels). In general, barriers to entry in international markets that differ from those in domestic markets include the following:

- cultural differences (i.e., the social system)
- language
- access to distribution channels
- customer switching costs
- government policy (i.e., taxes, licensing requirements,
  controls, import quotas, and export restrictions)
- product adaptation
- stability of the currency exchange rate
- expected local and global competition
- changes required in promotional activities
- nationalism
- political environment
- economic environment
- corruption
- cost advantages held by local companies

Cultural Differences

Cultural differences comprise probably one of the most important barriers to entry into international markets. This barrier, of course, results from the differences in people's beliefs, values, and customs. The ways of life are quite different in most countries, and consumers view product and service offerings quite differently than do most U.S. consumers. Therefore, it is important to study and understand the cultural differences in the countries of interest. It is also equally important to realize that there may be subcultures within cultures. Culture affects all areas of marketing: product design and acceptance, communication methods, the role of family members in the purchasing process, relations with distributors, and physical distribution (Kahler and Kramer 1977). Thus, the cultural differences barrier, in fact, creates or contributes to the formation of other barriers in international markets. It is almost impossible to eliminate this barrier since culture is learned and is a reflection of a society's adjustment to its environment. Furthermore, cultural changes come very slowly. Therefore, marketing strategies must be adjusted to the cultural environment.

Each country has its folkways, norms, and taboos (Kotler 1988). These translate into cultural differences among nations. These cultural differences are apparent not only among the consumers of different countries, but also among the business executives. Therefore, market research is a must before a firm makes a decision to enter a foreign market. For example, companies in Japan are usually "communal" organizations. Many of the large companies seem to exist for their workers; workers have lifetime ties to their firms for which they seem to work relentlessly (Ames 1986). Given the mind-set and the sociocultural characteristics of Japanese businesspersons and consumers, acquisition or joint venture may be the only successful entry mode in some Japanese markets.

Engel and Blackwell (1982) suggest the use of content analysis to determine the values, norms of behavior, and other elements of a culture by examining the verbal materials produced by the culture. The primary data-gathering techniques could also be used in examining the shopping and consumption patterns of consumers. However, the cost of gathering primary data could be prohibitive. Thus, purchasing data from market research firms or syndicated services may be a preferred alternative.

Language

This very common barrier for companies marketing their products in international markets has an impact on market entry from various perspectives. The marketing areas influenced by this barrier include

- branding
- packaging
- instructions for installing and using products
- warranty information
- communication with distribution channel members
- promotion (television, radio, and print advertising, as well as sales promotion activities such as coupons, rebates, entry into sweepstakes, point-of-purchase materials, etc.)

General Motors' experience with its Nova model in Mexico exemplifies the importance of language in international markets. In Spanish, the words *no va* means "no go" (Ricks 1983). Obviously, Mexican consumers did not want to drive a car that meant "no go." As a result, General Motors had to withdraw the Nova from the Mexican market. Similarly, Kotler (1988) presents some interesting examples of brand names that had to be modified in Germany. *Mist* means "manure" and *Scotch* (as in Scotch tape) means "schmuck" in German.

The advertisements used in domestic markets cannot be translated directly into other languages because they may mean different things, and sometimes they may even insult consumers in different cultures. An Electrolux vacuum cleaner advertisement was translated from Swedish into English and printed in a Korean magazine. advertisement was interpreted as "Nothing sucks like Electrolux" (Kotler 1988). Coca-Cola, on the other hand, has been very successful in advertising its principal product, "Coke," in other countries by using TV commercials that say very little or nothing. In fact, in some countries, the company uses the same commercial it uses in domestic markets. For example, the "Coke adds life" commercial has been used widely in international markets. Although Coca-Cola has been successful in using the same commercial in other countries, it is not always possible to employ this strategy. Thus, employment of a local advertising firm may be necessary if there is one. Some underdeveloped countries have no or only a few advertising agencies. In addition, in many countries, advertising is highly regulated, and advertisements have to pass strong censorship standards.

Access to Distribution Channels

Local companies in foreign countries have a definite advantage over their international rivals due to proximity and ease of communication. In addition, cultural differences influence the recruitment of channels and dealing with channel members. Japanese distribution channels provide a good example of the access to distribution channels barrier. Japan's distribution system is complex and thus acts as a barrier to entry. Alden (1987) reports that more than 1.7 million retailers serve Japan's population of 120 million, residing in 651 cities, 1,997 towns, and 607 villages scattered over the habitable 19 percent of the country's mountainous terrain.

Similarly, Shimaguchi and Lazer (1979) report that invisible barriers are imbedded in the mind-set and sociocultural characteristics of Japanese businesses, and particularly in the Japanese distribution system. The large number of small distributors and the length of the distribution channels appear to be the major causes of entry barriers in Japan.

Foreign distributors are not likely to handle products from other countries unless they can be assured of a continuous supply and are given large monetary incentives. Unless a firm can develop its own distribution channels or acquire other firms (i.e., vertical integration) to employ as its distributors, access to distribution channels will remain an important barrier to market entry. According to Porter (1980), a barrier to market entry can be created by the new entrant's need to secure distribution channels for its products. This barrier becomes especially important for firms in the international markets for four major reasons because it causes

1. difficulty in locating the appropriate channels of distribution
2. difficulty in selecting the right channels of distribution
3. difficulty in communicating effectively with the channels
4. difficulty in competing with other firms, either domestic or foreign, to secure good channels of distribution (i.e., firms are unable to provide adequate advertising allowances, etc.)

Customer Switching Costs

This barrier to entry can be especially high in international markets. Some cost is always involved in switching from one supplier or product to another in domestic and international markets. These switching costs usually include two major categories: (1) monetary costs (e.g., training employees, modifying products to match a supplier's product, providing assurance of supply); and (2) psychological costs (e.g., severing a relationship with one's present supplier) (Porter, 1980). Therefore, potential customers' perceptions of the switching costs influence their purchasing decisions. The perceived switching costs are even higher for the products of firms from other countries because of the lack of experience with these firms.

Providing training for potential buyers' employees, lower prices, and assurance of a continuous supply should lower the customer switching costs barrier. Creating a good image for the company and its products (i.e., following product differentiation strategy) can, of course, help the firm overcome this barrier. However, this strategy cannot be achieved overnight, and its benefits cannot be realized in the short run. Furthermore, this barrier does not apply to every product, and it may be very low for some products. For example, it is almost always high for industrial products where financial risks are usually considerable, but low for some consumer goods that present very little financial risk (e.g., chewing gum, socks).

Government Policy

This barrier is the most important in most international market entry situations. According to Walters and Monsen (1979), a growing competitive threat comes from state-owned companies abroad. These companies are heavily subsidized by their governments. Furthermore, they are not required to earn profits comparable to those of their privately owned competitors. More and more companies face such competition. In most industrialized nations, the telecommunication, railway, electrical, natural gas, steel, and shipbuilding industries are owned by the government. For example, the British Steel Corporation was underselling Japanese steel companies on the U.S. West Coast in 1977. Apparently, the decision to sell steel at a loss was a political one made in order to continue to employ steelworkers.

Governments establish most trade barriers to protect domestic companies or to reduce trade deficits. Japan has been very successful in constructing trade barriers for many products from the United States and Europe. Indeed, the Japanese government created high barriers to entry for foreign firms, including high tariffs and a set of complex trade regulations (i.e., product testing and recertification requirements) (Alden 1987).

Sometimes governments retaliate by building their own trade barriers. For example, the French government developed its own barrier against Japanese VCRs. All Japanese VCRs were allowed to land only at one port where only one inspector was employed. As a result, only 10 to 12 VCRs could enter the country each day. The United States also has a number of trade barriers that are designed to keep foreign competitors at a disadvantage in some markets. For example, high tariffs were imposed on certain Japanese electronic products. In addition, the United States has set import quotas for textile products coming from many Third World nations.

Interestingly, a new form of the government policy barrier to entry exists for firms marketing high technology products. In order to protect national security and national economies, many western nations have placed restrictions the type of high technology products that can be marketed to international markets. For example, the U.S. government has restricting various electronic equipment and parts that could end up in the wrong hands. In addition, governments try to limit or eliminate technology transfer so that they will not lose major international markets.

Product Adaptation

In most cases, depending on the product type, products must be adapted to meet local government requirements. In addition, they must often be changed to meet differing consumer needs in international markets. For example, McDonald's serves beer in Germany. Burger King serves French coffee, and their restaurants take the form of sidewalk cafes in France. Many U.S. household appliance manufacturers market smaller-size appliances in many European and Third World countries. Mercedes Benz and other European auto manufacturers have added pollution control devices to their automobiles that are marketed in the United States. These are all good examples of overcoming the product adaptation barrier in international markets. Therefore, it is necessary to study local government requirements and cultural differences in terms of product specifications.

Keegan (1980) suggests five strategies for adapting product or promotion for foreign markets: (1) product-communication extension, (2) product extension-communication adaptation, (3) product adaptation-communication extension, (4) product invention, and (5) dual adaptation. Of course, the easiest of these strategies is the product-communication extension since it requires very little change in the product. However, if this strategy is chosen, the firm must be careful in selecting the target market countries. Countries with similar cultures would require very little or no change in the product or promotion. Planning the necessary changes during the product or promotion development stages (i.e., designing the product or promotion in a way that will appeal to the cultures of the foreign countries in which the firm is interested) should make the modifications easier.

Stability of the Currency Exchange Rate

High indebtedness and political instability force a country's currency to depreciate or at least add to the volatility to the currency's value (Kotler 1988). This situation often causes such a country to have a very high inflation rate. This is true especially in developing and Third World nations. The U.S. dollar and other Western currencies often increase in value, sometimes from 50 to 100 percent. This increase usually results in price increases for the products that are being marketed. However, the firms marketing in international markets can get revenues that are lower in real value. In addition, many companies marketing in these markets are not used to increasing prices to keep up with the changing foreign currency rates, or sometimes they are not willing to increase prices frequently. This situation influences companies' decisions to enter foreign markets. Furthermore, price increases are not always welcomed by consumers in international markets. For example, a 70 percent increase in the price of Coca-

Cola resulted in a consumer boycott in Turkey. The Coca-Cola Company had to settle for a 30 percent increase instead.

While the volatility of the currency's foreign exchange rate can result in quick losses, it can also mean quick gains in international markets. One of the keys to success in such markets is to monitor foreign exchange rates and make adjustments in marketing strategies. Past experience with a particular market or the past history of the foreign exchange rate with a country can shed light in determining the price of a product or in deciding whether to enter that market. Firms might also consider targeting a market in a country that has a fixed exchange rate that has the home country.

Expected Local and Global Competition

This barrier is present in almost every international market unless the product being marketed is different from the products already being marketed there. Levis Strauss has marketed its line of blue jeans in many European and other markets. The Levis brand is well known, and the product line has probably been differentiated in many of the international markets. Indeed, in some countries, the Levis brand sometimes means status.

The competing products come from developed countries, underdeveloped countries, and developing countries. Oftentimes, products from the developing and underdeveloped countries are priced to undercut the prices of the products produced in domestic markets. The attractiveness of a market usually increases the number of competing firms. Thus, this barrier tends to be high in many Western world markets.

Changes Required in Promotional Activities

As indicated earlier in relation to the language barrier, many of the promotional activities must be adapted to the language and culture of the foreign country. The Ronald McDonald promotion of McDonald's failed in Japan because "white face" means death in Japan. Crest failed in Mexico when it used the U.S. campaign without any change. Apparently, either scientifically oriented advertising did not appeal to the Mexicans, or they did not care about cavity prevention (Kotler 1988).

Nationalism

Because of past or current political conflicts, entry into some international markets should not even be considered. The feeling of nationalism and the desire to retain local employment often influence consumers to patronize local companies. For example, Iranian consumers are not likely to favor U.S. products. Similarly, the "Buy American" campaign sponsored by many U.S. manufacturers and labor unions and the "Buy Japanese" attitude promoted by

Japanese firms are examples of barriers to entry that have their roots in nationalism (Alden 1987).

Political Environment

In some of the countries, governments change hands very often, and sometimes violently. American companies overseas have been taken over by foreign governments as a result of the changing political feelings of the government, or sometimes of the people. Therefore, companies marketing their products in countries with unstable political conditions often choose to export their products and keep a low inventory in the foreign country.

Economic Environment

The poor economic condition of a country naturally acts as a barrier to entry. This economic condition can be judged by examining the GNP, the per capita income and income distribution, the unemployment rate, and consumer expenditures. However, the size of the population is also very important and often enters into the picture. For example, some firms might be better off entering India than Switzerland.

Corruption

Government officials in some countries require bribes to allow foreign firms to enter their markets. While American businesspersons are banned from paying bribes by the Foreign Corrupt Practices Act of 1977, competitors from other countries do not have to obey any such law.

Cost Advantages Held by Local Companies

Local manufacturers often have advantages over their foreign rivals for several reasons. These reasons include transportation costs due to proximity to markets compared to exporting products into these markets; low labor costs because of the low wages paid, especially in developing and underdeveloped nations; and sometimes lower raw material costs. Companies marketing in international markets can overcome these barriers in two ways: (1) enter a foreign market by joint venture to enjoy the benefits of the local marketers, or (2) start a subsidiary firm in the foreign market, but make sure that many of the other barriers can be overcome.

A STUDY OF FIVE MAJOR BARRIERS IN INTERNATIONAL MARKETS

A market entry simulation study of 39 major U.S. firms marketing abroad revealed rather interesting results in terms of the importance of five barriers in international markets. The simulation exercise was designed in such a way that the participating executives' perception of the barriers to entry could be measured objectively (the market entry simulation exercise used in this study is presented in Appendix B). The cultural differences, product adaptation, access to distribution channels, political uncertainty, and foreign government policy barriers were studied. The importance of these barriers was tested for both early and late market entry situations in international markets. The results in terms of the relative importance of these barriers are summarized in Table 3.1. Relative importance was measured on a 100-point scale.

Table 3.1
Relative Importance of Market Entry Barriers

Barrier	Relative Weight in Early Market Entry	Relative Weight in Late Market Entry
Cultural Differences	13	11
Product Adaptation	17	15
Distribution Channels	26	24
Political Uncertainty	19	22
Government Policy	25	27
	n=39	n=39

Further analyses were performed to determine the percentage of respondents that consider these barriers important when making market entry decisions. The percentage breakdown of respondents that considered the market entry barriers significant is shown in Table 3.2. In determining the significance of each barrier, t-tests were performed on the beta weights of regression coefficients ($\alpha = 0.05$ level).

As can be noted from Table 3.2, the access to distribution barriers is considered important by 51 percent of the respondents in both early and late market entry situations. Thus, this barrier appears to be important to most respondents. Also, the government policy barrier is perceived as important for early and late market entry decisions by 41 and 49 percent of the respondents, respectively. Interestingly, the cultural differences barrier is perceived to be important by only 33 and 31 percent of the respondents in the study.

Very little difference is detected in terms of the importance of the five barriers when making early versus late market entry decisions into international markets. The cultural differences, product adaptation, and distribution channels barriers appear to be more important in early market entry situations. Similarly, the political uncertainty and government policy barriers appear to be somewhat more powerful in deterring late market entry. However, these differences are not statistically significant (using five paired t-tests). Therefore, one cannot reach the conclusion that the importance of the five barriers tested differs when making early versus late entry into international markets. Nevertheless, some barriers are considered more important than others when making early or late entry.

Table 3.2
Percentage of Respondents Who Consider Market
Entry Barriers Significant

Barrier	Early Market Entry	Late Market Entry
Cultural Differences	33%	31%
Product Adaptation	39	33
Distribution Channels	51	51
Political Uncertainty	39	41
Government Policy	41	49
	n=39	n=39

In early market entry situations, using statistical tests (ANOVA and Duncan's Multiple Range Tests), the importance of some of the international market entry barriers differs. The distribution channels barrier (relative weight = 26) and the foreign government barrier (relative weight = 25) are more important than the cultural differences barrier. Interestingly, there are no significant differences among the other barriers.

For late market entry conditions, based on statistical tests (ANOVA and Duncan's Multiple Range Tests), the cultural differences barrier is different from the distribution channels, political uncertainty, and government policy barriers. The cultural differences barrier (relative weight = 11) is perceived as less important than the distribution channels barrier (relative weight = 24), the political uncertainty barrier (relative weight = 22), and the government policy barrier (relative weight = 27).   Similarly, the government policy barrier (relative weight = 27) is more important than the product adaptation barrier (relative weight = 15).

The differences mentioned are based on the responding company executives' perceptions. Interestingly, none of the barriers is perceived as more important for early versus late market entry situations. The cultural differences barrier is not perceived to be as important as some of the other barriers (i.e., the government policy and distribution channels barriers) in both early and late market entry situations. This is interesting because most of the writings about international marketing usually place cultural differences at the top of the list of concerns. This finding in the market entry simulation study may be due to the other barriers' uncontrollable nature. While the product adaptation barrier is somewhat controllable by the entering firm, the other three barriers - government policy, distribution channels, and political uncertainty - are almost totally uncontrollable. It appears that marketing executives think they can research and learn the cultures of other countries or enter into a foreign market through a joint venture, but they may feel there is very little they can do about the other barriers.

IMPACT OF THE EUROPEAN ECONOMIC COMMUNITY

In 1992, the European Economic Community (EEC) will become a common market of more than 320 million people, with a gross domestic product of $2.7 trillion, exports of $680 billion, and imports of $708 billion annually (Barrett 1988). The unification of Belgium, Denmark, France, Germany, Greece, Ireland, Italy, Luxembourg, the Netherlands, Portugal, Spain, and the United Kingdom will remove the fiscal, physical, and technical barriers among these 12 nations. Specifically, the barriers eliminated are as follows (Quelch and Buzzell 1990, 16):

1. physical barriers
    a. frontier controls
    b. veterinary and plant health controls
    c. control of individuals including customs posts
2. technical barriers
    a. standards and regulations
    b. restrictions on the movement of individuals and professions
    c. restrictions on financial services
    d. restrictions on transportation services
    e. restrictions on new technologies
    f. capital controls
    g. differences in company law, intellectual and industrial property
       law, and taxation law
3. fiscal barriers
    a. differences in value-added tax rates and the goods to which
       they apply
    b. differences in excise duty rates and the goods to which they apply

Once the unification takes place, marketing in Europe will be somewhat different. Brimecomb (1988) suggests that distribution, especially for consumer products, probably will hold the key to a successful growth strategy for the European market. Also joint ventures might be profitable for higher-value products.

The 1992 unification may be a threat to or an opportunity for many U.S. firms, depending on the type of industry. Most EEC officials are trying to assure U.S. and Japanese businesses that the new single market will be as open to the outside world as it is to its members. In a communique´ from an EEC summit, officials declared that the unified market would be a "decisive factor" in liberalizing, rather than restricting, international trade (Grimes 1989). According to Goldbaum (1988), when it comes to major capital investments, many executives at U.S. chemical companies do not think there is any time to waste. In fact, strategic planners see significant untapped potential in the years ahead. Similarly, Kuttner (1988) believes that the single European market in 1992 will benefit many U.S. companies operating in Europe. For example, Europeans will treat foreign-owned companies with European facilities, such as IBM Europe, as full-fledged European companies and let them participate fully in the various research consortiums. Thus, Kuttner suggests that the United States should applaud the unification in 1992.

The 1992 unification certainly appears to favor many U.S. firms already operating in Europe. For example, many multinationals, such as Black & Decker, IBM, Gillette, Procter & Gamble, and Johnson & Johnson, will no longer be required to meet a number of the product standards set by the EEC countries (Asby 1988).

Regardless of the positive effects that the 1992 unification may bring, the changes in Europe will mean changes for U.S. and other firms marketing in Europe. In dealing with the changes in Europe, the 1992 unification should be closely examined and monitored by U.S. and other foreign firms that have stakes in the European market. Many marketing activities may need to be reorganized to meet the new regulations that have been set by the European Economic Commission. Quelch and Buzzell (1990, 370) suggest the following in response to changes associated with the 1992 unification:

- Assess the likely effects of the 1992 reforms on your specific industry.
- Make sure that your company's interests are adequately represented as new standards and regulations are developed in Brussels and, later, in individual national capitals.
- Consider, or reconsider, the strategic options open to your firm in light of the anticipated effects of market integration.

IMPACT OF THE TRADE TREATY BETWEEN THE UNITED STATES AND CANADA

In addition to the 1992 unification in Europe, Canada and the United States will lift many of the trade barriers between them. Burns (1988, F-3) explains the six highlights of this free-trade accord as follows:

1. *Tariffs:* a phased reduction over ten years, beginning January 1, 1989, of all tariffs between the two countries.
2. *Nontariff barriers:* elimination of customs user fees by 1994 and duty waivers linked to performance requirements by 1998; a phasing-out over ten years of most quantitative restrictions.
3. *Services:* establishes for the first time a set of rules governing trade in services. Each government agrees to treat each other's service businesses the way it treats its own. Regulations are relaxed to provide financial institutions with greater opportunities to do business on both sides of the border.
4. *Investment:* establishes a predictable investment climate so that investment will flow more freely in the future.
5. *Energy:* drops virtually all remaining restrictions on energy shipments such as quotas and export or import taxes.
6. *Institutions:* A Canada - United States Trade Commission, headed by cabinet-level trade officials, will have primary responsibility for carrying out the agreement. Either country may establish a binational panel to resolve disputes.

MARKET ENTRY INTO DEVELOPED COUNTRIES

Some of the market entry barriers are not equally important entering developed nations' markets. These barriers are access to distribution channels, stability of the currency exchange rate, nationalism, political environment, economic environment, and corruption. Distribution channels in the developed countries are usually similar to one another, excluding Japanese distribution channels. As indicated earlier in this chapter, Japanese distribution channels are quite different due to the vast dissimilarities between the American and Japanese cultures.

The currency exchange rate is relatively stable in most developed counties. Therefore, this barrier poses relatively less threat for new market entrants in the developed countries. However, as indicated earlier, in many of the developing and the Third World countries, the volatile currency exchange rate acts as a barrier to entry. For example, in Germany, Japan, England, France, and other developed nations, the value of the U.S. dollar changes only a few cents a day. This change is in favor of the U.S. dollar one day and against it the next day. Indeed, the value of the dollar in most developed countries have changed very little over the years. However, the situation is quite different in the developing and the Third World countries. In most cases, the U.S. dollar and the currencies of other developed nations have gained in value over the years. As the U.S. dollar gains in value, the U.S. goods sold in these countries become more expensive and not so competitive. Luckily, the amazing inflation rates make it possible for U.S. companies to remain somewhat competitive in these markets.

While the nationalism issue is prevalent, even in many of the developed countries, it is more important in some of the developing, and the Third World nations. In many of these nations, governments actively promote nationalism and use of nationally produced products. Of course, if a product does not exist in a country, then the nationalism barrier becomes negligible. Many multinational firms circumvent this barrier by marketing their products under a local brand name or by using a brand name in the host country's language. Thus, the citizens of the host country do not even know that the product they purchase comes from another country.

The economic environment of the developed nations is usually stable, and the consumers in these nations can usually afford many of the products marketed by the multinational corporations. However, the situation in the developing, the Eastern blocs, and the Third World countries is not the same. In many of these countries, only a handful of consumers can afford the products of the United States and other developed nations.

Although corruption may exist even in the developed countries, there is more of it in the developing and the Third World countries. This condition provides an opportunity to companies that are willing to break the ethical rules. However, it comes as a big shock to many company executives of the developed nations and often discourages market entry. In addition, the provisions of the Foreign Corrupt Practices Act of 1977 and the values of most executives in the developed countries give absolute advantage to those that are willing to give bribes to foreign officials to enter markets.

MARKET ENTRY INTO DEVELOPING COUNTRIES

Many of the market entry barriers in the developing countries are different from those in the developed countries. While some of the barriers are high, others are quite low, and sometimes some do not even exist. The barriers that are high in the developing nations include the following:

- cultural differences
- language
- access to distribution channels
- government policy (i.e., taxes, licensing requirements, controls, import quotas, and political risk)
- product adaptation
- stability of the currency exchange rate
- changes required in promotional activities
- nationalism
- political environment
- economic environment
- corruption
- local competition with relatively easy access to raw materials

On the other hand, some of the barriers are about equal in terms of deterring market entry into the markets of developing nations. For example, customer switching costs, expected local and global competition, and cost advantages held by local companies are about the same as they are in the developed and other nations. While the lists provided here are not exhaustive, they probably include the most important barriers. The differences in the importance of barriers rest in the developing countries' political, economic, and cultural status. Oftentimes, companies from the Western nations engage in joint ventures with local businesses in developing countries. In addition to marketing their products in the local markets, they also market their products in the Western world. As a result of this type of arrangement, they are usually able to price products below their competitors in the Western nations because of the low cost of labor in the developing countries. In addition, developing countries' governments often offer tax incentives to foreign companies starting a joint venture or owning a subsidiary company because they want to create employment for their citizens.

MARKET ENTRY INTO EASTERN BLOC COUNTRIES

Most executions from the United States and other Western nations know very little about the Eastern bloc nations' markets. The recent political changes in these countries provide many opportunities to market Western products. Although the true free-market economy is many years away in these countries, the height of the many market entry barriers has already been lowered. Therefore, the barriers in the Eastern bloc country markets are changing, and they will continue to change. The most important barrier in these countries will probably continue to be the affordability of Western products. While there is high demand for Western goods in these countries, the limited income earned by the consumers makes most of the Western products luxuries. This is mostly due to the foreign currency exchange rate. For example, in many of the Eastern bloc nations, the average monthly income is $30-$40. With such an income, the citizens of these countries can hardly afford to have a meal at McDonald's. A meal at McDonald's, which opened its doors in Moscow in 1989, is a luxury for most Soviet citizens. However, as trade between Western and Eastern bloc countries increases, the currency exchange rates and the wages in these countries are expected to change to provide a balance. However, it may be some time before high-ticket, discretionary-income items are affordable.

Government policy, changes required in promotional activities, and nationalism will probably continue to act as barriers to entry in the Eastern bloc nations for quite some time. For example, there are very few or no promotional activities in the Eastern bloc nations. However, most Western companies rely on their promotional activities to be successful. This condition will certainly influence the decision to enter these markets. The type and availability of the promotional media are not yet clear in the Eastern bloc nations. Therefore, companies wishing to market in these countries have to keep an eye on the developments and take advantage of the opportunities to come.

MARKET ENTRY INTO UNDERDEVELOPED COUNTRIES

Although many of the barriers discussed earlier are also present in the Third World markets, some of them gain significance. The most important barriers appear to be the political and economic environments, cultural differences, access to distribution channels, and corruption. These countries often face political and economic troubles. Thus, they are not target markets for many products that the Western world takes for granted. However, they are good markets for food, medicine, and military equipment. Because of the unattractiveness of these markets, there is very little competition. Therefore, if a company is willing to take risks, it will probably be the highest market share holder in the underdeveloped countries until other competitors follow suit.

OVERCOMING BARRIERS IN INTERNATIONAL MARKETS

Suggestions for dealing with specific entry barriers have been made throughout this chapter. The following suggestions, based on research on this topic, are general in nature and apply to many of the barriers in international markets. Kotler (1986) suggests that international marketers must often win the support of influential industry officials, legislators, and government bureaucrats in order to enter and operate in the target market. This may sometimes involve offering technological assistance, new jobs, and side payments to government officials. In addition, Kotler suggests that before entering an international market, companies must understand the community beliefs, attitudes, and values.

From a different perspective, Bartels (1968) suggests that more emphasis should be placed on the similarities of the marketing process in different countries instead of on their differences. Therefore, similar markets mean companies will use their domestic marketing strategies in international markets. For example, many U.S. companies marketing their products in Canada use the same strategy that they use in their domestic markets. In similar markets like Canada, U.S. marketers make very few changes, if any, in product, distribution, promotion, and pricing strategies.

As emphasized earlier, the Japanese have created various barriers to entry into their markets. More has been written about dealing with the barriers in Japan than any other country in the world. Alden (1987) suggests ways of breaking the barriers in Japanese markets, including the following:

- Keep probing the distribution system.
- Do not be afraid to end-run the distribution system.
- Find the best partner to work with in Japan.
- Be prepared to modify your products to conform with the local culture and conditions.
- Emphasize quality.
- Establish long-term links with the Japanese.

Kim and Mauborgne (1988) suggest a different approach in order to become successful in international markets. Instead of dealing with the barriers to entry, they recommend that the multinational corporation select the territory in which it is least costly to wage the battle or which is least likely to spark all-out war among global competitors. Furthermore, the multinational corporation can lower its costs by exploiting potential extranational economies of scale in R&D, manufacturing, and marketing through global resource sharing.

The most important step in successful international marketing strategy planning is conducting market research about the market entry barriers. This can be accomplished by several ways. To minimize the cost of market research, it is important to perform a situation analysis first. Preparing a situation analysis for market entry into international markets includes gathering information about the following:

● foreign government policies
● local and other competitors
● economic, social, and political conditions
● availability and type of distribution channels and retail outlets
● presence of any nationalist sentiments
● demographics
● history of company takeovers by the government
● size of the potential target market
● similarity of the potential target market to the markets already
  being served by the market entrant
● availability of advertising media and the restrictions placed on
  advertising
● the market entry mode(s) into the desired international markets

Information on most of the above areas can be obtained through secondary data sources. The best place to start is the U.S. Department of Commerce, which regularly gathers and analyzes data on many markets in other countries. These data are available to U.S. businesses at a nominal cost. Also, market research firms, regular media, and foreign embassies, including commerce attaches, are good sources.

If the secondary data search points toward market entry, then primary-data-gathering techniques can be utilized. While gathering primary data can be expensive and unnecessary in some cases, it is important to realize that international market research is different from domestic market research. Therefore, it may be imperative to employ a local market research firm or to study the market research techniques suitable in international markets.

CONCLUSIONS

The international markets certainly appear to be attractive. However, they also present high risks if the market entry barriers are not studied before making entry decisions. The market entry barriers must be measured and dealt with before and after entering markets because some barriers exist before entering markets, and others are created after entering markets. Therefore, firms entering international markets must also anticipate future entry barriers and be ready to adjust their marketing strategies.

The height of the barriers varies, depending on the nature of the market (i.e., industrial market consumer market) and the economic and social developmental stages of the country. Barriers are usually high in the developing and the Third World countries. In the developed nations, the barriers also are high, but the types of high barriers are different. For example, in some of the developed countries, the language barrier does not even exist (e.g., in England and the United States), but the government policy and cost advantages of local companies barriers can be very high. On the other hand, it is difficult to pass sound judgment on the height of the barriers in the Eastern bloc nations because of recent political developments. These developments appear to lower the barriers in these countries, but it is still too early to be sure.

In conclusion, to reduce their risk of failure in international markets, firms must perform market research. However, market research in international markets is different from research in domestic markets, and companies should focus on the present and future market entry barriers. While it is difficult to forecast the future, an attempted forecast is always better than no forecast at all.

REFERENCES

Alden, Vernon R. 1987. "Who Says You Can't Crack Japanese Markets?" *Harvard Business Review* (January-February): 52-56.

Ames, Walter L. 1986. "Buying a Piece of Japan, Inc.: Foreign Acquisitions in Japan." *Harvard International Law Journal* 27 (special issue): 541-96.

Asby, Janice. 1988. "European Unification in 1992 Challenges U.S. Export Packaging." *Marketing News* 22 (October 10): 12.

Barrett, M. 1988. "A New Chapter for Europe." *Euromoney* (UK) (September): 2-5.

Bartels, Robert. 1968. "Are Domestic and International Marketing Dissimilar?" *Journal of Marketing* 32 (July): 56-61.

Berlew, Kingston F. 1984. "The Joint Venture—A Way into Foreign Markets." *Harvard Business Review* 62 (July-August): 48-51.

Brimecomb, I. 1988. "1992—Single Market, Smaller Premium?" *Reactions* (UK) (September): 13-14.

Burns, John F. 1988. "On Guard of Thee Imperils Trade Treaty." *Providence Journal*, November 13, F-3.

Engel, James, and Roger Blackwell. 1982. *Consumer Behavior*. New York: Dryden Press.

Goldbaum, D. E. H. 1988. "Chemical Companies Reposition for a Freer European Market." *Chemical Week* 143 (15): 30 (October 12).

Grimes, Charlotte. 1989. "U.S. Could Benefit If It's Ready for European Trade Market." *Standard Times* (New Bedford, Mass.), November 8, 6.

Hout, Thomas, and Michael E. Porter. 1982. "How Global Companies Win Out." *Harvard Business Review* 60 (September - October): 98-108.

Kahler, Ruel, and Roland Kramer. 1977. *International Marketing*. Cincinnati: South-Western.

Keegan, Warren. 1980. *Multinational Marketing Management*. 2d Ed. Englewood Cliffs, N.J.: Prentice-Hall.

Kim, Chan W., and R. A. Mauborgne. 1988. "Becoming an Effective Global Competitor." *The Journal of Business Strategy* 9 (January-February): 33-37.

Kotler, Philip. (1986). "Megamarketing." *Harvard Business Review* (March-April), 117-24.

_____.1988. *Marketing Management*. Englewood Cliffs, N.J.: Prentice-Hall.

Kuttner, Robert. 1988. "The U.S. Should Applaud the Coming of Europe Inc." *Business Week,* July 11, 16.

Porter, Michael. 1980. *Competitive Strategy: Techniques for Analyzing Industries and Competitors*. New York: Free Press.

Quelch, John A., and Robert D. Buzzell. 1990. *The Marketing Challenge of 1992*. Reading, Mass.: Addison-Wesley.

Ricks, D. 1983. *Big Business Blunders: Mistakes in Multinational Marketing*. Homewood, Ill.: Dow Jones-Irwin. 37-47.

Shimaguchi, Mitsuaki, and William Lazer. 1979. "Japanese Distribution Channels: Invisible Barriers to Market Entry." *MSU Business Topics* 27 (Winter): 49-62.

Simon, Hermann. 1986. "Market Entry in Japan." *International Journal of Research in Marketing* 3 (2): 105-16.

Wall Street Journal. 1987. "As EC Markets Unite, U.S. Exporters Face New Trade Barriers." February 7: A4.

Walters, Kenneth D., and R. Joseph Monsen. 1979. "State-Owned Business Abroad: New Competitive Threat." *Harvard Business Review* (March April): 160-67.

Chapter 4

Product Life Cycle and Market Entry Barriers

PRODUCT LIFE CYCLE THEORY AND STRATEGIC ACTIONS

Barriers to market entry vary in influencing firms to enter markets at different stages of the product life cycles (PLC). Thus, it is important to consider this concept here as it relates to market entry and barriers to entry.

The product life cycle theory has been around for many years. Dean (1950) was among the pioneers of the theory. He explained the implications of PLC theory for pricing strategies for new products. According to Dean, all new products eventually lose their competitive advantages. Contrary to the four classic life cycle stages, Dean described three stages in a product's life cycle: (1) introduction into the market, (2) the rapid expansion due to acceptance, and (3) maturity due to increased competition. Most research on the PLC concept speaks of four stages: introduction, growth, maturity, and decline (Rink and Swan 1979).

Another PLC stage is suggested by Wasson (1978). This additional stage is the "competitive turbulence" stage, which precedes the maturity stage. This stage is characterized by a slowdown in the growth rate and the presence of excess capacity, which creates intense competition. Thus, prices start to decline as promotional activities increase and profits begin to erode. Usually, early market entrants or pioneers start intensive competitive activities to minimize reduction in their market shares.

A complete literature review of the PLC concept was conducted by Rink and Swan (1979). They discovered the presence of 12 types of PLC patterns and concluded that more research is needed on the PLC concept. Rink and Swan have reached the following four conclusions:

1. The evidence for the existence of the classical bell-shaped PLC curve is strong, as a number of studies have found such a pattern.
2. Some successes have been claimed for methods designed to forecast the

transition from one PLC stage to another.

   3. Very limited evidence suggests that the usual PLC concept applies to periods of either economic stability or economic growth. How recession might influence the PLC questionable.

   4. Almost no research has been reported on how different characteristics of the firm might influence the PLC.

   The classic PLC stages and their relationship to industry sales and profits in different stages are shown in Figure 4.1. As shown in the figure, industry sales reach a peak toward the end of the growth stage and stabilize in the maturity stage. Toward the end of the maturity stage, sales start to decline and continue to decrease in the decline stage. Interestingly, profits are highest in the growth stage, but start to go down in the maturity stage, even though sales continue to increase during the early part of the maturity stage. This is because the competition usually becomes intense in the maturity stage as many firms enter the market at the end of the growth stage. Thus, firms increase their expenditures on promotion and other competitive activities.

Figure 4.1
Classic Product Life Cycle Stages and
Industry Sales and Profits

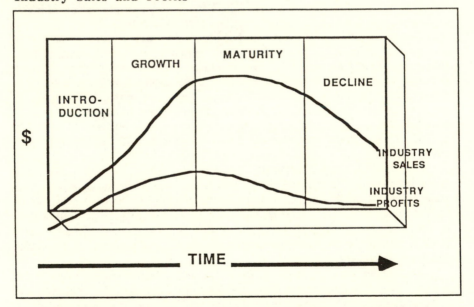

   When considering the PLC and barriers relationships, it is also important to include the length of the PLC stages. The time span is very long for some products and short for others. The length of the PLC is a function of the rate of technological change, the rate of market acceptance, and the ease of competitive entry into markets (Dean 1950). If a PLC stage is long, then barriers tend to get lower in the middle and toward the end of each stage, excluding the introduction stage. Therefore, it is necessary to forecast the length of each PLC stage. Although there is no perfect model to forecast the time span of each PLC stage, some researchers have developed new product models that forecast the growth and maturity phases of a new product on the basis of test market data (Bass 1969; Crawford 1966; King 1966; Urban 1968). However, these models have not been totally successful, particularly in predicting beyond the beginning of the maturity stage. Henderson (1984) suggests that the interaction between the experience curve and the price elasticity curve defines the shape of the sales volume in product life cycle. Therefore, if price elasticity can be predicted correctly, then it should be possible to forecast the life cycle of a product with some confidence. From a different view, Wilson (1969) suggests investigating the following variables to determine the PLC stages: number of new triers versus replacement sales, growth or decrease in profit, capacity in industry, elasticity in advertising, customer consumption rate, and price elasticity.

The importance of the PLC concept has been also pointed out by Hofer (1975). According to Hofer, the stage of the PLC is the most fundamental variable in determining an appropriate business strategy, and major changes in business strategy are usually required in three stages of the PLC introduction, maturity, and decline. Thus, Hofer considers the PLC a contingency factor that should be utilized in strategy formulation.

Anderson and Zeithaml (1984) have made a major recommendation that growth businesses should consider the implication of their objectives and strategies for later stages of the PLC (i.e., they should consider projections of market conditions and competitor strategies). Trying to predict market conditions and competitors' strategies is associated with creating market entry barriers or with sizing up the height of the present barriers. If firms can measure the height and length of the market entry barriers, they can develop strategies accordingly. Furthermore, if firms can deter other firms from entering their markets, they can lengthen the PLC. These researchers' conclusions support Hofer's propositions.

Research conducted by Thietart and Vivas (1984) shows that firms employ different strategies at different stages of the PLC, supporting the premise that the PLC is a contingency factor. These researchers' conclusions indicate that the use of a salesforce is very important during the introduction stage, while price cutting and an increased emphasis on R&D are important in later stages.

Camillus (1984) points out that technological innovation and social change are two very different motivating forces in terms of the demands they place on organizations that seek to link their strategies to the PLC concept. Accordingly, organizations that base their strategies on leadership in technological innovation, in keeping with the primary driving force of the relevant product/industry life cycle, are quite different from those organizations that base their strategies on their sensitivity and responsiveness to changes in the market.

A study conducted by Simon (1979) has suggested developing optimal pricing strategies over the PLC and has estimated price elasticity for brands at different stages in their life cycles. Simon's conclusions indicate that price elasticity tends to start at a low level during a brand's introductory and growth stages, reaches a minimum in the maturity stages, and then increases in the decline stage. Although Simon's contribution to the study of the PLC is noteworthy, his findings have been criticized by some researchers. For example, Shoemaker (1986) claims that the elasticity estimator used by Simon is not sufficiently flexible under certain conditions and may lead to incorrect tests of the hypotheses on price theory.

Day (1977) suggests that barriers to market entry should be included in any specific analysis of the product portfolio. Most business have stars (products with a high growth rate and a high market share) and sometimes wildcat (those with a high growth rate and a low market share) during the introductory and growth stages. Cash cows (products with a high market share and a low growth rate) and dogs (those with a low growth rate and a low market share) are typically found during the maturity and decline stages. Star products have high growth potential; they are mostly differentiated products that may deter entry of new competitors into markets. However, the wildcats and the dogs do not offer barriers to entry, usually, because of competitors' entry into markets with newer and better products. Yet, cash cows possess high market shares and continue to act as barriers to entry in most cases.

Until 1981, most research related to the PLC had included consumer goods. Using the Profit Impact of Marketing Strategy (PIMS) database, Thorelli and Burnett (1981) developed and tested a set of hypotheses that concerned the existence and the nature of the PLC for industrial goods businesses. Their results indicate that PLC behavior is clearly evident in industrial goods markets.

Dhalla and Yuspeh (1976) have challenged the existence of the PLC concept by giving various examples. According to these authors, the PLC concept has little validity and has done more harm than good by persuading top executives to neglect existing brands and place undue emphasis on new products. However, as indicated earlier, Rink and Swan's (1979) review of the literature on the PLC concept rejects the suggestions made by Dhalla and Yuspeh. Most researchers accept that four distinct PLC stages Cox 1967; introduction, rapid growth in sales, maturity, and decline exist for most products (see Buzzell 1966; Hinkle 1966; Patton 1959) With these in mind, the relationship between the PLC and barriers to entry are discussed for four stages of the PLC.

MARKET INTRODUCTION STAGE AND BARRIERS TO ENTRY

The introduction stage of the PLC starts when a new product is introduced into a market. Therefore, there is usually a single firm in the market until competitors follow with the same or similar products. Often times, the pioneers or the early entrants enjoy monopolies in their markets mostly because they hold a patent or because the product is innovative. Also, firms not in the market are reluctant to decide on entry in the introduction stage because they are not certain of the demand for a new product introduced by their competitor. Demand for some products does not increase in a short period of time. It usually takes a considerable amount of informative advertising and customers persuasion. For example, it took a long time for consumers to accept instant coffee. In one study, Haire (1950) found that housewives were reluctant to purchase instant coffee because they associated brewing coffee with being good housewives.

Although some of the market entry barriers do not exist during the introduction stage of the PLC, others are quite high. Thus, many firms hesitate to enter markets. In different stages of the PLC, consumers make purchasing decisions differently. Depending of the life cycle stage, they face extensive, limited, or and routine problem-solving situations. In most cases, consumers do extensive problem solving in the introduction stage of the PLC. This condition contributes to market entry barriers' height because consumers resist trying new products without careful thinking.

Depending on the product type, the monopoly secured in the market introduction stage can last throughout the growth stage of the PLCO. However, as products move toward the end of the growth or maturity stage, barriers to market entry usually get lower (Yip 1982a) and other firms with improved products enter the market. Again, depending on the type of product and the strength of the potential competitors, the pioneers charge high or low prices. Figure 4.2 shows two pricing strategies. Pioneer or early follower firms sometimes follow a short-run pricing strategy in which they attempt to maximize profits by charging high prices, although, the marginal cost of production declines with increased production. Another reason for using this pricing strategy is the desire for the pioneers or early followers to recover their sunk costs. This pricing strategy is shown as period A in the left part of Figure 4.2. If such strategy is employed for long, competitors are likely to enter the market because they perceive such market as profitable. This may result in a steep price decline. Such a pattern is shown in period B in the left part of Figure 4.2. As a result of increased competition, profit margins remain thin in period C.

Pioneer or early entrant firms may choose a barrier pricing strategy in which the firms aggressively lower prices as costs decline with increased cumulative volume. By charging low prices, pioneers or early followers try to create a barrier that is difficult to overcome. By using this strategy, firms may have low profit margins in the short run, but the long-term profits tend to be stable. Such a strategy is demonstrated in the right half of Figure 4.2. Potential entrants must not only be ready to match the prices of incumbents, but also understand the strategy employed by them. Thus, forecasting demand and cost of production using the experience curve effect becomes increasingly important.

Figure 4.2
Two Pricing Strategies and Learning

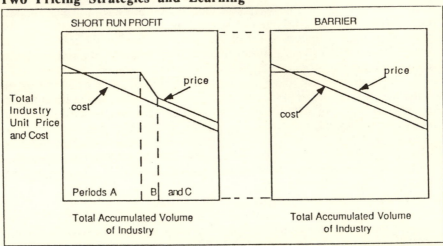

In the introduction stage, another barrier that is extremely important barrier is the access to distribution channels barrier because middlemen are often afraid to take chances with new products. Many middlemen wait until a new product proves itself or require the manufacturer to pay a fee to carry the new product. For example, some supermarkets charge as much as $15,000 to $20,000 to place a new product on their shelves for a month. The following barriers are usually important in deterring new competition from entering markets:

- incumbents' superior production processes
- customer switching costs
- access to distribution channels
- research and development
- price
- trade secrets held by competitors
- selling expenses;
- incumbents, proprietary product technology
- capital requirements to enter markets
- capital intensity of the market
- government licensing requirements
- incumbents' government subsidies
- number of competitors
- technology and technological change
- sunk costs
- incumbents' expected reaction to market entry
- incumbents' relatively easy access to raw materials
- possession of strategic raw materials

Although all of the barriers listed above are important in the introduction stage, some of them are more important than others. The more important barriers usually deal with the financial loss if the entering firm is not successful and the ability of the entering firm to match the quality of incumbents' products. For example, the sunk costs, capital requirements, and high promotional expenditures required to enter markets are usually more important in the introduction stage because of the uncertainty of demand for the entering firm's product. In addition, possession of strategic raw materials, proprietary product technology, trade secrets held by competitors, government licensing requirements, and government subsidies are barriers that firms cannot overcome easily, even if they have the financial resources.

The advantages and disadvantages of early market entry were described in Chapter 2. The major benefits of entering a market at this stage include higher market share, brand awareness, and lower cost due to economies of scale. These conditions also occur when entering international markets. For example, Ryans (1987) has found that the captured firms that entered early in the product life cycle in Japan captured a larger market share.

MARKET GROWTH STAGE AND BARRIERS TO ENTRY

The market growth stage is characterized by a rapid increase in sales and entry of new competition into the market. In the growth stage, most of the barriers that exist during the introduction stage still remain high. However, some of the uncertainties, such as product performance and demand for a product, usually diminish. Depending on the type of industry, most companies attempt to enter markets at this stage to get their own shares of the pie, characterized by Buzzel and Gale (1987) as the phenomenon of "jumping on the bandwagon". Market entry for these firms usually takes place toward the end of the growth stage. Thus, the competitors and their activities to create barriers to entry are noticeable. Therefore, the cost advantages of incumbents become especially important at this stage because they are likely to deter competition and work as a competitive weapon once the new entrants find their way into the market. The price charged during the introduction stage also remains the same, but costs decrease due to experience curve effects and economies of scale. Toward the end of this stage, some newcomers avoid barriers by segmenting markets and entering markets that have been selected carefully. Of course, this usually requires product modification or the use of a promotional campaign than differs from those of the incumbent firms or sometimes both. The following barriers are especially important in this stage:

- incumbents' cost advantages due to economies of scale
- incumbents' cost advantages due to experience or learning curves
- incumbents' with absolute cost advantages
- incumbents' with superior production processes

● customer switching costs
● research and development
● price
● trade secrets held by competitors
● selling expenses
● incumbents with proprietary product technology
● capital requirements to enter markets
● capital intensity of the market
● technology and technological change
● high profit rates earned by incumbents
● sunk costs
● incumbents' expected reaction to market entry
● incumbents with relatively easy access to raw materials
● possession of strategic raw materials

The length of the growth stage depends on the type of product. While it can be very long for some products, it is very short for others. Buzzell (1966) has found that the length of time from growth to maturity is rather long. For example, for instant coffee and frozen orange juice, the time span was about 12 years. Similarly, Buzzel reports that this stage for breakfast cereals, dessert mixes, and peanut butter could be longer.

MARKET MATURITY STAGE AND BARRIERS TO ENTRY

Sales reach a peak in the maturity stage while profits start to decline due to increased expenditures in promotional activities. In this is stage, the market is saturated and the competition is almost always intense. As Figure 4.1 showed, this stage also tends to last longer than any other PLC stage.   Some firms introduce different versions of essentially the same products. In fact, some claim to introduce new and improved products. Often what is improved is the package and what is new is an accessory to the product. However, many firms do indeed find ways of introducing new values for customers, as shown by Japanese firms that compete in such mature markets such as autos, motorcycles, televisions, watches, and cameras (Kotler 1988).

In this stage of the PLC, cost-related barriers become extremely important in deterring market entry as well as in competing with the firms already in the market.   Thus, in the maturity stage, building production capacity in anticipation of demand has been a particularly effective method of creating market entry barriers. Antitrust courts have noted this phenomenon since the decisions of 1947 (Harrigan 1981). In fact, mature markets are usually less concentrated as the larger firms lose market shares because they cannot sustain their original cost advantages. Firms attempt to differentiate their products, but price wars are also common for some products. Furthermore, firms do not have much choice when selecting a pricing strategy because failure to reduce prices usually leads to a significant loss of market share to competitors. In particular, the following barriers gain momentum in the maturity stage:

- incumbents' cost advantages due to economies of scale
- incumbents' cost advantages due to experience or learning curves
- incumbents' absolute cost advantages
- product differentiation and customer loyalty
- customer switching costs
- access to distribution channels
- heavy advertising by incumbent firms
- price
- selling expenses
- capital requirements to enter markets
- capital intensity of the market
- number of competitors
- seller concentration and the magnitude of market shares held by incumbent
- sunk costs
- incumbents' expected reaction to market entry

One should note that, in addition to the cost-related barriers, other barriers such as product differentiation, customer loyalty, customer switching costs, access to distribution channels, incumbents' expected reaction to market entry, and number of competitors become rather important in the maturity stage of the PLC.

Although barriers are usually high in this stage, entering a market early at this stage can pay off if appropriate marketing strategies are employed. If a firm decides to enter a market at the maturity stage, there are three marketing strategy alternatives can work: segmenting the markets, entering the market with an improved product, and identifying new uses for a product.

The first strategy requires market segmentation studies before entering the market.   Through market segmentation studies, it is possible to identify unserved markets or markets that require slightly different products. This relates to Porter's (1980, 1985) business-level strategy of focus. By using this strategy, new market entrants need not compete head on with the incumbent firms. The second strategy is somewhat related to the first, but new entrants usually face competition from incumbent firms once they have entered the market. The reason is that incumbents also introduce improved versions of their products during this stage. Thus, the competition can get fiery. The third strategy, identifying new uses for a product, also requires market research and includes competing with the incumbent firms. Once a new entrant enters a market, targeting its product for a specific market (i.e., nonusers), the incumbent firms will soon modify their marketing strategies to include this new market. One example is the recent change in Jockey International's marketing strategy. For many years, Jockey underwear had been targeted for men, but the company recently added women customers to its market by successfully marketing women's' underwear.

SALES DECLINE STAGE AND BARRIERS TO ENTRY

In the sales decline stage, new firms are not expected to markets. Rather, some firms drop out, introduce new or improved products to the same markets, or do nothing. Thus, during the decline stage, the competitor-activated barriers to entry are nonexistent or very weak. Some of the advantages held by market pioneers slowly deteriorate over time. Advantages based on product quality, product line breadth, price and absolute cost, distribution, advertising, and consumer information are areas for potential deterioration (Robinson and Fornell 1985). Thus, these barriers are especially weak in the decline stage. The decline stage for some products may last for a long time. In addition, a sales decline is sometimes followed by a resurgence in sales (Hinkle 1966). As in the maturity stage, this resurgence of sales is due usually to improvements made to renew an old product and sometimes to low prices designed to attract nonusers.

Only a few firms try to take advantage of the low barriers to entry in the sales decline stage and enter the market with the same or slightly improved products. One should note, however, that many of the barriers may still be high, regardless of the stage of the PLC.

PRODUCT LIFE CYCLE THEORY AND MARKETING STRATEGY

Several researchers have suggested that the PLC theory should be used for strategic planning (Hofer 1975; Polli and Cook 1969; Wasson 1978). Wasson suggests that firms should focus on minimizing learning requirements in manufacturing, reducing defects, increasing publicity, and offering trade discounts in the introduction stage. During the growth stage, Wasson (1978) proposes that firms should attempt to build strong brand names and distribution channels and to segment markets, using price as a segmentation criterion. The objective during the maturity stage should be to maintain market share through product improvements, efficiency in production, and customer relations. However, in the decline stage, harvesting by way of using a profitable pricing strategy is recommended. In fact, most marketing strategy texts and articles on the PLC concept suggest reducing promotional expenditures and charging lower prices to diminish the inventory in the decline stage.

PRODUCT LIFE CYCLE AND THE RELATIVE IMPORTANCE OF SIX MAJOR BARRIERS

The study of the PLC concept by itself does not provide insights into understanding the competitive behavior of firms. Since the importance of barriers differs in different stages of the PLC, the study of barriers in different stages of the PLC should provide information on firms' competitive activities. Having this in mind, differences in the importance of barriers among firms at different stages of the PLC were examined in a study of 137 marketing executives. This investigation was performed from two perspectives: (1) how the life cycle stage of a firm's principal product or product line influences the importance of market entry barriers in deciding to enter consumer and industrial goods markets, and (2) how the life cycle stage of an industry's major products influences the importance of market entry barriers in deciding to enter consumer and industrial goods markets.

The same market entry simulation exercise mentioned in earlier chapters was utilized to test the importance of barriers in different stages of the PLC. The following six market entry barriers were tested: cost advantages, product differentiation, capital requirements, customer switching costs, access to distribution channels, and government policy (Porter 1980). The executives made market entry decisions based on these six market entry barriers. The executives were asked to indicate the life cycle stage of their principal product or product line and of their industry.

Approximately 96 percent of the respondents revealed that their products were in the growth or the maturity stage (i.e., n = 43 for the growth stage and n = 85 for the maturity stage). Therefore, only the responses for growth and maturity stages were compared (using t-tests).

Influence of the Product's Life Cycle Stage on the Importance of Barriers

The relative weights associated with market entry barriers to early and late entry into consumer and industrial markets were compared for firms in the growth and the maturity stages of the product life cycle. The relative weights were mathematically transformed in such a way that the barriers could be compared because they add up to 100 points or 100 percent. The results are presented in Tables 4.1 through 4.4. The average relative weights for only two of the barriers cost advantages and customer switching costs (Table 4.1) differ significantly for the growth and the maturity stages of the PLC, based on statistical tests. Executives perceive the cost advantages barrier as more difficult to overcome in the market maturity stage than in the growth stage (average relative weight of 21.7 versus 17.3). However, the customer switching costs barrier is perceived to be more important in the growth stage of the PLC than in the maturity stage (average relative weight of 16.2 versus 12.0).

Table 4.1
Comparison of Barriers between Firms in Growth and
Maturity Stages for Early Entry into Consumer Markets

BARRIERS	MEAN RELATIVE WEIGHT (GROWTH STAGE)	MEAN RELATIVE WEIGHTS (MATURITY STAGE)
Cost Advantages	17.3	21.7*
Product Differentiation	20.2	19.7
Capital Requirements	18.6	21.7
Customer Switching Costs	16.2	12.0*
Access to Distribution Channels	13.4	14.3
Government Policy	14.2	11.1
TOTAL	100	100

*indicates difference (using two-tail t-test)
n=43 for growth stage
n=85 for maturity stage

Table 4.2 shows the importance of barriers for firms in the growth and the maturity stages when deciding to make a late entry into consumer markets. Two barriers, capital requirements and customer switching costs, differ significantly (using t-tests). The capital requirements barrier is perceived to be more important for firms in the maturity stage than for those in the growth stage (average relative weight of 21.8 versus 16.9), while the customer switching costs barrier is more important for firms in the growth stage of PLC than for those in the maturity stage (average relative weight of 17.5 versus 13.4).

For early-entry decisions into industrial markets, only a single barrier, the cost advantages of incumbents, is significantly different for firms in the growth and the maturity stages (Table 4.3). The cost advantages of incumbents barrier is perceived to be more important for firms in the maturity stage of the product life cycle than for those in the growth stage (average relative weight of 26.2 versus 19.1).

Examination of the differences between firms in the growth stage and those in the maturity stage in terms of the importance of barriers to entry in industrial markets revealed that two barriers differ significantly (Table 4.4). Specifically, the cost advantages barrier appears to be more important for firms in the maturity stage than for those in the growth stage (average relative weight of 26.6 versus 19.2). Similarly, the customer switching costs barrier is more critical for firms in the growth stage of product life cycle than for those in the maturity stage (relative weight of 20.6 versus 15.5).

Table 4.2
Comparison of Barriers Between Firms in Growth and Maturity Stages for Late Entry into Consumer Markets

BARRIERS	MEAN RELATIVE WEIGHT (GROWTH STAGE)	MEAN RELATIVE WEIGHTS (MATURITY STAGE)
Cost Advantages	21.0	22.3
Product Differentiation	17.2	20.7
Capital Requirements	16.9	21.8*
Customer Switching Costs	17.5	13.4*
Access to Distribution Channels	14.5	12.0
Government Policy	12.5	10.7
TOTAL	100	100

*indicates difference (using two-tail t-test)
n=43 for growth stage
n=85 for maturity stage

Table 4.3
Comparison of Barriers between Firms in Growth and Maturity Stages for Early Entry into Industrial Markets

BARRIERS	MEAN RELATIVE WEIGHT (GROWTH STAGE)	MEAN RELATIVE WEIGHTS (MATURITY STAGE)
Cost Advantages	19.1	26.2*
Product Differentiation	18.5	15.6
Capital Requirements	17.1	21.1
Customer Switching Costs	17.3	14.3
Access to Distribution Channels	12.5	12.1
Government Policy	15.7	11.5
TOTAL	100	100

*indicates difference (using two-tail t-test)
n=43 for growth stage
n=85 for maturity stage

Table 4.4
Comparison of Barriers between Firms in Growth and
Maturity Stages for Late Entry into Industrial Markets

BARRIERS	MEAN RELATIVE WEIGHT (GROWTH STAGE)	MEAN RELATIVE WEIGHTS (MATURITY STAGE)
Cost Advantages	19.2	26.6*
Product Differentiation	18.7	15.0
Capital Requirements	16.6	20.2
Customer Switching Costs	20.6*	15.5
Access to Distribution Channels	12.1	11.9
Government Policy	13.3	11.1
TOTAL	100	100

*indicates difference (using two-tail t-test)
n=43 for growth stage
n=85 for maturity stage

Influence of the Industry's Stage of Life Cycle on the Importance of Barriers

The influence of an industry's life cycle stage on the importance of barriers was tested in the same way. For the early entry into consumer markets decision, the product differentiation barrier was perceived to be more important for the firms in industries with most products in the maturity stage than for the firms industries with most products in the growth stage (average relative weight of 21.4 versus 16.2) (Table 4.5).

For late entry into consumer markets, the importance of four barriers differs significantly (Table 4.6). The cost advantages and product differentiation barriers are more important in the maturity stage than in the growth stage (average relative weights of 23.9 versus 18.4 and 21.3 versus 14.9, respectively). However, customer switching costs and access to distribution channels are perceived to be more important for firms in an industry whose life cycle is in the growth stage (average relative weights of 18.9 versus 13.1 and 16.0 versus 11.3, respectively).

Comparison of the barriers for early entry into industrial markets showed that only the cost advantages barrier is more important in the maturity stage than the growth stage (average relative weight of 26.6 versus 17.3). As Table 4.7 shows, the other barriers do not differ significantly.

Table 4.5
Comparison of Barriers for Firms in Industries with
Most Products in Growth and Maturity Stages for
Early Entry into Consumer Markets

BARRIERS	MEAN RELATIVE WEIGHT (GROWTH STAGE)	MEAN RELATIVE WEIGHTS (MATURITY STAGE)
Cost Advantages	18.9	21.4
Product Differentiation	16.2	21.4*
Capital Requirements	19.1	21.2
Customer Switching Costs	15.7*	12.5
Access to Distribution Channels	15.5	13.2
Government Policy	14.5	11.0
TOTAL	100	100

*indicates difference   n=37   n=92
(using two-tail t-test)

Table 4.6
Comparison of Barriers for Firms in Industries with
Most Products in Growth and Maturity Stages for
Late Entry into Consumer Markets

BARRIERS	MEAN RELATIVE WEIGHT (GROWTH STAGE)	MEAN RELATIVE WEIGHTS (MATURITY STAGE)
Cost Advantages	18.4	23.9*
Product Differentiation	14.9	21.3*
Capital Requirements	18.5	20.9
Customer Switching Costs	18.9*	13.1
Access to Distribution Channels	16.0*	11.3
Government Policy	12.9	10.3
TOTAL	100	100

*indicates difference (using two-tail t-test)
n=37 for growth stage
n=92 for maturity stage

Table 4.7
Comparison of Barriers for Firms in Industries with
Most Products in Growth and Maturity Stages for
Early Entry into Industrial Markets

BARRIERS	MEAN RELATIVE WEIGHT (GROWTH STAGE)	MEAN RELATIVE WEIGHTS (MATURITY STAGE)
Cost Advantages	17.3	26.6*
Product Differentiation	18.4	16.4
Capital Requirements	18.3	20.4
Customer Switching Costs	17.3	14.3
Access to Distribution Channels	12.3	12.1
Government Policy	15.8	11.2
TOTAL	100	100

*indicates difference (using two-tail t-test)
n=337 for growth stage
n=91 for maturity stage

Table 4.8
Comparison of Barriers for Firms in Industries with
Most Products in Growth and Maturity Stages for
Late Entry into Industrial Markets

BARRIERS	MEAN RELATIVE WEIGHT (GROWTH STAGE)	MEAN RELATIVE WEIGHTS (MATURITY STAGE)
Cost Advantages	15.1	28.0*
Product Differentiation	19.0	15.5
Capital Requirements	17.9	19.5
Customer Switching Costs	22.1*	15.2
Access to Distribution Channels	12.6	11.7
Government Policy	14.0	10.4
TOTAL	100	100

*indicates difference (using two-tail t-test)
n=37 for growth stage
n=91 for maturity stage

For late entry into industrial markets, the importance of the cost advantages and customer switching costs barriers differs significantly (Table 4.8). The cost advantages barrier is perceived to be more important for the firms in an industry whose life cycle is in the maturity stage (average relative weight of 28.0 versus 15.1) . The opposite is true for the customer switching costs (average relative weight of 22.1 versus 15.2).

Although the importance of only a few barriers differs for firms in the growth and the maturity stages of the PLC, these differences are important. The differences vary depending on early or late market entry into consumer and industrial markets. For firms with principal products or product lines in the maturity stage of the PLC, the cost advantages barrier is perceived as being more important for early and late entry into industrial markets and for early entry into consumer markets. Therefore, cost advantages are more important for firms in the maturity stage of the PLC than the firms in the growth stage. This finding supports the suggestion made earlier that cost advantages become an extremely important competitive weapon in the maturity stage. Similarly, the capital requirements barrier is more important for firms in the maturity stage when making late entry into consumer markets. Interestingly, the customer switching costs barrier is perceived to be more important for firms in the growth stage, with the exception of early entry decisions into industrial markets where the PLC did not have any influence.

An industry's life cycle stage also has an impact on market entry decision makers. This influence exists for the cost advantages and product differentiation barriers in the market maturity stage. Cost advantages appear to be more important for late entry into consumer markets and for early and late entry into industrial markets. However, the industry PLC influences the importance of product differentiation only in consumer markets in the maturity stage. Interestingly, the customer switching costs barrier is different only for late entry into both consumer and industrial markets. This barrier is perceived as more important for respondents in the growth stage of the industry PLC. Also, the access to distribution channels barrier is perceived as more important by respondents where the industry PLC is in the growth stage. It is noteworthy that for late entry into consumer markets, four of the six barriers tested vary in importance.

Conclusions of the Study of Six Major Barriers

As noted above, the life cycle stage of both the firm's principal product or product line and the industry's product lines has some influence on how executives perceive barriers. Therefore, a relationship exists between the PLC and the importance of entry barriers as perceived by marketing executives. Considering this relationship when making market entry decisions will prove beneficial. The PLC influence is dominant for the overall cost advantages and customer switching costs barriers in the maturity and the growth stages of PLC. Thus, these two barriers should be investigated thoroughly before any market entry decision is made. Yelle (1980) provides strong support for estimating the cost advantages of a market entrant so that the height of this barrier can be lowered. Yelle suggests that firms estimate their costs using the learning curve concept since the cost per unit of product declines as the output is increased.

OVERALL CONCLUSIONS

Based on the PLC literature and the study conducted, The PLC does influence market entry decisions because the barriers in different stages take different shapes and reach different heights. Although the barriers activated by competitors are almost nonexistent in the introduction stage of the PLC, many other important barriers, such as demand uncertainty, technical production capability, sunk costs associated with market entry, and capital requirements, do influence firms' decisions to enter markets. Most of the barriers present in the introduction stage continue to exist in the growth stage, but the competitor-activated barriers gain importance toward the end of this stage. However, firms must enter the market in this stage if they expect to gain substantial market shares and compete effectively because a firm that enters after this stage usually is a follower and often termed a "me too" entry.

Occasionally, firms can create a competitive niche, even in the maturity stage, if they follow marketing strategies appropriate for the maturity stage. In fact, many small companies enter the market in this stage and become quite successful, but their success is often due to having some type of competitive niche. Since competition is very intense in the maturity stage, cost cutting becomes very important in order to compete effectively and attract customers that are cost conscious. Therefore, the cost advantages barrier is the most important in this stage. For some products, especially mass-marketed consumer products, access to distribution channels also becomes extremely important because middle-men require incentives to carry new entrants' products.

In the decline stage, only a few firms, if any, enter the market because demand is very low and customers are likely to buy the well-known brands that have proved themselves. Therefore, while it really does not make sense to enter a market at this stage, some firms do enter markets with improved products and become somewhat successful.

REFERENCES

Anderson, Carl R., and Carl P. Zeithaml. 1984. "Stage of the Product Life Cycle, Business Strategy, and Business Performance." *Academy of Management Journal* 27 (1) 5-24 (March).

Bass, Frank, 1969. "A New Product Growth Model for Consumer Durables." *Management Science* 15 (January): 215-27.

Buzzell, Robert. 1966. "Competitive Behavior and Product Life Cycles." In *New Ideas for Successful Marketing*, ed. J. Wright and J. Goldstucker. Chicago: American Marketing Association.

_____. 1981. "Are There 'Natural' Market Structures?" *Journal of Marketing* 45 (Winter): 42-51.

Buzzell, Robert, and Bradley T. Gale. 1987. *The PIMS Principles: Linking Strategy to Performance*. New York: Free Press.

Camillus, John C. 1984. "Technology-Driven and Market-Driven Life Cycles: Implications for Multinational Corporate Strategy." *Columbia Journal of World Business* 19 (Summer): 56-60.

Cox, William, Jr. 1967. "Product Life Cycles and Marketing Models." *Journal of Business* 40 (October): 375-84.

Crawford, C. Merle. 1966. "The Trajectory Theory of Goal Setting for New Products." *Journal of Marketing Research* 3 (May): 117-26.

Day, George S. 1977. "Diagnosing the Product Portfolio." *Journal of Marketing* 41 (April): 29-38.

Dean, Joel. 1950. "Pricing Policies for New Products." *Harvard Business Review* 28 (November-December): 45-53.

Dhalla, Nariman, and Sonia Yuspeh. 1976. "Forget the Product Life Cycle Concept." *Harvard Business Review* 54 (January-February): 102-11.

Haire, Mason. 1950. "Projective Techniques in Marketing Research." *Journal of Marketing* 14 (April): 649-56.

Hambrick, Donald C., Ian C. MacMillan, and Diana L. Day. 1982a. "Strategic Attributes and Performance on the BCG Matrix-A PIMS Based Analysis of Industrial Product Businesses." *Academy of Management Journal* 25 (September): 510-31.

_____. 1982b. "The Product Portfolio and Profitability - A PIMS Based Analysis of Industrial Product Businesses." *Academy of Management Journal* 25 (December): 733-55.

Harrigan, Kathryn Rudie. 1981. "Barriers to Entry and Competitive Strategies."*Strategic Management Journal* 2 (4): 395-412.

Henderson, Bruce D. 1984. *Henderson on Corporate Strategy*. Cambridge, Mass.: Abt Books.

Hinkle, Joel. 1966. *Life Cycles*, New York: Nielsen

Hofer, Charles W. 1975. "Toward a Contingency Theory of Business Strategy."*Academy of Management Journal* 18 (4): 784-809.

Karakaya, Fahri, and Michael J. Stahl. 1989. "Barriers to Entry and Market Entry Decisions in Consumer and Industrial Goods Markets." *Journal of Marketing* 53 (April): 80-91.

King, William. 1966. "Early Prediction of New Product Success." *Journal of Advertising Research* 6 (June): 3-13.

Kotler, Philip. 1988. *Marketing Management*. 6th ed. Englewood Cliffs, N.J.: Prentice-Hall

Mann, Michael H. 1966. "Seller Concentration, Barriers to Entry and Rates of Return in Thirty Industries, 1950-1960." *Review of Economics and Statistics* 48 (August): 296-307.

Patton, Arch. 1959. "Stretch Your Product's Earning Years: Top Management's Stake in the Product Life Cycle Management." *Management Review* 48 (June): 9-14, 67-79.

Polli, Rolando, and Victor Cook. 1969. "Validity of the Product Life Cycle." *Journal of Business* 42 (October): 385-400.

Porter, Michael. 1980. *Competitive Strategy: Techniques for Analyzing Industries and Competitors*. New York: Free Press.

_____. 1985. *Competitive Advantage*. New York: Free Press

Rink, David R, and John E. Swan. 1979. "Uncertain Innovation and the Persistence of Monopoly." *Journal of Business Research* 73 (September): 219-242.

Robinson, William T, and Cleas Fornell. 1985. "Sources of Market Pioneering Advantages in Consumer Goods Industries." *Journal of Marketing Research* 22 August: 305-17.

Ryans, Adrian B. 1987. *"Entry Marketing Strategies and Market Share Achievement in Japan."* Working Paper Series No. 86-42. London, Ontario: University of Western Ontario.

Shepherd, W. G. 1979. *The Economics of Industrial Organization*. Englewood Cliffs, N.J.: Prentice-Hall.

Shoemaker, Robert W. 1986. "Comment on Dynamics of Price Elasticity and Brand Life Cycles: An Empirical Study." *Journal of Marketing Research* 23 (February): 78-82.

Simon, Herman. 1979. "Dynamics of Price Elasticity and Brand Life Cycles: An Empirical Study." *Journal of Marketing Research* 16 (November): 439-52.

Slovic, P., and S. Lichtenstein. 1971. "Comparison of Bayesian and Regression Approaches to the Study of Information Processing in Judgement." *Organizational Behavior and Human Performance* 6 (4): 649-744.

Slovic, P., B. Fischhoff, and S. Lichtenstein. 1977. "Behavioral Decision Theory." *Annual Review of Psychology* 28 (1): 1-39.

Stahl, Michael J., and A. M. Harrell. 1981. "Modeling Effort Decisions with Behavioral Decision Theory: Toward an Individual Differences Version of Expectancy Theory." *Organizational Behavior and Human Performance* 27: 303-25.

Stahl, Michael J., and A. M. Harrell. 1982. "Evolution and Validation of a Behavioral Decision Theory Measurement Approach to Achievement, Power and Affiliation." *Journal of Applied Psychology* 67 (December): 744-50.

Stahl, Michael J., and Thomas W. Zimmerer. 1984. "Modeling Strategic Acquisition Policies: A Simulation of Executives' Acquisition Decisions." *Academy of Management Journal* 27 (June): 369-83.

Thorelli, Hans B., and Stephen C. Burnett. 1981. "The Nature of Product Life Cycles for Industrial Goods Businesses." *Journal of Marketing* 45 (Fall): 97-108.

Thietart, R. A., and R. Vivas. 1984. "An Empirical Investigation of Success Strategies for Businesses Along the Product Life Cycle." *Management Science* 30 (December): 1405-23.

Urban, Glen. 1968. "A New Product Analysis and Decision Model." *Management Science* 14 (April): 490-517.

Wasson, Chester R. 1978. *Dynamic Competitive Strategy and Product Life Cycles.* St. Charles, Ill.: Challenge Books.

Wilson, Aubrey. 1969. "Industrial Marketing Research in Britain." *Journal of Marketing Research* 6 (February): 15-28.

Yelle, Louis E. 1980. "Industrial Life Cycles and Learning Curves: Interaction of Marketing and Production." *Industrial Marketing Management* 9: 311-18.

Yip, G. S. 1982a. "Gateways to Entry." *Harvard Business Review* 60 (September-October): 85-92.

_____. 1982b. *Barriers to Entry: A Corporate Strategy Perspective.* Lexington, Mass.: D. C. Heath.

Chapter 5

Barriers to Market Exit
and Market Exit Decisions

DYNAMICS OF MARKET DECLINE

Over the past couple of decades, U.S. firms have faced increasing foreign competition. For many, increased competition has brought the problem of decreasing demand for their products. However, foreign competition is certainly not the sole reason for declining demand. It can also be caused by technological obsolescence, better advertising by competitors, and poorer quality, to name a few other reasons. Decline, according to the product life cycle theory, is an inevitable stage in the life of a product. Declining sales can be dealt with in a variety of different ways, depending on the cause of decline, market conditions, the response of the competitors, and the financial position of the firm facing the decline. "Turnaround" strategies may be followed, investing more resources to capture a larger market share of whatever demand is left. A retrenchment strategy may also be pursued, reducing cost in order to improve the firm's competitive position. A harvesting strategy, in which the business is milked for what it is worth, with no additional investment, can be followed. Finally, divestiture of the business unit is also an alternative. The strategy to be followed depends on the various factors mentioned above. For instance, if the industry as a whole is declining due to new technology, a firm would not attempt a revitalization strategy, but would be inclined to exit the business rapidly. On the other hand, if the decline in sales is due to the lack of competitive strength, an attempt can be made to rebuild that strength or exit slowly. Thus, it is critical to know the reasons for the decline. Competitor response is also important. If most competitors leave the market early, a firm may stay on longer and make profits, even in a declining industry (Harrigan 1980; Lambert 1985).

The last decade has seen a wave of restructuring in corporate America, especially due to increased global competition. The emphasis seems to have shifted from growing for growing's sake to having a more focused strategy and being streamlined and efficient (Lynch 1980). The restructuring of corporations has been an effort to concentrate on related businesses. This means that firms that diversified into several fields have to redefine their goals and divest those businesses that are unrelated to their core of businesses. Divestiture is thus seen more as a necessary corporate strategy than an embarrassment to the executives (Christoph 1985). Unlike diversification, not enough attention has been paid to the divestment decision-making process. How is a divestment decision made? What alternatives are considered?

Divestiture is a tough decision to make. Several factors deter the divestment of a failing business unit. Porter (1976) discusses three major types of barriers - namely, economic, strategic, and managerial barriers. Economic barriers refer to the costs associated with selling a business as a unit that will be run by someone else or with dismantling a business and then selling the pieces. In either case, a buyer is essential, and the selling price may be less than the book value of the assets. Technological change can decrease the number of potential buyers since a business unit with the old technology would be less efficient to operate. The capital intensity of a unit also raises a barrier. In a capital-intensive business, management may be reluctant to divest due to the sunk costs. Strategic barriers are also created by the strategic posture of the firm. For instance, a firm following a single business strategy would cease to exist if divested. A less extreme case is that of a relatedly diversified firm, which would face a barrier to divesting a business that shares resources with other businesses in the firm. The economies created due to sharing are lost if the business is divested. In addition, personal barriers are a potent force. Managers may perceive severe damage to their image of competence if their business is divested. This may translate into losing their jobs or having to take a reduction in pay.

Which of these factors do decision makers really take into account while making the exit decision? What is the relative importance of the factors that are considered? How do these differ across industries? Some researchers have attempted to answer some of these questions, notably Porter (1976) and Harrigan (1980; 1985). However, the studies conducted so far have relied on some combination of historical databases and interviews. Historical databases restrict the scope of the research simply because all the relevant data are usually not available. A researcher is often forced to use improper operationalization of constructs. Using interviews and traditional questionnaires, on the other hand, is known to create potential biases in the data (Arnold and Feldman 1981; Hyman 1954; Stahl 1986, 1989; Stahl and Harrell 1982). The research to date has not been able to satisfactorily include enough of the relevant factors that deter exit, especially the personal barriers. Clearly, a study using a different methodology is called for.

With the above questions in mind, a study was conducted to identify the determinants of divestiture behavior from the literature and find their relative importance to decision makers, using a market exit simulation exercise. The most important factors that potentially deter exit were identified from the literature. These were then used at different levels to simulate several divestiture candidates with different degrees of exit barriers. This decision-modeling exercise was mailed to executives, and their responses were used to test the hypothesized relationships of the exit decisions to the variables representing the barriers to exit.

Causes of Divestiture or Exit from a Market

Most products do face a decline in demand somewhere in their lifetime. The principal causes for decline mentioned in the PLC literature (Wasson 1978) are discussed below. First, a distinction must be made between decline of the industry as a whole and decline in sales for a particular firm. The following three reasons apply to decline in the industry:

1. *Obsolete technology*: This causes the product or service to be inferior in quality and the cost of production is usually higher than if thelatest technology were used. The decline in demand here is thus not for the entire product class itself, but for specific products produced by inferior methods.

2. *Changing consumer tastes*: Changing cultural values or fashions reduce demand for products, a phenomenon most evident in clothing.   Once again, demand for certain types of clothing can diminish, but hardly for clothing itself.

3. *Lack of need*: Conditions may change in some way to make a product unnecessary. For example, a smallpox vaccine would be unnecessary in a country where smallpox has been eradicated. Also, the creation of perfect substitutes due to a change in technology that makes the substitutes cheaper or better can cause a lack of   need for a product. The lack of demand is thus for the product itself, regardless of the competitive strengths of the firms producing it.

Decline can occur at the firm level, too. The major cause of this is the loss of competitive strength of the firm.

1. *Competition*: Vigorous competition can reduce demand for a firm's product. Competitors can, through aggressive marketing or underpricing, capture a large market share. This idea has been   proposed by several researchers. Better advertising by competitors not only reduces the demand for less aggressive firms, but also forms an effective entry and mobility barrier (Demetz 1982; Harrigan 1981b; Spence 1980). Here, again, the decline is due not to an overall decrease in demand for the product, but to a decrease in demand for the product of certain firms.

2. *Consumer tastes*: Fashions can sometimes affect the demand for the product of a specific firm instead of the entire industry. Some firms may not be able to respond appropriately to changing fashions,   causing a decline in sales for those firms alone. Perhaps the best-known example of failure to respond to changing consumer taste was the failure of Ford Motor Company to manufacture different models   of cars when the popularity of the Model T was waning.

Other causes that are not based on the PLC or any other theory can be found that affect the demand for a product. The political and social situations, for instance, are potential factors. A politically induced boycott of a product or set of products obviously shuts off the demand in the region concerned. Political or religious interference, however, can have the reverse effect. The controversy involving Salman Rushdie's novel *The Satanic Verses* served to advertise it and probably contributed to its sales in some countries.

A product that harms humans due to a flaw in production or due to sabotage obviously makes consumers wary of it. The alleged sabotage of Tylenol capsules and the traces of cyanide found in some Chilean grapes are examples of at least a temporary loss of demand.

Knowing the cause of decline can be invaluable in strategy formulation (Levitt 1965). Certain causes indicate a possibility of regaining market share and bouncing back, while others indicate that a quick departure from the business is the best strategy. For strategy formulation, it is important to know if the industry as a whole is declining or if the problem is with the competitive strength of the firm. The projected rate of decline is also an important factor to consider in making such decisions.

STRATEGIC OPTIONS FOR DECLINING BUSINESSES

Harrigan (1980) criticizes the PLC literature for neglecting various factors when suggesting strategies for declining businesses. Generalized strategic alternatives that do not take into account industry differences are of little use to the manager. Instead of the two broad strategies of "revitalize" and "harvest," Harrigan suggests the following five alternatives, to be used appropriately based on the environmental conditions surrounding the declining business:

1. Increase investment to capture market share.
2. Maintain the current level of investment.
3. Reduce investments in certain parts of the business to focus on the others.
4. Harvest, or "milk the cash cow."
5. Exit from the business immediately.

Choosing the right alternative from among the above depends on an analysis of various factors. As mentioned earlier, the perception of the firm about the rate of decline in demand has a great influence on the decision. A firm that forecasts a quick decline in demand would be more eager to exit from the business. Therefore, if another firm takes a more optimistic view, and if it is right, it can increase its market share through acquisition and reap profits through dominance. Good forecasting is thus a definite asset. To increase market share through acquisition, however, the firm's competitive position needs to be strong. That is, the firm must have a well-established name, along with relatively lower investment levels and higher returns than the competitors. Only such a firm can afford the risk of increasing the investment level to capture market share. A firm that does not have a low cost of production cannot gain from increasing its investment level, as the competitors could squeeze their profit margin by starting a price war (Rafferty 1987). To follow the strategy of increasing investment, the firm would have to know, or at least expect, that it will be able to get back what it invests through an increase in the cash flow. Further, should the prediction about the rate of decline of demand be wrong, it must have a market in which to sell its assets. That is, the decline should not be due to a change in technology, where the assets may be useless to anyone else (Harrigan 1980).

If there is a good possibility that a firm may not recover its extra investment, but if it has good brand name recognition and the market is not too price sensitive, the strategy of holding the current investment level is more appropriate. This strategy is really one of waiting for more information. If the rate of decline cannot be forecast with any certainty, the firm must wait until it can follow a definite direction. Thus, this is a defensive strategy a firm follows when it believes it may still be profitable to compete, yet not profitable enough to be aggressive. Harrigan (1980) also notes that such a firm would have to be in a good competitive position, so it can match any price changes or other strategic moves made by its competitors.

Even in an otherwise declining industry, a firm can carve itself niches in the market and hope for continuing demand. This demand may continue because customers in that segment of the market have not switched to new technologies along with the rest of the industry due to, say, a high cost of switching (Harrigan 1982). In such a case, a firm can benefit from continuing to serve such profitable parts of the market, while cutting off investments to the other parts where demand is declining. This is a focus strategy, where certain parts are selectively harvested and the cash flow used in other parts of the business. MacMillan (1982, 53) calls this a strategy of "selectively serving where it best can do so, but with minimum additional resource deployments." To follow this strategy effectively, it is necessary, of course, that the products not be commodity-like. Only a differentiated product or service can hold its own in a declining market and provide the firm with a profitable niche.

When the forecast for demand is pessimistic, it is time for the firm to recover as much of its earlier investments as it can by "milking the cash cow." No new investment is made, and cash flows are inward only. This cash may be used elsewhere for new investments by the firm. This is the "harvest" strategy and is followed when a firm's competitive position is not strong enough to survive a price war. A firm that has a higher ratio of investment level to returns compared to its competitors will not be able to generate enough cash for continuing investment in the event of a downward price spiral.

An unfavorable competitive position combined with unfavorable industry conditions would make it difficult for a firm to stay in business. Unless there are any major barriers to exit, the business should be divested (MacMillan 1982). Unfavorable conditions would include a steep decline in demand due to perfect substitutes, which do not present significant switching costs for customers. Further, commodity-like products with a price-sensitive market would make any strategy other than divestment ineffective if the firm does not have competitive strengths.

Divestiture as a Strategy

For several years divestiture was regarded not as a strategy, but as a helpless response to a failure to compete. This view, however, has changed over the past decade or two, which saw a trend toward leaner businesses that focused their attention on related industries (Lynch 1980). Since Rumelt's (1974) classification of firms according to their diversification strategy, several studies have shown that relatedly diversified firms, especially those in the related-constrained category, are more profitable and less risky.

The decision to divest does not have to be connected with a decline in the industry, but may simply represent a change in the corporate goals concerning the industry in which to compete. A business unit may be far too unrelated to the main operations of the firm, so that the top management does not have sufficient knowledge about its operations, and hence it gets divested (Dubin 1986). Lynch (1980) has noted that many firms are selling off their unrelated acquisitions in order to lift their stock price by improving their image as firms with a clear sense of the direction they are taking in the future.

Size is another possible contributor to the exit decision (Miles and Rosenfeld 1983). A business unit may be too small, and its contribution to the overall profit of the firm may be negligible compared to the effort it requires on the part of management. Thus, it can be more effective to simply sell the unit, which is profitable, since it will generate cash that can be used elsewhere.

Benefits of Divesting

There are at least six benefits to divesting; it

1. may create wealth for the firm (i.e., it may increase the stock price),
2. transfers wealth from the bondholders to the stockholders,
3. reduces financial risk,
4. may obtain more investment,
5. get rid of a firm with an unfavorable labor contract, and
6. may improve public image.

Several studies have focused their attention on the financial impact of divestitures (Alexander et al. 1984; Klein 1986; Miles and Rosenfeld 1983; Rosenfeld 1984; Zaima and Hearth 1985). When a firm voluntarily announces a divestment, it is a reasonable assumption that the decision was reached in order to create wealth for the firm. This assumption by the market about the future increase in the firm's wealth causes the stock price to go up, starting the day of the announcement. Further, the common stock of a subsidiary is usually distributed among the stockholders of the parent firm in a voluntary divestment. This causes part of the collateral of the bondholders to be given away to the stockholders, thus bringing about a transfer of wealth from the bondholders to the stockholders of the firm (Galai and Masulis 1976). In an empirical investigation, Miles and Rosenfeld (1983), have found a statistically significant increase in the stock prices around the date a divestiture is announced. They also have found a positive relationship between the size of the divested business and the increase in the stock price of the firm. Stewart and Glassman (1988) argue that selling unprofitable or unsuitable business units creates value for both the divestor and the acquirer. The divestor receives cash for something of little or no value to itself, while the acquirer gets a unit that is presumably of value to it in the future. The divestor also has the benefit of being rid of the responsibility of running the unit, and the risk associated with it, and can focus its attention on the other businesses.

Feinberg (1988) notes that many small firms sometimes divest the entire firm as a financing strategy. There may be several reasons for such an extreme strategy, argues the author. Public offerings of stock may not be selling, entrepreneurs may not want to borrow in order to grow or they may expect to do better under a larger corporation that could provide more money for research expenses, and so on.

There are other reasons-legal, political, social, and moral-that may persuade a firm to divest businesses. Alexander, Benson, and Kampmeyer (1984) noted that voluntary spinoffs may be made in order to rid a firm of some labor contracts that it does not want or to change its tax status. Hite and Owers (1983) found that while gains were positive in voluntary spinoffs, the returns were negative when firms divested as a response to legal difficulties. Most of the firms studied, however, divested units that were not very large compared to the parent company. A good example of a large firm breaking up due to legal difficulties is the breakup of AT&T over a period of two years. Chen and Merville (1986) have studied the effects of the breakup of AT&T and have found that existing financial theory satisfactorily explains the events connected with the breakup. There was an increased riskiness in the shares of AT&T during the breakup. There was no transfer of wealth from the bondholders to the stockholders because the bondholders regained any potential losses from third parties (the government and the customers).

Social, moral, and political issues also force divestments, as in the case of politically motivated sanctions against certain countries. Social and moral issues are at the heart of disinvestment by U.S. firms in South Africa. Hall (1986) discusses the issue of ethics in investment and divestment and questions the principles and prudence of the divestments in South Africa. Ennis and Parkhill (1986) also discuss the United States' South African policy. American corporate investment in South Africa, they argue, is only a small fraction of the South African economy. Several experts agree that divestment is unlikely to help black South Africans and is therefore an ineffective strategy for achieving the social goals desired. The authors also argue that divestment is expensive to manage and increases the firm's risk of failure to earn the expected rate of return. On the other hand, few people argue with the idea that it is the "right" thing to do from a moral standpoint. Whatever the pros and cons of such divestment activity, there can be no doubt that ethics, morals, and politics can play an important role in corporate divestiture plans.

EXIT BARRIERS

Divestiture can be an appropriate and profitable strategy, but the decision to divest is complicated by the presence of several barriers. Firms often find themselves involved with running businesses that are earning well below the expected rate of return and, thus, they are unable or unwilling to divest them due to these exit barriers. Porter (1976) classifies the barriers into three broad categories: structural or economic, strategic, and managerial. Table 5.1 summarizes Porter's market exit barriers.

Table 5.1
Barriers to Exit

Type of Barriers	Components
Economic Barriers	Asset specificity and durability, capital intensity, sunk costs, severance regulations
Strategic Barriers	Operating and marketing fit, vertical integration (backward and forward), buyer and supplier power
Managerial Barriers	Personal attachment, perceived loss of image and compensation

Economic Barriers

The economic barriers represent the costs associated with divestiture, which can force a firm to operate a business, even when the returns are less than desired (Harrigan 1981a). These include the costs of dismantling a plant and the possibility of not finding a market in which to sell the assets. The extent to which these form a barrier depends on the characteristics of the assets of the business. Porter (1976) considered the following three factors to be determinants of the height of economic exit barriers: (1) durability and specificity of assets, (2) capital investment, and (3) regulations regarding severance.

Porter (1976) argued that if the reason for exiting the business is because a new technology has made the present assets obsolete, then it is hardly likely that competing firms that can use these assets would be interested in them. Thus, the already thin market for business-specific assets becomes almost nonexistent. A possible customer for obsolete equipment may be a firm in another region (a less-developed country) where the technology is not obsolete and may even be better than the technology currently available there. An example is some "long wall" mining equipment sold by Britain to an Indian coal mining company. While becoming obsolete in Britain, it was new to the Indian firm, where the bulk of the mining was done using manual labor. While it may not be impossible to sell obsolete assets, in general, the probability of selling assets to other firms is higher if the reason for exiting is a lack of competitive strength rather than a change in technology.

Capital intensity is another important factor to consider during decline. The more capital intensive the industry is, the more likely it is that a greater volume of sales is necessary to break even with the cost of running the business. This makes it tougher to handle a fluctuation in demand. The huge investment also makes it difficult to divest since it is likely that such a capital intensive business forms a substantial portion of the firm's total sales and income. The bigger the business unit, the greater the exit barrier, because divesting a large part of the firm can alter the firm's structure and goals in a significant manner. In the case of a single-business firm, it may also mean an end to its existence. The decision to divest a large business unit is thus dependent on its effect on the firm, rather than on the cost of solving the internal problems of the business unit (Duhaime and Baird 1987).

The portions of the capital investment that cannot be recovered are called *sunk costs*, and these also create a barrier to exit. Several researchers have studied the effect of sunk costs on entry and exit decisions (Bernheim 1984; Dixit 1980; Kleindorfer and Knieps 1982; Macleod 1987). It has been argued by some researchers (Baumol et al. 1982) that the amount of capital invested by itself does not form a barrier to entry. Rather, entry is deterred by the extent to which the costs are sunk upon entry. Entry and exit barriers are thus closely related in this case. Sunk costs are a barrier to exit, and they form a barrier to entry because firms are less likely to enter a business if it means they cannot leave if necessary. Why do sunk costs deter exit? Economists would argue that sunk costs are irrecoverable and should in no way interfere with the decision making. Holcomb and Evans (1987) have studied the effect of sunk costs on decision making behavior. They argue that contrary to the claims of the economists, sunk costs do affect the decision making of individuals. Common experience is cited to confirm this. For example, a person wanting to sell a possession (say, a painting) is unable to sell it for a long time. This indicates that it is overpriced, but the person refuses to lower the price since he/she had paid more for it and would lose money. From the economist's point of view, the money that he/she paid is already lost and is a sunk cost. It has nothing whatsoever to do with the current market price. However, as the authors found, people do let sunk costs affect their decision making since decision makers, being human, are not completely rational. Thus, a decision maker is less likely to exit from a business if a lot of capital has been sunk into it.

Contracts that protect employees in case of severance can raise a significant economic exit barrier. When a firm becomes aware of a takeover threat, its employees realize that there is a good chance that the acquiring firm may divest some of the businesses of the acquired firm. Employees can expect to get fired. To protect against such an occurrence, the firm may enter into agreements about compensation in the event of termination. This raises the cost of termination of employees and hence is a barrier to exiting from the business.

Strategic Barriers

The most important strategic barrier to divesting a business is its relationship with the other businesses in the firm. If different business units share production facilities or marketing channels, the economies so achieved could be lost when one or more of the business units are divested. Further, one business may build up an image, a reputation for the company, that helps the sales of the other businesses. Divesting such a business, if it shows subnormal earnings, may seem economically justified, but one must take into account the damage that it might do to the sales of the other business units (Porter 1976).

The relatedness of a business unit may also be due to vertical integration, either forward or backward. Harrigan (1985a) studied the effect of vertical integration on exit barriers and concluded that the greater the degree of vertical integration, the greater the exit barriers. A similar argument was made by Porter (1980). When a business unit is the major customer for another unit's product, the latter will be bound to suffer if the downstream business unit is divested. Thus, the degree of internal transfers of resources and products in a vertically integrated firm is directly proportional to the height of exit barriers.

Buyer and supplier power also determines a firm's strength during decline. If the firm is not vertically integrated and a business unit faces decline, it will be in a good competitive position if it is a strong buyer. When the unit represents a large portion of the sales of another firm, then the supplier is in a sense a partner. It is in the best interests of the supplier to see that the buyer does not go out of business. Hence, the supplier would be willing to help the declining business achieve economies by reducing prices, transportation costs, etc., in order to ensure its own survival. A similar argument can be made when the supplier is more powerful. When the supplier is powerful, the downstream business would have a lower exit barrier.

Harrigan (1985a) pointed out yet another disadvantage of a vertically integrated firm. If there is a change in technology that causes a unit to change its inputs or operations, it will be greatly hindered if the same firm owns the supplier, which now supplies obsolete products. Buzzell (1983) listed the disadvantages of vertical integration which put a firm in a weaker competitive position: capital requirements, unbalanced throughput because each stage has a different "minimum efficient scale" of operation, and the loss of flexibility and specialization.

A highly differentiated product is another source of a barrier to exit. Firms often strive to differentiate their products as a means of creating entry and mobility barriers (Caves and Porter 1977). This strategy is effective in keeping a set of customers loyal to the brand name, due to its image of better quality of product or service or both. The importance of having an established brand name cannot be overemphasized. The cost of introducing a new brand name in the market can be extremely high. A well-known name, on the other hand, is less risky to use and can bring in quick profits. An example is that of Budweiser. Finding no success with Natural Light brand beer, the Bud Light brand was introduced, using a name already known to customers. The increase in sales due to the brand name was significant (Evans 1988). Hollywood film makers use the same principal when they make sequels to films. The result of this strategy in businesses, however, is higher exit barriers. The firm may continue to operate a business with poor returns for the sake of goodwill, so it will not lose customers in other businesses.

Just as relatedness, meaning horizontal or vertical integration, raises exit barriers, the lack of strategic fit lowers them significantly. In an effort to restructure, firms are likely to divest units that are not related to achieving the corporate mission. This is especially true when one firm acquires another and divests the unrelated businesses of the acquired firm (assuming other exit barriers are taken care of). Porter (1988) has studied acquisitions and divestitures made between 1950 and 1986 by 33 large firms chosen at random. The study showed that 50 to 70 percent of acquired businesses were divested by the acquiring firms when the businesses were in entirely different fields or in different industries within the same field. This indicates much lower exit barriers for unrelated businesses.

While highly diversified firms seem to have lower exit barriers for their businesses, the opposite is true of single businesses since exiting for them implies the end of the firm itself. Given a single-business firm in a poor competitive position in a declining industry, either it will be taken over by a competitor, or it will "bloody the entire industry in a bitter endgame price war to regain lost sales volumes if it cannot move resources to another business venture smoothly" (Harrigan 1980, 107).

Some multibusiness firms stay in a declining business for another strategic reason. A firm may have a business unit that is a poor competitor, but its competitors also compete with the firm in other businesses. The firm can use such a business unit to play the role of a "competitive harasser." The objective of such a unit is to constantly harass the competition with price wars, even though the business unit sustains losses. This achieves the purposes of distracting the competitors from the other businesses and preventing them from getting substantial cash flows that can be used to fund other businesses. The competitive harasser thus pulls the competition down along with itself (MacMillan 1982).

Managerial Barriers

Hilton (1972) calls divestiture the "single most unpalatable decision" that a manger has to make. The normal human tendency is to try to improve a bad situation, and the situation of business units is no exception. Before considering exit, managers are more likely to use more resources to rebuild the business. The greater such an investment is, the harder it gets to divest the unit.

Porter (1976) classified managerial exit barriers according to the type of firm the managers belonged to-single business or multibusiness. In a single-business firm, divestment would be regarded by the manager as a personal failure, and external observers would also question his or her competence. The manager may have been with the firm for several years, perhaps even helping build the unit in question from scratch. This creates a bond between the manager and his or her business that is difficult to sever. Even if there is no loss of reputation for the manager, whether real or perceived, he or she may still find it hard to find personal employment or employment for the other employees. This is especially true if the business was specialized, so that the special skills acquired by the employees are of little use elsewhere. The manager does feel responsible for the loss of jobs of the employees and may not want that burden on his or her shoulders. This feeling of social responsibility is stronger when the business unit is located in a town where it is the major employer, and its closing would adversely affect the town's economy. That feeling can deter the decision makers from divestment.

In a multibusiness firm, since there are operations in more than one business, there is likely to be more objectivity in the decision making. The presence of corporate planners at the top level is perhaps more objective due to less direct involvement in any of the business units. However, as in a single-business firm, exit may still be perceived as a failure. Although it may not be the failure of the top management, the ultimate responsibility does lie with them. As Porter (1976) argues, the longer the present corporate management has been associated with the business, the less the likelihood of their divesting it. It is also possible that even in a multibusiness firm the decision is not objective, for the business unit in question may have been the brainchild of one or more of the corporate planners. It is therefore easier for a new management to divest businesses as a restructuring effort than for the current management to do so.

Multibusiness firms do have the advantage that they can use some or all of their employees from the divested unit elsewhere or retain them for a new business venture. The social responsibility is thus not necessarily compromised due to divestiture. In spite of that, managers of the divestiture candidate are likely to oppose exit since their compensation and position may be adversely affected. In other cases, the failure of the business may not be the fault of the manager of the unit or the employees. However, they may see the divestiture as indicating a lack of confidence in them by the top management and cause them to resign. The firm thus loses valuable trained employees.

Corporate executive compensation may itself be tied in with growth in the sales or profits of the firm. The pressure to show sales in the short term may force them not to divest certain units, although it may be a good long-term strategy.

Information barriers can also prevent timely exit decisions. If only aggregate data from a set of business units are reported to the top management, the poor performance of one unit may be offset by the better performance of another.

EMPIRICAL STUDIES DEALING WITH MARKET EXIT

While most of the discussions about exit barriers found in the literature make intuitive sense, not many researchers have made empirical examinations. The studies that have empirically tested hypotheses have had some weaknesses in the methodology that make it difficult to interpret and generalize the results.

Porter (1976) reports a study based on 310 businesses that earned less than average returns on investment over a four-year period between 1970 and 1973. It was argued that they were in business because of the presence of exit barriers. In this study, Porter performed statistical analyses on ten different exit barriers; four of those were measures of structural barriers and six of strategic barriers. Eight of the ten variables significantly influenced the firm's decision to exit from market. These exit barriers were:

1. investment intensity
2. product differentiation intensity
3. capital utilization
4. relative price
5. relative cost
6. shared facilities
7. backward and forward integration
8. overall diversity

All of the above were operationalized using data from the Profit Impact of Marketing Strategy (PIMS) database. The major drawback of the study was that managerial barriers, which cannot be quantified in any database, could not be studied. The results of the study are thus limited by the fact that these barriers were, in effect, assumed absent, or at least equal for all cases.

Harrigan (1980) studied 61 firms from 8 different industries. The industries were chosen for having different levels of product differentiation, economic exit barriers (capital intensity), and competitor concentration. Executives from 36 of the 61 firms were interviewed to obtain their perceptions of the different barriers. The results of the study indicate that production and advertising related barriers are less important to the exit decision when the business unit is of lower strategic importance than when the business unit is of higher strategic importance. The problem with this conclusion is that the "high" and "low" degrees of strategic importance of business units were decided based on the interviews. It is natural that a business unit will be considered strategically important by the executives only when it is strongly related in some way to the other businesses of the firm, for example, because of shared production and marketing facilities. There thus seems to be a circular argument. Production and advertising barriers are by definition nonexistent when the business unit is unrelated. However, the study does show that relatedness and cost of divestment are important factors in the exit decision.

Duhaime and Grant (1984) have studied 40 large diversified firms to find factors that influence the decision to divest. Their results show that divesting firms are in a weaker competitive position and that the divested units themselves show a lack of financial and competitive strengths. Further, divested units are not highly related to other business units of the firm while managerial commitment is not found significant. This could be due to the biases created by the fact that data were collected through interviews.

Harrigan (1985a) studied the effect of vertical integration on the decision to exit from a business. Data were obtained by interviews, documents, and Delphi techniques for 192 firms in 16 industries. The study found that having many stages of vertical integration raised the height of exit barriers. Also, if a business unit is a captive customer - that is, downstream in the chain of vertical links-it is more difficult to divest than a unit that is upstream in the chain. Businesses down the line can switch suppliers more easily, so the exit barrier is not as high for the supplying unit.

BARRIERS TO EXIT AND MARKET EXIT DECISIONS

Having the literature review on divestiture and barriers to exit in mind, a study of exit barriers was performed using a market exit simulation exercise. The major advantage of such a study is that all of Porter's major exit barriers could be included in the study, without the biases involved with using databases, interviews, and traditional questionnaires. The relative importance of the factors is inferred from the market exit decisions made. This has a definite advantage over asking the decision maker to indicate the importance of the factors directly since the decision makers may have poor insight into their own decision-making process (Stahl 1989; Stahl and Zimmerer 1984).

Specifically, the study uses six factors: (1) cost of divestment relative to the firm's asset base (2) operating fit (3) marketing fit (4) degree of forward vertical integration (5) degree of backward vertical integration, and (6) number of years the unit has been with the firm. The selection of these factors was based on Porter's (1976) classification of exit barriers as economic, strategic, and managerial. The first variable, cost of divestiture, is obviously the economic barrier faced by the firm. Absolute cost is not a meaningful variable since different firms are of different sizes. Hence, the variable used represents a cost relative to the firm's asset base.

Strategic exit barriers are the barriers a firm faces due to the interrelationships between the business unit and the rest of the firm. Such relationships are both horizontal and vertical. Research on diversification generally refers to the horizontal relationships as the relatedness between the units. In Rumelt's (1974) classification of diversification strategies, relatedness is essentially an assessment of the operating or marketing fit between the various business units of the firm. Thompson and Strickland (1978) and Shepherd (1979) discuss the two types of fit as being components of strategic fit. Caldwell and Harrison (1986) operationalize operating and marketing fits and test their relationship with a firm's profitability. It was clear from earlier research that operating and marketing fits have different effects on a firm's performance. It could therefore be expected that they may raise exit barriers of different heights.

Hence, the operating fit and the marketing fit variables are used in this study to represent the strategic exit barriers raised by horizontal relationships.

Vertical integration is the other dimension of strategic exit barriers. Harrigan (1985a) discusses both forward and backward integration and concludes that the height of the exit barrier for a downstream unit is different from that of an upstream unit. Therefore, forward vertical integration and backward vertical integration variables are used in this study. The former refers to the degree to which a unit buys from other units of the firm, while the latter refers to the degree to which the unit sells to other units of the firm.

Finally, managerial exit barriers, which were defined by Porter as the psychological barriers that managers face in getting rid of a business due to emotional attachment to the unit, are measured by the number of years the unit has been with the firm. This is a proxy for emotional attachment, but is used since managerial emotional barriers are nearly impossible to measure directly. The advantage of using the proxy of the number of years is that it is an objective measure. Duhaime and Grant (1984) use as a proxy the number of years that the decision maker has been associated with the unit. It is possible that a decision maker may have been associated with a unit for a short time, but that the firm as a whole (the decision-making committee) has a strong attachment to a unit that has been with the firm for a number of years. Thus, the number of years that a unit has been in the firm is perhaps a better proxy to use than the length of time that any individual decision maker has been associated with the unit. This is especially true since a decision to divest is not likely to be made by a single decision maker in a firm.

Harrigan (1980) argues that the impact of the stage of the product life cycle and the rate of decline in demand are important considerations in making the exit decision and cannot be ignored. For this study, the effects of the exit barriers were studied for two separate cases: when the units belong to industries in the mature stage, and when the units belong to industries in the decline stage. Also, to control for the projected rate of decline, it was made clear in the market exit simulation exercise that the forecast was for a slow rate of decline, not a rapid rate of decline caused by a major technological change. Specifically, the study attempted to answer the following major questions:

- What is the relative importance of the various factors to the decision makers considering exit?
- Are all the major factors discussed in the literature even considered by the decision makers?
- What is the relationship between the stage of the product life cycle that the business is in and the decision to divest it?
- Does the relative importance of the factors change in making the divestment decision for a mature industry as opposed to a declining industry?

Fortune 500 executives in 1989 were targeted to receive the market exit simulation exercise (Figure 5.1). Table 5.2 describes the market exit barriers and the two decisions that were made by executives who participated in the study.

The executives selected were those most likely to be involved in making divestment decisions, typically the vice presidents of finance and corporate planning, senior vice presidents, group vice presidents, and presidents. The list of the executives involved in strategic planning and development was obtained from the 1989 <u>Standard & Poor's Register of Corporations, Directors, and Executives</u>. Eighty-two executives participated in the study.

Figure 5.1
An Example of Market Exit Simulation Exercise

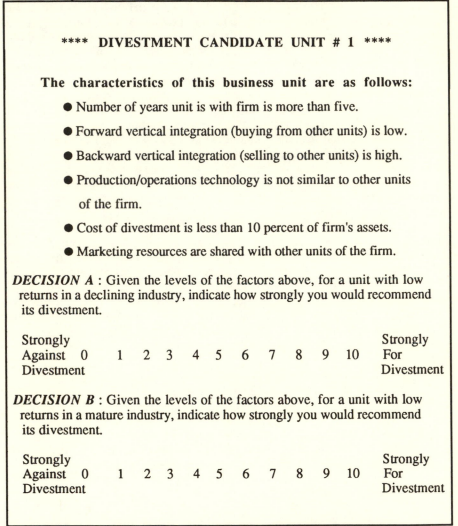

**** DIVESTMENT CANDIDATE UNIT # 1 ****

The characteristics of this business unit are as follows:

- Number of years unit is with firm is more than five.

- Forward vertical integration (buying from other units) is low.

- Backward vertical integration (selling to other units) is high.

- Production/operations technology is not similar to other units of the firm.

- Cost of divestment is less than 10 percent of firm's assets.

- Marketing resources are shared with other units of the firm.

DECISION A : Given the levels of the factors above, for a unit with low returns in a declining industry, indicate how strongly you would recommend its divestment.

Strongly   Strongly
Against   0   1   2   3   4   5   6   7   8   9   10   For
Divestment   Divestment

DECISION B : Given the levels of the factors above, for a unit with low returns in a mature industry, indicate how strongly you would recommend its divestment.

Strongly   Strongly
Against   0   1   2   3   4   5   6   7   8   9   10   For
Divestment   Divestment

Table 5.2
Definition of the Variables

VARIABLE	DEFINITION
YDEC	The decision to divest the unit, assuming it belongs to a declining industry
YMAT	The decision to divest the unit, assuming it belongs to a mature industry
YEARS	The number of years the unit has been with the firm
FVI	Forward vertical integration of the unit (degree to which it buys from other units of the firm)
BVI	Backward vertical integration of the unit (degree to which it sells to other units of the firm)
OPFIT	Operating fit between the divestment candidate unit and other units of the firm
COST	Cost of divestment, including dismantling, selling, and sunk costs
MKTFIT	Marketing fit between the divestment candidate unit and other units of the firm

Relative Importance of Exit Barriers

The relative importance of each exit barrier was calculated for the decision to divest in declining and in mature industries individually. These relative weights were also tested for statistical significance. Not all executives considered each of the exit barriers tested as important. Table 5.3 gives such results for the declining industry. Forward vertical integration was considered important by 64 of the 77 executives in making the divestment decision, while the variable

YEARS was applied by only 15 of the respondents in making market exit decisions. Table 5.4 shows the results of a similar count for the mature industry. Here, the total number of respondents is 76, having dropped the six respondents with inconsistent responses.

The most significant feature of Tables 5.3 and 5.4 is the difference in the importance of forward vertical integration. While 64 respondents thought it important for the declining industry, only 53 considered it important in the mature industry. This indicated that while forward integration and backward integration were considered equally important in the mature stage, forward integration was definitely considered more important in the decline stage.

Table 5.3
Consideration of Barriers in the Exit Decision -
Declining Industry

Exit of Barriers[a]	No. of executives who thought it significant	Percentage total (77) executives
COST	39	50.65
OPFIT	41	53.25
MKTFIT	36	46.75
FVI	64	83.12
BVI	51	66.23
YEARS	15	19.48

a. Exit Barriers are defined in Table 5.2.

Table 5.4
Consideration of Barriers in the Exit Decision -
Mature Industry

Exit of Barriers[a]	No. of executives who thought it significant	Percentage total (76) executives
COST	41	53.95
OPFIT	39	51.32

Table 5.4 (continued)

Exit of Barriers[a]	No. of executives who thought it significant	Percentage total (76) executives
MKTFIT	37	48.68
FVI	53	69.74
BVI	53	69.74
YEARS	19	25.00

a. Exit Barriers are defined in Table 5.2.

Differences in the Importance of Exit Barriers

As Table 5.5 shows, forward vertical integration was the most important deterrent to divestment of a business in a declining industry, while the number of years the business is with the firm was found to be the least important. No significant difference was found between the average relative importance of backward vertical integration and the cost of divestment, or between operating fit and marketing fit.

Table 5.5
Average Relative Weights - Declining Industry[a]

Exit Barriers[b]	Avg. Relative Weight Declining Industry (n=77)	Grouping[c]
FVI	27.43	A
BVI	20.07	B
COST	19.53	B
OPFIT	15.62	B,C
MKTFIT	12.97	C
YEARS	04.37	D

Table 5.5 (continued)
a. Relative weights were multiplied by 100.
b. Exit Barriers are defined in Table 5.2.
c. Same letters indicate no significant difference.

Table 5.6 shows the average relative weights and the differences for the mature industry. The results in Table 5.6 show that both types of vertical integration and the cost of divestment are not significantly different from each other. These three factors are the major barriers to exit. Vertical integration is a bigger barrier than operating fit, marketing fit, and the number of years.

As discussed earlier regarding Tables 5.3 and 5.4, the significant point about Tables 5.5 and 5.6 is the importance of forward vertical integration. In a mature industry, forward and backward integration and the cost of divestment are not significantly different from each other in terms of the barriers they pose to divestment. However, in a declining industry, forward integration is significantly more important. This is not surprising since a captive customer is more difficult to let go of during decline when other buyers are more difficult to find for the upstream units.

Table 5.6

Average Relative Weights - Mature Industry[a]

Exit Barriers[b]	Avg. Relative Weight Mature Industry (n=76)	Grouping[c]
FVI	24.09	A
BVI	21.55	A
COST	20.00	A,B
MKTFIT	14.24	B,C
OPFIT	13.50	C
YEARS	06.61	D

a. Relative weights were multiplied by 100.
b. Exit Barriers are defined in Table 5.2.
c. Same letters indicate no significant difference.

Market Exit Decision: Differences in Declining and Mature Industries

To test whether executives use different models in making divestment decisions for the declining and the mature stages, a statistical test known as "Chow's F-test" was performed for each respondent. A significant difference in the two models was found for 36 of the 82 respondents. Another test was also performed to examine whether there is an overall difference for declining and mature industries (with 77 and 76 respondents, respectively). The significance of the F-test indicates that there is a statistically significant difference in the divestiture decision models used for the two stages of the product life cycle. The nature of the difference can be seen in tables 5.3, 5.4, 5.5, and 5.6. They all indicate the greater importance of forward vertical integration during decline.

Discussion and Conclusions

The statistical analyses performed show that except for the number of years a business has been with the firm, all the factors are important in the case of a declining industry. For a mature industry, all six factors were found significant in the overall regression. Each factor deterred the decision to divest and hence is an exit barrier.

The relative importance of the factors was not contrary to expectations. Forward vertical integration of the business unit was the most important deterrent to its divestment, followed by backward vertical integration, cost of divestment, and operating and marketing fit. The results are consistent with Harrigan's (1985b) argument that vertical integration is an important exit barrier and that a downstream unit faces a greater exit barrier than does an upstream one. Forward vertical integration was found to raise a greater barrier than backward vertical integration in a declining industry. This seems logical since divesting a captive customer, especially during decline, leaves the upstream units with no customers. Also, the presence of a captive buyer can lead to the upstream unit's being less efficient, and, consequently, the divestment of the downstream unit can seriously affect the sales of the upstream unit. Divestment of the upstream unit, however, is perhaps not as great a threat to the downstream unit since the likelihood of finding another supplier during decline is greater than that of finding a buyer.

As Harrigan (1985b) pointed out, however, the phase of the product life cycle is important and can change the relative importance of forward and backward vertical integration. While forward integration raised a greater barrier during decline, there was no significant difference between forward and backward integration during the mature phase. This can be explained by the fact that more options are available to the upstream units during maturity than during decline. Hence, the divestment of a downstream unit is a greater problem during decline than during the mature phase. In general, vertical integration creates greater interdependence between business units of a firm than does horizontal relatedness. While relatedness due to shared production or marketing resources is important, the divestment of a related unit does not have as much of a direct impact on sales as does the divestment of a vertically integrated unit.

The lack of significance of the number of years a unit has been with the firm suggests that managerial barriers, as measured by the number of years of association with the firm, do not play as important a role in divestment decision making, as indicated in the arguments of Porter (1976). The lack of significance of this factor for the declining industry and its significance for the mature industry suggest that the economic considerations for the declining industry would be too strong to permit personal attachments to get in the way of divestment. In a mature industry, however, there is a greater chance that revitalization will be the corporate strategy, instead of divestment, and personal attachment may be a deciding factor in the decision.

Thirty-six respondents (about 45 percent of the total number of respondents) used different decision-making models for declining and mature industries. Thus, on an individual basis, executives do seem to make decisions differently depending on the business unit's life cycle stage. As mentioned before, there are two notable differences in the models. First, forward vertical integration is a more important factor during decline than during maturity. Second, the variable YEARS changes from being insignificant for the declining industry to being significant for the mature industry. The relative weight of this factor is still very low (1.11 percent) indicating that while managerial barriers may be present, their influence on the decision is very small compared to other factors.

The study confirmed the presence of the major barriers to exit and found their relative importance to executives in making a divestment decision. It also showed the difference in the importance of these barriers to divestment decision making in two different stages of the product life cycle, maturity and decline. The results support earlier literature that proposes that the stages of the product life cycle determine, at least in part, corporate strategies. An objection to the product life cycle theory in the literature is that executives cannot tell accurately when an industry is in a certain stage, and, hence, the theory cannot be used accurately to formulate strategy. While there is some truth to that argument, this study shows that when the life cycle stage is known, executives do use that information for strategy formulation.

BARRIERS TO EXIT AND THEIR IMPLICATIONS

The relative importance of the exit barriers has some implications for strategic management and marketing. The finding that vertical integration is the most important barrier to exit raises a question about the pros and cons of following that strategy. Opinion is divided about the benefits of vertical integration. While the strategy can provide better control over raw materials and distribution networks and can raise entry barriers for potential competitors (Harrigan 1984), there are disadvantages, too. The capital requirements are high, the firm is less able to respond to changing market conditions, and exit barriers are raised.

Empirical studies relating vertical integration to performance do not show much agreement. Rumelt (1974) and Buzzell (1983) have found that highly vertically integrated firms are less profitable than other kinds of diversified firms. Harrigan (1986), however, has found the reverse to be true. Balakrishnan and Wernerfelt (1986) propose that vertical integration can be profitable if certain market conditions are present.

The results of this study confirm the contention that vertical integration has a major disadvantage in that it raises exit barriers. No case can be made, however, about the overall impact of the strategy on the performance of a firm. It obviously depends on several other factors.

An important area of study that is closely related to market exit barriers is that of market entry barriers. Many of the barriers that prevent timely exit are usually caused by strategies implemented during the growth phase to raise entry barriers against potential competitors (Porter 1980). Vertical integration and capital investment are both deterrents to market entry (Harrigan 1981a; Karakaya 1987). There is thus a tradeoff that firms must consider between the added advantage during the growth and the maturity phases and the potential cost of running an unprofitable business during decline.

The second major finding of this study was the difference in the models used for divestment decision making in the mature and the declining stages of the product life cycle. This brings up the question of cause and effect, which has been discussed in the literature (Wind and Claycamp 1976). Do the strategies differ based on the stage of the life cycle, or do the strategies followed determine the stage of the life cycle and the longevity of the product? A distinction between the life cycle for an industry and for an individual firm and a specific product is required to answer the question. If by the product life cycle one refers to the industry as a whole, then it is more likely that the strategy is a response to the stage of the life cycle. Environmental factors, such as the economic conditions and consumer tastes, can affect the life cycle, but it is unlikely that an individual firm's strategy would change the characteristics of the life cycle, except in the case of a monopoly or perhaps an oligopoly. However, an individual firm's sales may grow, level out, and decline independent of the stage of the industry life cycle. This is where the strategy of the firm determines the stage of the life cycle that the firm is in.

This chapter was authored by Satish Nargundkar of Clemson University, Fahri Karakaya and Michael J. Stahl.

REFERENCES

Alexander, G. J., P. G. Benson, and J. M. Kampmeyer. 1984. "Investigating the Valuation Effects of Announcements of Voluntary Corporate Selloffs." *Journal of Finance* 19 (June): 503-17.

Arnold, H. J., and D. C. Feldman. 1981. "Social Desirability Response Bias in Self-Report Choice Situations." *Academy of Management Journal* 24: 377-85.

Balakrishnan, S., and B. Wernerfelt. 1986. "Technical Change, Competition, and Vertical Integration." *Strategic Management Journal* 7: 347-59.

Baumol, W., J. C. Panzar, and R. Willig. 1982. *Contestable Markets and the Theory of Industry Structure*. San Diego: Harcourt Brace Jovanovich.

Bernheim, B. D. 1984. "Strategic Deterrence of Sequential Entry into Industry." *Rand Journal of Economics* 15: 1-11.

Bettis, R. A. 1981. "Performance Differences in Related and Unrelated Diversified Firms." *Strategic Management Journal* 2: 379-93.

Buzzell, R. D. 1983. "Is Vertical Integration Profitable?" *Harvard Business Review* 61 (January-February): 92-102.

Caldwell, L. G., and J. S. Harrison. 1986. "The Content of Corporate Level Strategy in Highly Diversified Firms." *Proceedings of the Decision Sciences Institute National Conference*. Hawaii.

Caves, R. E., and M. E. Porter. 1977. "From Entry Barriers to Mobility Barriers." *Quarterly Journal of Economics* (May): 241-62.

Chen, A. H., and L. J. Merville. 1986. "An Analysis of Divestiture Effects Resulting from Deregulation." *Journal of Finance* 39 (December): 997-1010.

Christoph, R. T. 1985. "Divestiture Decision Modeling Utilizing the Capital Asset Pricing Model." Ph.D. diss., Clemson University.

Demsetz, H. 1982. "Barriers to Entry." *American Economic Review* 72 (March): 47-57.

Dixit, A. 1980. "The Role of Investment in Entry Deterrence."*Economic Journal* 90: 95-106.

Dubin, R. N. 1986. "Divestments, Some Practical Thoughts on How to Sell a Division." *Financial Executive's Manual* 2 (November): 37-39.

Duhaime, I. M., and I. S. Baird. 1987. "Divestment Decision-Making: The Role of Business Unit Size."*Journal of Management* 13: 483-98.

Duhaime, I. M., and J. H. Grant. 1984. "Factors Influencing Divestment Decision-Making: Evidence from a Field Study."*Strategic Management Journal* 5: 301-18.

Ennis, R. M., and R. L. Parkhill. 1986. South Africa Divestment: Social Responsibility or Fiduciary Folly?" *Financial Analysts Journal* (July-August): 30-38.

Evans, H. 1988. "What's in a Brand Name?" *Management Review* (June): 33-35.

Feinberg, P. 1988. "The Ultimate Financing : Putting the Company on the Block." *Corporate Cashflow Magazine* (Sept.): 60-61.

Galai, D., and R. W. Masulis. 1976. "The Option Pricing Model and the Risk Factor of Stock." *Journal of Financial Economics* 3 (January-March): 53-81.

Hall, J. P. 1986. "Ethics in Investment: Divestment." *Financial Analysts Journal* (July-August): 7-10.

Harrigan, K. R. 1980. *Strategies for Declining Businesses*. Lexington, Mass.: Lexington Books.

_____. 1981a. "The Effect of Exit Barriers upon Strategic Flexibility." *Strategic Management Journal* 1: 165-76.

_____.1981b. "Barriers to Entry and Competitive Strategies." *Strategic Management Journal* 2 (4): 395-412.

_____. 1981c."Deterrents to Divestiture." *Academy of Management Journal* 24 (2): 306-23.

_____. 1982."Strategic Planning for Endgame." *Long Range Planning* 15 (6): 45-48.

_____. 1984. "Formulating Vertical Integration Strategies." *Academy of Management Review* 9 (4): 638-52.

_____. 1985a. "Exit Barriers and Vertical Integration." *Academy of Management Journal* 28: 686-97.

_____. 1985b. "Vertical Integration and Corporate Strategy." *Academy of Management Journal* 28: 397-425.

_____. 1986. "Matching Vertical Integration Strategies to Competitive Conditions." *Strategic Management Journal* 7: 535-55.

Hilton, P. 1972. "Divestiture: The Strategic Move on the Corporate Chessboard." *Management Review* (March): 16-19.

Hite, G., and J. Owers, 1983. "Security Price Reactions Around Corporate Spinoff Announcements."*Journal of Financial Economics* 12 (December): 409-36.

Holcomb, J. H., and D. A. Evans. 1987. "The Effect of Sunk Costs on Uncertain Decisions in Experimental Markets." *Journal of Behavioral Economics* (Fall): 59-64.

Hrebiniak, L. G., and C. C. Snow. 1982. "Top Management Agreement and Organizational Performance." *Human Relations* 35: 1139-58.

Hyman, H. 1954. *Interviewing in Social Research*. Chicago: University of Chicago Press.

Karakaya, F. 1987. "Modeling Market Entry Decisions: A Test of Porter's Market Entry Barriers." Ph.D. diss., Clemson University.

Klein, A. 1986. "The Timing and Substance of Divestiture Announcements: Individual, Simultaneous and Cumulative Effects." *Journal of Finance* 41 (July): 685-96.

Kleindorfer, P., and G. Knieps. 1982. "Vertical Integration and Transaction Specific Sunk Costs." *European Economic Review* 19: 71-87.

Lambert, D. M. 1985. *The Product Abandonment Decision*. Montval, N.J.: National Association of Accountants.

Levitt, T. 1965. "Exploit the Product Life Cycle." *Harvard Business Review* 43 (November-December): 81-94.

Lynch, M. C. 1980. "Many Firms Are Selling Off Acquisitions to Clarify Their Images, Lift Their Stocks."*Wall Street Journal*, December 4: 48.

MacLeod, W. B. 1987. "Entry Sunk Costs and Market Structure." *Canadian Journal of Economics* (February): 140-52.

MacMillan, I. C. 1982. "Seizing Competitive Initiative." *Journal of Business Strategy* 2 (Spring): 43-57.

Miles, J. A., and J. D. Rosenfeld. 1983. "The Effect of Voluntary Spin-Off Announcements on Shareholder Wealth." *Journal of Finance* 38 (December): 1597-1606.

Missirian, A. K. 1988. "Current and Future Utilization of Quantitative Methods in Strategic Management Research." *Proceedings of the Annual Meeting, DSI* (November): 1282-84.

Porter, M. E. 1976. "Please Note Location of Nearest Exit: Exit Barriers and Planning." *California Management Review* (2): 21-33.

_____. 1980. *Competitive Strategy: Techniques for Analyzing Industries and Competitors*. New York: Free Press.

_____. 1988. "Managing Value: From Competitive Advantage to Corporate Strategy."*McKinsey Quarterly* (Spring): 35.

Rafferty, J. 1987. "Exit Barriers and Strategic Position in Declining Markets." *Long Range Planning* 20: 86-91.

Rosenfeld, J. D. 1984. "Additional Evidence on the Relation Between Divestiture Announcements and Shareholder Wealth." *Journal of Finance* 39 (December): 1437-48.

Rumelt, R. P. 1974. *Strategy, Structure, and Economic Performance*. Boston: Division of Research, Graduate School of Business Administration, Harvard University.

Shepherd, W. G. 1979. *The Economics of Industrial Organization*. Englewood Cliffs, N.J.: Prentice-Hall.

Sherer, P. D., D. P. Schwab, and H. G. Heneman. 1987. "Managerial Salary-Raise Decision: A Policy Capturing Approach." *Personnel Psychology* 40: 27-38.

Spence, M. A. 1980. "Notes on Advertising, Economies of Scale, and Entry Barriers." *Quarterly Journal of Economics* 95 (November): 493-507.

Srivastava, A. 1986. "The Roles of Strategic Fit, Profitability, and Risk in Acquisitions." Ph.D. diss., Clemson University.

Stahl, M. J. 1986. *Managerial and Technical Motivation: Assessing Needs for Achievement, Power, and Affiliation*. New York: Praeger.

_____. 1989. *Strategic Executive Decisions*. Westport, Conn.: Quorum Books.

Stahl, M. J., and A. M. Harrell. 1982. "Evolution and Validation of a Behavioral Decision Theory Measurement Approach to Achievement, Power, and Affiliation." *Journal of Applied Psychology* 67: 744-50.

Stahl, M. J., and T. W. Zimmerer. 1984. "Modeling Strategic Acquisition Policies: A Simulation of Executives' Acquisition Decisions." *Academy of Management Journal* 27: 369-86.

Standard & Poor's Register of Corporations, Directors, and Executives, 1989. New York: McGraw-Hill.

Stewart, G. B., and D. M. Glassman. 1988. "Why Restructuring Adds Value: When Subtracting Is a Goal." *Cashflow Magazine* (February): 48-50.

Thompson A. A., and A. J. Strickland. 1978. *Strategy and Policy: Concepts and Cases*. Plano, Tex.: Business Publications.

Wasson, C. R. 1978. *Dynamic Competitive Strategy and Product Life Cycles*. St. Charles, Ill.: Challenge Books.

Wind, Y., and H. Claycamp. 1976. "Planning Product Line Strategy: A Matrix Approach." *Journal of Marketing* 40 (January): 2-9.

Zaima, J. K., and D. Hearth. 1985. "The Wealth Effects of Voluntary Spinoffs: Implications for Divesting and Acquiring Firms." *Journal of Financial Research* 8 (Fall): 227-36.

Chapter 6

Managerial Consensus and Market Entry Strategy

Market entry decision making usually involves a group of executives. Marketing executives infrequently take the risk of making market entry decisions alone. The question of interest here is whether a market entry decision agreed on by marketing executives leads to more profits. Previous research concerning consensus on strategic decisions and firm performance has yielded mixed results.

The notion of "groupthink" (Janis 1972, 1982) is well known and suggests that early consensus leads to suboptimal decisions that restrain organizational performance. In contrast, the literature on groups provides support for a positive relationship between managerial consensus and organizational performance (Blake and Mouton 1967; French and Bell 1973; Schein 1969). Environmental complexity and uncertainty (Lawrence and Lorsch 1967; Thompson 1967; Van de Ven and Ferry 1979) and the social context in which the decisions are made (Tjosvold and Field 1983) are likely to influence the relationship between consensus and performance. Child (1974) and Tilles (1963) suggest that consensus among executives concerning corporate goals and policies is one of the necessary ingredients of success.

Several empirical studies have attempted to examine the relationship between consensus among corporate executives on strategy and corporate performance. While the areas of consensus have varied, the variable of interest in these studies has usually been firm profitability or performance. The areas of consensus on strategic issues studied were goals (Bourgeois 1980), perceived environmental uncertainty (Bourgeois 1985), environmental goals and strategies (Bourgeois and Singh 1983), means for innovation activities (DeWoot, Heyvaert, and Martou 1977-1978), objectives and role perceptions (Grinyer and Norborn, 1977-78) strengths and weaknesses of firms (Hrebiniak and Snow 1982), and company objectives and competitive methods (Dess 1987). While some of these studies suggest that positive relationships exist between consensus and firm performance, others indicate the opposite.

The different findings concerning performance and consensus may be separately categorized into strategy formulation and strategy implementation studies. The concept of "groupthink" (Janis 1972, 1982) may explain the findings of a negative relationship between consensus and performance in strategy formulation (Bourgeois 1980; Grinyer and Norburn 1977-1978; DeWoot, Heyvaert, and Martou 1977-1978; Whitney and Smith 1983). Bourgeois (1985) again has established that lack of consensus on goals is positively related to performance. Hrebiniak and Snow (1982) have found that consensus among executives about the strengths and weaknesses of their firms is positively related to company performance.

Ansoff's (1965) concept of the critical role that executives play in strategy implementation may be responsible for the suggestion of Dess (1987) and Dess and Origer (1987) that there is a positive relationship between consensus on strategy implementation and performance. Bourgeois (1980) has found that consensus on strategies is more strongly related to performance than is consensus on company goals. In fact, when executives agree on goals without agreement on strategies, there is a negative relationship with profitability. Similarly, Dess (1987) has studied 19 companies in the paint industry and has found that consensus strategies are positively correlated with company performance.

Although the findings about consensus and company performance are mixed, the relationship between consensus on company strategies and company performance is positive. The literature on consensus applies to both strategy formulation and strategy implementation. First, executives must decide whether or not to enter a market. Second, they must decide how to enter a market (i.e., through acquisition or direct entry by way of internal development) and when to enter a market. In formulating a market entry strategy, executives usually consider and discuss the following areas:

1. target market selection, including market segments
2. design of the marketing mix
   a. product or classes of products
   b. branding and packaging
   c. service and warranty offer
   d. distribution strategy, including the type of
      distributors, degree of distribution (i.e., intensive
      selective or exclusive), and strategy to recruit
      middlemen (i.e., push vs. pull strategy)
   e. promotion strategy
   f. pricing strategy (i.e., skimming vs. penetration strategy
3. competition
4. uncontrollable environment

Of course, the barriers to entry originate either directly or indirectly from the above considerations. Marketing executives usually reach a consensus in terms of formulating the entry strategy and implementing it. However, there is usually considerable disagreement before reaching a consensus. In some situations, there is never a full consensus, but the market entry decision is made because the executive in charge favors market entry. With this in mind, the authors examined the relationship between consensus on the importance of barriers when making market entry decisions and company financial performance.

In order to measure the degree of consensus, several statistical techniques were employed. (Discussion of the consensus measures developed and their mathematical properties is beyond the scope of this book. For information on these measures, contact the authors.) Two consensus measures were used: (1) composite index of consensus, which measured the degree of consensus on market entry considering the importance of barriers simultaneously, and (2) single index of consensus, which measured the degree of agreement on the importance of each barrier individually when entering markets. The return on assets was used as the performance variable in order to examine its relationship to the consensus on market entry. The data from the market entry simulation exercise explained in Chapter 1 (and also presented in Appendix A) were utilized. The six barriers studied were (1) cost advantages, (2) product differentiation, (3) capital requirements, (4) customer switching costs, (5) access to distribution channels, and (6) government policy barriers (Porter 1980). Since these decisions are made in the context of strategy implementation, positive relationships among the barriers and firm performance were hypothesized.

CONSENSUS AND CORPORATE PERFORMANCE RELATIONSHIP CONSIDERING SIX BARRIERS TO ENTRY SIMULTANEOUSLY

The relationship between consensus on the importance of barriers and company performance was tested for four market entry decisions: early and late entry into both consumer and industrial markets. Positive relationships were found for three decisions, early and late entry into consumer markets and early entry into industrial markets (the correlation coefficients were .35, .35, and .33, respectively). There was no relationship between consensus and company performance for the late entry into industrial markets decision. As it can be noted from the correlation coefficients, the degree of relationship was about the same for the three decisions. For these three decisions, as consensus increases, so does company performance.

Consensus on the Importance of Individual Barriers and Corporate Performance

Although executives consider more than a single barrier when making market entry decisions, they are likely to find some barriers more important than others. The relative importance of the barriers was discussed in Chapter 2. To examine the impact of consensus on the importance of individual barriers, six separate statistical tests were performed for each of the four market entry decisions. One should note that the calculated indices cannot be greater than 100 or smaller than 0. Relatively speaking, larger values mean consensus, and smaller values mean disagreement.

Consensus in Early Entry into Consumer Markets and Performance

For early entry into consumer markets, consensus is highest for the customer switching costs barrier (Table 6.1). Interestingly, this barrier is considered the fourth most important and is significantly less important than the cost advantages, product differentiation, and capital requirements barriers. The lowest consensus is on the importance of the cost advantages barrier, followed by the capital requirements and product differentiation barriers. As can be noted from the relative weights, these three barriers are more important than the other three barriers for which the executives more often reach consensus. It appears the executives agree that these barriers are weak in deterring market entry. In terms of the relationship between consensus and company performance, from the table, it looks as if the importance of barriers on which the executives disagreed the most are related to performance. However, as agreement on the importance of barriers increases so does company performance. Thus, in the sample used to study the relationship between consensus and performance, some firms agree on the weaknesses or importance of the first four barriers in the table, but the return on assets is low. Therefore, one can conclude that as consensus on the importance of the capital requirements and cost advantages barriers increases, company performance also increases.

Table 6.1
Consensus Indices and Relationships with Company Performance for Individual Barriers in Early Entry into Consumer Markets

Barriers[a]	Mean Relative Weights	Mean Consensus Index for Early Entry into Consumer Markets	Correlation
CSC	.130	69	.24
ADC	.141	63	.09
GP	.118	62	.16
PDI	.196	52	.11
CR	.204	50	.33**
CAI	.208	49	.34**
MEAN		58	

Table 6.1 (continued)
n = 29 corporations
**p<0.05, one-tailed significance
a. CAI = Cost Advantages of Incumbents
    PDI = Product Differentiation of Incumbents
    CR = Capital Requirements
    CSC = Customer Switching Costs
    ADC = Access to Distribution Channels
    GP = Government Policy

Consensus in Late Entry into Consumer Markets and Performance

Table 6.2 shows the relationship between consensus and the importance of six barriers, including the consensus indices and the relative importance of each barrier. Again, the consensus is higher for the barriers with lower relative importance. However, since this is a late market entry situation, consensus on the importance of the customer switching costs barrier is related to company

Table 6.2
Consensus Indices and Relationships with Company Performance for Individual Barriers in Late Entry into Consumer Markets

Barriers[a]	Mean Relative Weights	Mean Consensus Index for Early Entry into Consumer Markets	Correlation
CSC	.149	73	.38**
ADC	.124	67	.17
GP	.128	65	.06
CAI	.237	58	.33**
CR	.193	58	.45*
PDI	.165	51	.09
MEAN		62	

n = 29 corporations
* p<0.01, one-tailed significance
**p<0.05, one-tailed significance
a. Barriers are defined in Table 6.1.

performance. In other words, as the marketing executives agree on the importance of customer switching costs, company performance increases. This would mean that the executives in more profitable firms choose not to enter markets late when the customer switching costs are high. In late entry into consumer markets, the cost advantages and capital requirements barriers appear to be the most important (mean relative weights of .217 and .203, respectively) and the consensus on the importance of these two barriers is related to company performance.

Consensus in Early Entry into Industrial Markets and Performance

As Table 6.3 shows, consensus on two of the barriers, access to distribution channels and capital requirements, is related to company performance. Although access to distribution barriers is not as important as some of the barriers, it has the highest consensus score. Of course, one might suggest that the executives agree on the weakness of this barrier in deterring early entry into industrial markets.

Table 6.3
Consensus Indices and Relationships with Company Performance for Individual Barriers in Early Entry into Industrial Markets

Barriers[a]	Mean Relative Weights	Mean Consensus Index for Early Entry into Consumer Markets	Correlation
ADC	.128	69	.30**
CSC	.148	68	.27
GP	.107	59	.07
PDI	.193	52	.04
CR	.203	52	.31**
CAI	.217	41	.18
MEAN		57	

n = 29 corporations
**$p<0.05$, one-tailed significance
a. Barriers are defined in Table 6.1.

The capital requirements barrier is considered the most important barrier and is associated with company performance. However, the consensus score is not as high for the capital requirements barrier. It appears that in certain companies executives agree on the importance of this barrier strongly, and the performance variable, return on assets is also high in these firms. Therefore, the relationship between consensus and performance is still positive.

Consensus on the customer switching costs barrier is almost as high as on the access to distribution channels barrier, which has the highest mean consensus score (mean consensus scores of 68 and 69, respectively). Interestingly, the same pattern that was observed earlier is also present in early entry into industrial markets. As one notes from the table, the barriers with higher relative importance have lower consensus scores. A closer examination of the data indicates that the executives in the companies with a higher return on assets actually agree on the importance of these barriers and that executives in the companies with a lower return on assets disagree.

Consensus in Late Entry into Industrial Markets and Performance

Consensus on three barriers is related to company performance for the late entry into industrial markets decisions. As Table 6.4 shows, these three barriers are customer switching costs, access to distribution channels, and capital requirements. The consensus scores on customer switching costs and access to distribution channels are equal, but these barriers differ in relative importance. The customer switching costs barrier is perceived to be more important than the access to distribution channels barrier, and its correlation coefficient is higher. However, as the consensus on these barriers increases, so does the company performance.

The consensus score on the capital requirements barrier is rather close to the other two barriers that are related to company performance. As consensus on the importance of capital requirements increases, company performance increases as well. Interestingly, there is very little consensus among the executives about the importance of the cost advantages barrier for late entry into industrial markets. Furthermore, consensus on this barrier is not related to company performance. In fact, the correlation coefficient is close to zero. However, one should note that this situation does not mean that disagreement on this barrier leads to higher company performance. Indeed, if the correlation coefficients are not significant, it simply means that there is no relationship one way or the other.

Table 6.4
Consensus Indices and Relationships with Company
Performance for Individual Barriers in Late Entry into
Industrial Markets

Barriers[a]	Mean Relative Weights	Mean Consensus Index for Early Entry into Consumer Markets	Correlation
CSC	.170	70	.38**
ADC	.121	70	.32**
CR	.193	68	.35**
GP	.113	63	.07
PDI	.161	58	.06
CAI	.238	57	.03
MEAN		64	

n = 29 corporations
**p<0.05, one-tailed significance
a. Barriers are defined in Table 6.1

CONCLUSIONS

Three significant relationships were discovered when executives consider the six barriers simultaneously in making market entry decisions. Consensus was found on three barriers that relate to firm performance - customer switching costs, access to distribution channels, and capital requirements to enter markets. Only the consensus on six barriers when making late entry into industrial markets was not related to company performance. Similarly, ten significant associations were found when considering barriers individually in market entry decisions. Table 6.5 shows these significant relationships.

Table 6.5
Correlations of Return on Assets and Consensus Using Single Index of Consensus

Barriers[a]	Decision A[b]	Decision B	Decision C	Decision D
CAI	.34**	.33**	.18	.03
PDI	.11	.09	.04	.06
CR	.33**	.45*	.31**	.35**
CSC	.24	.38**	.27	.38**
ADC	.09	.17	.30**	.32**
GP	.16	.06	.07	.07

n = 29
* p<0.01, one-tailed significance
** p<0.05, one-tailed significance

a. CAI   = Cost Advantages of Incumbents
    PDI   = Product Differentiation of Incumbents
    CR   = Capital Requirements
    CSC   = Customer Switching Costs
    ADC   = Access to Distribution Channels
    GP   = Government Policy

b. Decision A = Early Entry into Consumer Goods Markets
   Decision B = Late Entry into Consumer Goods Markets
   Decision C = Early Entry into Industrial Goods Markets
   Decision D = Late Entry into Industrial Goods Markets

The cost advantages and capital requirements barriers are related to company performance when there is consensus for these barriers in both early and late market entry decisions. These two barriers were considered the two most important barriers in both early and late entry into consumer markets. Similarly, in the late entry decision into consumer markets, consensus on the customer switching costs barrier is associated with company performance.

For early and late entry into industrial markets, consensus on the capital requirements and access to distribution channels barriers leads to higher company performance. The same is true for the customer switching costs barrier in the late market entry situation. The capital requirements barrier is considered the third most important barrier in both early and late market entry situations. The access to distribution channels barrier is considered the fifth most important barrier, but consensus on this barrier as being a weaker barrier is associated with higher company performance. The customer switching costs barrier is perceived as the fourth most important barrier in late entry into industrial markets, and consensus on this barrier is related to higher company performance.

Overall, consensus on some of the barriers is not related to company performance when considering these barriers individually. One should note that they are related to firm performance in three of the market entry decisions when considering the six barriers simultaneously. The facts that executives are likely to consider more than one barrier at a time, and that significant relationships exist between consensus and firm performance for three market entry situations (early and late entry into consumer markets and early entry into industrial markets) are important and should be considered in market entry decisions. Furthermore, when only a few barriers exist, it is suggested that executives consider consensus on the individual barriers that are related to company performance. Finally, it should be noted that consensus does not mean agreement on decisions without discussion. Indeed, a lack of early consensus simply indicates a diversity of opinions that may lead to better-quality decisions (Janis 1982; Wanous and Youtz 1986).

REFERENCES

Ansoff, H. I. 1965. *Corporate Strategy: An Analytical Approach to Business Policy for Growth and Expansion.* New York: McGraw-Hill.

Blake, R. R., and J. S. Mouton. 1967. "Reactions to Intergroup Competition Under Win-Lose Conditions." *Management Science* 7: 420-35.

Bourgeois, L. 1980. "Performance and Consensus." *Strategic Management Journal* 1 (July-September): 227-48.

_____. 1985. "Strategic Goals,Perceived Uncertainty, and Economic Performance in Volatile Environments." *Academy of Management Journal* 28: 548-73.

Bourgeois, L., and H. Singh. 1983. "Organizational Slack and Political Behavior within Top Management Teams." *Academy of Management Proceedings,* 43-47.

Child, J. 1974, "What Determines Organizational Performance? The Universals vs. It-all-depends." *Organizational Dynamics* 3 (Summer): 2-18.

Dess, G. G. 1987. "Consensus on Strategy Formulation and Organizational Performance: Competition in a Fragmented Industry." *Strategic Management Journal* 8: 259-77.

Dess, G. G., and N. K. Origer. 1987. "Environment, Structure, and Consensus in Strategy Formulation: A Conceptual Integration." *Academy of Management Review* 12: 313-30.

DeWoot, P., H. Heyvaert, and F. Martou. 1977-1978. "Strategic Management: An Empirical Study of 168 Belgian Firms." *International Studies of Management and Organization* 7: 60-75.

French, W. L., and C. H. Bell. 1973. *Organization Development.* Englewood Cliffs, N.J.: Prentice-Hall.

Grinyer, P., and D. Norburn. 1977-1978. "Planning for Existing Markets: An Empirical Study." *International Studies in Management and Organization* 7: 99-122.

Hrebiniak, L. G., and C. C. Snow. 1982. "Top Management Agreement and Organizational Performance." *Human Relations* 35: 1139-58

Janis, I. L. 1972. *Victims of Groupthink.* Boston: Houghton Mifflin.

_____. 1982. *Groupthink.* 2d ed. Boston: Houghton Mifflin.

Lawrence, P. R., and J. W. Lorsch. 1967. "Differentiation and Integration in Complex Organizations." *Administrative Science Quarterly* 12: 1-47.

Porter, M. E. 1980. *Competitive Strategy: Techniques for Analyzing Industries and Competitors.* New York: Free Press.

Schein, E. 1969. *Process Consultation.* Reading, Mass.: Addison-Wesley.

Thompson, J. D. 1967. *Organizations in Action.* New York: McGraw-Hill.

Tilles, S. 1963. "How to Evaluate Corporate Strategy." *Harvard Business Review* 41 (July-August): 111-21.

Tjosvold, D., and R. H. G. Field. 1983. "Effects of Social Context on Consensus and Majority Vote Decision Making." *Academy of Management Journal* 26: 500-6.

Van de Ven, A., and D. Ferry. 1979. *Measuring and Assessing Organizations.* Wiley-Interscience.

Wanous, J. P., and M. A. Youtz. 1986. "Solution Diversity and the Quality of Group Decisions." *Academy of Management Journal* 29 (1): 149-59.

Whitney, J. C., and R. A. Smith. 1983. "Effects of Group Cohesiveness on Attitude Polarization and the Acquisition of Knowledge in a Strategic Planning Context." *Journal of Marketing Research* 20: 167-76.

Chapter 7

Profitability and Barriers to Entry

Empirical evidence suggests that barriers to entry and market share are principal determinants of profit margins. Economic analysis of market structure, particularly of market share and company-specific barriers, is of dominating importance in explaining high profit margins (Grinyer, et al. 1988). In attractive (profitable) industries, however, entry barriers are high, and the high cost of entry may consume potential profits (Porter 1980). Although the relationship between barriers to entry and profitability varies from industry to industry, and even sometimes from company to company, in general, a positive relationship exists.

EARLY MARKET ENTRY AND PROFITS

When opportunities exist for early market entry, many of the barriers, especially those that are activated by competitors, are low or nonexistent. Entry barriers can be considered as costs of competing for late entrants not experienced by the market pioneers (Kerin, et al. 1990) and sometimes by early followers. Furthermore, early entrants or pioneers usually enjoy the long-term benefits of early entry, such as brand loyalty, cost advantages due to economies of scale and learning curve effects, access to distribution channels, and high market shares (Lambkin 1988; Robinson 1988; Robinson and Fornell 1985). Of course, in most situations, these advantages translate into long-term profits.

In early market entry situations, the competitor-created or activated barriers are usually low. As a result, early followers in emerging product markets show higher profitability than do pioneers because of larger market shares and lower marketing and R&D expenditures (Srinivasan 1988). The barriers such as selling expenses and R&D costs are usually high for the pioneering firms. The early entrants who follow the pioneers into markets benefit from the experiences of these pioneers.

Since there is ample evidence of the relationship between market pioneering and various long-term benefits, including market share and profits, one may conclude that creating or overcoming barriers to entry is associated with profitability. While many of the barriers are present even when the pioneers enter markets, many others are created by the pioneers - and sometimes by customers. By building barriers, pioneer and early entrant firms stop or slow down other firms from entering markets. Thus, they obtain large market shares in an attempt to monopolize the market and, consequently, get higher returns on investment. This situation is true in the markets where barriers are high so that potential entrants remain out of the markets. Thus, one should note that each industry is unique and that barriers affect industries differently. For example, there are very few or no customer switching costs in a snack food market, as compared to a computer market.

LATE MARKET ENTRY AND PROFITS

In some markets, however, most firms enter late and still become profitable. In fact, oftentimes, late entrants are more profitable than the pioneers or early entrants are. These late entrants know how to deal with barriers and create their own barriers. In fact, some choose to enter markets late because they want to evaluate the product(s), the market potential, and customer needs and wants. This situation often helps late entrants find niches that provide competitive advantages. Therefore, pioneering or early entry does not always lead to high profits. Several examples of profitable late entry were presented in Chapter 2.

Late market entrants benefit in many ways from the experiences of the pioneering and early follower firms. For example, they are not likely to repeat the mistakes of the incumbent firms. Indeed, they use the marketing and production experiences of incumbent firms. In addition, the height of some barriers is lowered as the incumbent firms' products enter the growth stage of the product life cycle. Therefore, some late market entrants are more profitable than the pioneering and early follower firms.

Low Barriers in Late Market Entry

Research and Development. Since the incumbent firms' products have been in the market for some time in late market entry conditions, this barrier may become less important in deterring entry. Potential new market entrants benefit from the already existing products' design and other related components. Thus, the late entrants do not have to invest as much money in research and development as do the pioneers and early followers.

Trade Secrets Held by Competitors. If any trade secrets exist, they have a tendency to leak out over time. Thus, for late entrants, this barrier sometimes may not exist, or it may not be as important as it is in the early market entry situation. As a result, late entrants profit from the knowledge and experience of the pioneers or early entrants with little or no investment.

Incumbents' Proprietary Product Technology. As with the trade secrets barrier, proprietary product technology may also become known to competitors over time. Although many firms patent their products and their technology, competition will usually find ways to learn about product technology and weaken this barrier as time goes on.

Government Licensing Requirements. As some products (e.g., foods) remain in markets, safety issues often become less of a concern because the passage of time indicates that the products are safe. The government eases up on licensing requirements, making market entry easier for late entrants. However, one should note that, in some industries (e.g., the trucking industry), the government wants to limit the number of companies present. In such industries, then, this barrier becomes even higher for late entrants.

Technology and Technological Change. Technological changes continue to occur after incumbent firms have been in a market for some time. However, the changes slow down eventually, and customers as well as firms with interests in the same markets adapt to these changes. Thus, the technology barrier becomes lower as the products progress in the product life cycle. In some industries, such as the electronic equipment industry (e.g., computers), technological changes happen continuously. In this type of technologically volatile industry, this barrier remains high, even in late market entry conditions.

Possession of Strategic Raw Materials. This barrier becomes less important over time because competitors try to find ways of acquiring strategic raw materials that they do not have. Therefore, time is on the side of the potential market entrants in dealing with this barrier, and the strategic raw materials become nonstrategic once the competition acquires them.

Sunk Costs. Because later entrants learn from the experiences of pioneers or early entrants, the sunk costs barrier becomes lower. In addition, later entrants do not have to educate potential buyers about products or services that have been around for some time. Their primary goal is to motivate customers to switch brands (i.e., to create selective demand).

Selling Expenses. Since incumbent firms experiment and often establish successful methods of selling their products, later entrants usually follow the same strategies or find even more cost-efficient selling techniques to use. Indeed, by the time later entrants attempt to enter markets, products being marketed are usually mass marketed. Thus, later entrants do not have to use much personal selling to attract distribution channels.

Incumbents' Expected Reaction to Market Entry. When pioneers or early entrants first enter markets, one of their major objectives is to recover their investments. Thus, they are willing to compete aggressively. Once incumbent firms recover their investments, the battle they are willing to fight is not as fierce. Thus, this barrier is not as important in the later stages of the product life cycle (i.e., maturity and decline) as it is in the early stages.

High Barriers in Late Market Entry

Incumbents' Cost Advantages Due to Experience or Learning Curves. As time goes on, incumbent firms reduce their costs because of learning curve effects. Simply put, they learn more cost efficient ways of producing and marketing their products. Therefore, the cost per unit produced decreases as the volume of production increases (i.e., the cost per unit decreases by about 20 to 30 percent as the quantity produced is doubled). In addition, incumbent firms increase their production volumes, resulting in economies of scale. Pioneers or early entrants use the cost reductions that result from economies of scale and learning curve effects to create barriers to market entry.

Incumbents' Superior Production Processes. Again, as with the trade secrets and proprietary product technology barriers, the superior production process barrier becomes less important as time goes on because potential market entrants are likely to investigate the best methods of production for a product that already exists. In addition, information about the incumbents' production capabilities also become public, whether legally or illegally.

Product Differentiation and Customer Loyalty. Two of the major long-term benefits of market pioneering or early entry are product differentiation and customer loyalty. Pioneer or early brands often become the standard against which customers judge the later entrants. Furthermore, customers develop loyalty to the brands that they already use. Thus, it becomes difficult to motivate the loyal customers to switch from the existing brands that they use to new brands that they have not had any experience with. In late market entry conditions, this barrier is high, even for well-known companies that enter markets. Companies that have achieved product differentiation or customer loyalty are usually the pioneers or the early followers (Robinson and Fornell 1985) and usually have higher market shares and high profits.

Customer Switching Costs. Once customers purchase products and become familiar with using certain brands of products, they resist trying other brands. This is because of perceived risks associated with trying other brands the amount of resistance and will vary from product to product. The height of the customer switching costs barrier also depends on the the type of perceived risk (i.e., whether functional, physical, financial, social, or psychological risk). Regardless, there is usually some cost involved in switching from one brand or product to another. Pioneers or early entrants attempt to create switching costs to ensure that they will continue to sell their products to the same customers. The switching costs, however, are not high for all products. For many low-priced consumer goods, switching costs are low or nonexistent, but for industrial products and high-priced consumer goods, the switching costs are almost always high.

Access to Distribution Channels. Market pioneers and early entrants have advantages in selecting or making arrangements with a large number of available distribution channels in early market entry situations. However, the choice for later entrants is usually limited. Thus, this barrier becomes higher in late market entry conditions.

Heavy Advertising by Incumbents. If a potential entrant cannot match the advertising expenditures of incumbent firms, then heavy advertising by incumbents becomes a barrier to entry. Furthermore, by heavy advertising, pioneers and early followers sometimes create product differentiation and brand loyalty. Thus, heavy advertising by incumbents serves to create other barriers for late entrants that translate into profits.

Price. This barrier usually results from having cost advantages. As pioneers or early followers remain in their markets, they are likely to reduce their costs due to economies of scale and learning curve effects. This condition allows them to lower prices, especially when the threat of market entry by competition exists. Since most late entrants enter markets during the maturity stage of the product life cycle, prices are almost always lower in this stage because of intense competition. Sometimes firms charge low prices when they enter markets because they have calculated the future costs and revenues rather than the short-term costs and revenues. Charging low prices, of course, discourages new competition from entering markets, thus creating a barrier to entry.

Incumbents' Government Subsidies. Since the government limits the amount of subsidies, later entrants are at a disadvantage in getting them. The government usually uses the first come, first served rule. Thus, in industries that the government subsidizes, the early entrants have a clear advantage.

Number of Competitors. As time goes on, the number of firms present in a market increases. This reduces the size of the pie available for late market entrants and can make it unattractive for firms to enter the market. The number of competitors in a market is usually greatest in the maturity stage of the product life cycle when some firms actually start dropping out of the market.

High Profit Rates Earned by Incumbents. Although the high profits earned by incumbents motivate market entry by others, these profits also act as a barrier to entry in late market entry conditions. This is because the incumbents with high profits can afford to wage price wars and increase promotional expenditures to maintain their current market positions.

Seller Concentration and the Magnitude of Market Shares Held by Incumbents. In some markets, incumbents tend to be located in certain geographical areas of the country. This condition acts as a barrier to entry in later stages of the product life cycle. In addition, some incumbent firms obtain large market shares that give them cost advantages due to economies of scale or other factors. Thus, the later entrants find themselves at a disadvantage and often choose not to enter markets.

WHY ARE BARRIERS RELATED TO PROFITABILITY?

Market Share and Economies of Scale and Profits

The barriers that are present in most markets and the barriers that are created by incumbent firms keep the competition out of markets or slow down their entry. Thus, incumbent firms often enjoy high market shares and consequently produce in large quantities that allow them to achieve low costs due to economies of scale. In order for new entrants to achieve economies of scale, they must also be able to produce in large volumes. This may be risky and it may require large investments in production, distribution, and promotion.

Based on previous research, the economies of scale advantages that pioneers or early entrants have appear to be the most important source of profitability. Of course, pioneers or early entrants also have high market shares. In fact, firms generally must have large market shares to enjoy the cost advantages of economies of scale. However, achieving economies of scale may require incumbent firms to increase their outputs. In fact, companies sometimes have to produce in such high volumes that they create excess capacity (Lieberman 1987). Having excess capacity may force firms to lower their prices so that they can sell the products produced. However, if demand exists, profits can increase due to increased sales volume.

Schmalensee (1981) shows that in the presence of scale economies entry deterrence is profitable. However, he also concludes that if the minimum scale is less than 10 percent of the market demand, then under demand certainty, scale-economy entry barriers can account for a rate of monopoly profits that exceeds the competitive rate by less than 10 percent. Perrakis and Warskett (1986) list the following U.S. industries in which economies of scale are thought to be important: aircraft, refrigerators and freezers, computers, passenger cars and trucks, electric motors, turbo generators, diesel engines, breweries, and cigarettes.

Cost Advantages Barriers and Profits

In addition to the economies of scale effect, incumbent firms experience lower costs per unit as they increase production. These cost reductions can result from learning curve effects and/or sometimes from superior production processes (often trade secrets). Of course, having cost advantages means having price advantages in the marketplace. If potential entrants cannot match the prices charged by incumbent firms, then they may choose not to enter markets. If they enter, however, without being able to match incumbent firms' costs, they are not likely to make as much profit as incumbent firms do.

If incumbent firms have some kind of know-how or technical capability that allows them to produce high-quality or low-cost products that are difficult for the competition to match, this situation may present itself as a barrier to entry. The low-cost position, of course, presents an advantage in acquiring high market shares and higher profits. The ability to produce high-quality products that the competition has difficulty matching usually creates product differentiation, which leads to brand loyalty.

Customer Switching Costs and Profits

Some barriers, such as customer switching costs, work as competitive tools in fighting competition before and after the competition enters the market. When customer switching costs are high, potential market entrants are likely to hesitate to enter markets. This barrier is usually high in most industrial markets and in some consumer markets, such as personal computers and household appliances. Switching long distance telephone services is a recent example of customer switching costs. Although the switching costs are not very high, they still present monetary and other costs to consumers (e.g., learning how to use the new dialing system). Therefore, firms that are already in the market are sometimes able to create somewhat of a monopoly that causes inelasticity of demand and consequently higher profits.

Customer switching costs, however, do not always increase profits. Klemperer (1987) has shown that competition among sellers for the initial sale causes sellers to compete away future switching cost rents in the price of the initial purchase. However, buyers still find it necessary to acquire as large a market share as possible in the initial buy-in period.

Price Barrier and Profits

Of course, prices charged by incumbent firms are related to their costs. When prices are so low that the potential entrants are afraid to match them, incumbent firms dominate the markets and enjoy high profits resulting from their high volume of sales. In addition, incumbent firms often attempt to deter competitors' entry by threatening to cut prices (MacLeod 1987).

Heavy Advertising by Incumbents and Profits

High levels of advertising lead to increased monopoly power and eventually to high profits (Comanor and Wilson 1979). Advertising, in addition to creating a barrier to entry by building brand loyalty, increases market share and hence profits (Waterson 1984). High advertising expenditures also create sunk costs, which act as barriers to market entry. In a study of 53 Canadian manufacturing industries, Kardasz and Stollery (1984) have determined that advertising raises the overall barrier to entry. Furthermore, higher profitability leads to advertising intensity, especially in industries producing mainly consumer goods.

Kessides (1986) suggests that advertising by incumbents may reflect profit maximization behavior. The need to invest money in advertising leads to incremental cost and incremental risk for potential entrants (Kessides 1986). This situation causes potential entrants to consider advertising expenditures as sunk costs.

Research and Development and Profits

High R&D expenses often influence firms' market entry decisions. This barrier is related to the sunk costs barrier because the amount of money spent on R&D cannot be recovered unless the firm is successful. Also, from a different perspective, firms that can afford to spend the necessary funds on R&D are likely to be the pioneers or early followers. Therefore, they may be able to enjoy the benefits associated with pioneering or early market entry, which include profits. The R&D barrier is high primarily in industries that develop technical products, and it cannot be an advantage if the product developed can be copied by the competition. In fact, if competitors can copy the product, they will have an advantage in the market because their R&D expenses are not as high as those of the pioneers or the early followers.

Product Differentiation, Customer Loyalty, and Profits

Firms try to differentiate their products from competitors' products because this leads to customer loyalty and sometimes to price inelasticity. Firms with loyal customers and highly differentiated products charge premium prices for their products that produce high profits. There are many examples in the clothing and cosmetics industries and in several industrial markets. A well-known clothing manufacturer, Polo Inc., charges very high prices for its clothes and cosmetic products. For example, the price of a wool sweater that carries the Polo logo, but is actually made in China, ranges from $150 to $300. A similar sweater with a different brand name can be purchased for $30 to $70. Consumers are willing to pay the high price for the Polo logo because it provides status in the sense that only the more fortunate and the successful can afford it (an image created by Polo). In the meantime, Polo enjoys high profits. Of course, Polo appeals to a very small market segment. Other clothing manufacturers could attempt to enter the same market, but they would have to invest a lot of money in promotion directed at consumers and develop promotional programs designed to attract the appropriate retailers to carry their products. Because this might prove to be risky, many choose to stay out of such markets.

Capital Requirements, Capital Intensity, and Profits

The high financing needed to meet capital requirements serves as an independent barrier to entry. However, this situation occurs mostly in capital-intensive markets, rather than labor-intensive markets. The costs involved can be considered as sunk since they are required to enter into capital-intensive markets. However, MacLeod (1987) has found that the existence of sunk costs by itself does not mean that the incumbent firms will necessarily earn supernormal profits. Grinyer, McKiernan, and Yasai-Ardekani (1988) have measured the capital intensity of a market by calculating the amount of fixed assets per employee. They claim that capital intensity acts as a barrier to entry and it is an important determinant of profitability. In capital-intensive markets that require large amounts of financing, the number of firms is usually small. As a result, companies in such markets have large market shares, and enjoy economies of scale and other benefits that contribute to profits.

Government Policy and Profits

Government policy affects profits in two ways: (1) Through licensing requirements, government limits the number of firms in a market. This situation is likely to provide important advantages to those firms that receive licenses. Simply put, they are likely to enjoy somewhat of a monopoly. (2) Government subsidizes certain industries, but the amount of such subsidies is not limitless. Therefore, firms in industries that receive subsidies have an additional competitive weapon to keep their rivals out of the market. This barrier is especially evident in international markets. For example, some subsidized companies in other countries are not required to earn profits. In addition, some foreign governments subsidize companies in certain markets so that these companies can keep their market shares.

Number of Competitors and Profits

As the number of companies in any given market increases, profit per company decreases. This is mainly due to lower market shares, which affect the ability of firms to achieve economies of scale because they are limited in increasing the production volume. Therefore, firms unwilling to accept low market shares and profits perceive the number of competitors in any given market as a barrier to entry.

Technology, Technical Changes, and Profits

Technology and technological change are two barriers that are likely to be present in all high technology industries (e.g., the computer industry). Entry into high technology markets usually requires large initial investments. Furthermore, once a firm has entered a high technology market, maintaining the required technology and adapting to changes in technology also require high levels of investment. Sometimes technology changes so rapidly that firms have to change their technologies without recovering their initial investments. Thus, only the successful and financially sound companies are likely to remain competitive in markets that require frequent technological changes.

Incumbents' Expected Reaction, High Profit Rates Earned by Incumbents, and Profits

Although common sense dictates that high profits earned by incumbent firms should motivate potential market entrants, they often do the opposite. The reason for this is the fact that incumbent firms are in a strong position to battle any new entrant by reducing prices, increasing promotion, etc. Potential entrants consider how incumbent firms will react to their market entry. When the incumbents earn high profits, the potential entrants expect the incumbent firms to compete fiercely and often choose not to enter markets.

Incumbents' Relatively Easy Access to Raw Materials and Profits

This barrier can favor incumbent firms in two ways: (1) incumbents' proximity to raw material suppliers and (2) contracts held by incumbent firms with raw material suppliers. Therefore, potential entrants may easily be at a disadvantage due to their locations or the contracts held by incumbents with suppliers. The location advantage, of course, creates costs advantages that can translate into higher profits. The contracts with raw materials suppliers assure continuity of supply at prices that are sometimes below market. Again, this condition provides cost advantages to incumbent firms, which often lead to higher profits.

Possession of Strategic Raw Materials and Profits

Sometimes incumbent firms own or acquire suppliers that possess strategic raw materials. Strategic raw materials are those that are not easily available and that are sometimes in short supply. Therefore, these firms have an advantage that can last as long as the supplies last, and they can monopolize markets without any contest for long periods of time. Ultimately, the firms with strategic raw materials create a barrier to entry that is almost impossible to overcome, and they earn substantial profits.

CONCLUSIONS

Almost all barriers are created by incumbent firms so they can prevent the competition from entering markets and can enjoy monopoly profits. However, some barriers lead the way to higher profits than do others. In both consumer and industrial markets, most barriers provide cost advantages to incumbents that are used to battle new competition or to discourage the entry of potential competitors into markets. As cost advantages and other barriers keep the new competition out of the market, the successful incumbent firms enjoy high profits by monopolizing the markets.

In addition to the cost advantages barrier, customer switching costs, product differentiation, customer loyalty, sunk costs, superior production processes, and the possession of strategic raw materials are the barriers that mostly relate to profitability. Profits result mainly from the fact that barriers limit the number of competitors in any given market.

REFERENCES

Comanor, William S., and Thomas S. Wilson. 1979. "The Effect of Advertising on Competition: A Survey." *Journal of Economic Literature* 17 (July): 453-76.

Grinyer, Peter H., Peter McKiernan, and Masoud Yasai-Ardekani. 1988. "Market, Organizational and Managerial Correlates of Economic Performance in the U.K. Electrical Engineering Industry." *Strategic Management Journal* 9 (July-August): 297-318.

Kardasz, Stanley W., and Kenneth R. Stollery. 1984. "Simultaneous Equation Models of Profitability, Advertising and Concentration for Canadian Manufacturing Industries." *Quarterly Journal of Business and Economics* 23 (Winter): 51-64.

Kerin, Roger A. P., Rajan Varadarajan, and Robert A. Peterson. 1990. *First Mover Advantages: A Synthesis and Critique.* Working Paper. Dallas: Southern Methodist University, 1-47.

Kessides, Ionnis N. 1986. "Advertising, Sunk Costs, and Barriers to Entry." *Review of Economics and Statistics* (Netherlands) 68 (February): 85-95.

Klemperer, Paul. 1987. "Markets with Consumer Switching Costs." *Quarterly Journal of Economics* (May): 375-94.

Lambkin, Mary. 1988. "Order of Entry and Performance in New Markets." *Strategic Management Journal* 9 (Summer): 127-40.

Lieberman, Marvin B. 1987. "Excess Capacity as a Barrier to Entry." *Journal of Industrial Economics* 35 (June): 607-27.

MacLeod, Bentley W. 1987. "Entry, Sunk Costs, and Market Structure." *Canadian Journal of Economics* 20 (1): 140-51.

Perrakis, Stylianos, and George Warskett. 1986. "Uncertainty, Economies of Scale, and Barrier to Entry." *Oxford Economic Papers* (UK) 38 (November): 58-74.

Porter, Michael. 1980. "From Competitive Advantage to Corporate Strategy." *Harvard Business Review* 58 (May-June): 43-59.

Robinson, William T. 1988. "Sources of Market Pioneer Advantages: The Case of Industrial Goods Industries." *Journal of Marketing Research* 25 (February): 87-94.

Robinson, William T., and Cleas Fornell. 1985. "Sources of Market Pioneering Advantages in Consumer Goods Industries." *Journal of Marketing Research* 22 (August): 305-17.

Schmalensee, R. 1981. "Economies of Scale and Barriers to Entry." *Journal of Political Economy* 89 (December): 1228-38.

Srinivasan, Kannan. 1988. "Pioneering Versus Early Following in New Product Markets." Ph. D. diss., University of California, Los Angeles.

Waterson, M. J. 1984. "Advertising Facts and Advertising Illusions." *International Journal of Advertising* 3 (4): 207-21.

Chapter 8

Creating and Overcoming
Barriers to Entry

Some barriers are not always created by competition. They exist even before a single firm enters a market. This type of barrier (i.e., capital requirements, government policy, technology, and technological change, etc.) is especially difficult to deal with. Nevertheless, there is a second group of barriers that are created by competitors after they successfully enter markets (i.e., product differentiation and customer loyalty, cost advantages, customer switching costs, heavy advertising, etc.), and they can be overcome if potential market entrants are willing to commit the necessary resources.

A third group of barriers also exists before and after the market entry of pioneering and follower firms (i.e., government policy, customer switching costs, capital requirements, sunk costs, etc.). For example, the customer switching costs barrier may exist before any pioneering firm enters a market because customers usually have products that perform the same or similar functions as the products of new market entrants, the pioneer and follower firms. A large number of companies that owned expensive typewriters (e.g., IBM electric typewriters) resisted buying computer word processors. In addition to losing the money invested in the typewriters, these companies also faced costs for the training that the new word processors required. Presently, however, most companies that own these expensive typewriters use them for typing addresses on envelopes or large labels or for typing some office forms. Additionally, in some offices, these once-expensive typewriters have been collecting dust because laser printers can type addresses, etc.

HOW TO CREATE BARRIERS TO ENTRY

Attain the Lowest Delivered Cost Position Relative to the Competition

As suggested in the previous chapter, incumbent firms can lower their costs by achieving economies of scale, using superior production processes, and experiencing learning curve effects. Firms with the lowest cost positions relative to the competition are not just profitable firms; they are often market leaders with the largest market shares. Hall (1980) suggests that achieving the lowest cost position relative to the competition should be coupled with both an acceptable delivered quality and a pricing policy intended to capture profitable volume and increase market share.

Use a Penetration Pricing Strategy

In order to discourage market entry by potential competitors, some firms employ a penetration strategy, charging low prices, to appeal to a mass market. Using this strategy, however, may require calculation of future costs, using the learning curve and the economies of scale effects. Of course, firms sometimes take risks in employing this strategy because it may take longer than expected to recover sunk costs or initial investments. However, potential market entrants are likely to view the low prices changed by incumbents as unprofitable and decide to stay out of the market.

Attain the Highest Product   Differentiated Position
Relative to the Competition

Product differentiation provides long-term benefits, as explained in earlier chapters. Achieving such a position usually requires high-quality products, service, and promotion. Of course, positive customer experience in the past is also an important factor in achieving product differentiation. Sometimes firms achieve such positions due to their past reputations. For example, IBM personal computers have achieved a significant market position relative to the competition, even though IBM entered the personal computer market late. This is mainly due to IBM's image as a producer of quality computers and other office equipment. Hall (1980) suggests that a firm's product differentiation position should be linked with both an acceptable delivered cost and a pricing policy intended to gain profits adequate for reinvestment in product differentiation.

Determine Your Distinctive Competence and Use It

Distinctive competence is defined by Webster (1979, 255) as "that set of capabilities that translates into a product-market strategy distinguishing the firm from its competitors in a way that is important to its customers." Distinctive competence can be found in a firm's variety of operations such as production, engineering, R&D, marketing, distribution, finance, public relations, and government relations.

Empirical evidence suggests a significant relationship between distinctive competence and firm profits. Hitt and Ireland (1985), after examining the relationship between profitability and distinctive competence in 185 companies, conclude that firms using their distinctive competences in developing their corporate strategies are successful. The importance of using distinctive competence is also evident from the experiences of companies that have done so successfully. For example, IBM has been successful in the computer market for many years, but it had principally manufactured and marketed mainframe computers. Its entry into the personal computer market led to a change in its customers, but the product was still a computer. Nevertheless, IBM also entered and failed in the duplicating machines business. Apparently, duplicating machines are not the kind of product that IBM has been used to manufacturing and marketing for years. Interestingly, Xerox, which has been in the duplicating business for a long time, entered and failed in the computer market (Sheth and Ram 1987).

Be Ready to Invest Large Sums of Money in Promotion

It is a known fact that products that are promoted through personal selling, advertising, publicity, or sales promotion do better in the marketplace than do those that are not promoted. Although the promotion techniques used depend on the product type (i.e., consumer product versus industrial product) and the target market, promoted products are likely to obtain differentiated positions. For example, many brands of bleach are indistinguishable; yet Clorox dominates the market despite the fact that its price is much higher than those of other brands of bleach. Similarly, ReaLemon reconstituted lemon juice is not much different from other brands that are much cheaper, but it controls 80 percent of the market (Wiggins and Lane 1983). These advantages are mainly the result of advertising campaigns launched by Clorox and ReaLemon. Consumers are likely to purchase advertised brands because they feel that the advertised brands are of better quality. Furthermore, many consumers feel that they reduce risks associated with the purchase of such products. This condition holds true for most consumer products, even though other brands may be better buys.

Previous research has shown that advertising increases brand loyalty and reduces the number of perceived product substitutes by enhancing product differentiability and by creating brand loyalty (Kessides 1986). This condition poses a high degree of risk of failure for potential market entrants. For potential entrants, the need to advertise leads to an unrecoverable entry cost in case of failure, creating the sunk costs barrier to entry (Kessides 1986).

Create Customer Switching Costs

This barrier is probably one of the most common barriers to entry in most industrial and some consumer markets. Firms, knowingly or unknowingly, create customer switching costs to keep their customers loyal. Customer switching costs are usually higher in industrial markets and in consumer markets for technical products because these products often require learning new skills (e.g., training) and abandoning products representing substantial initial investments (as when companies switch from typewriters to computer word processors). Sometimes companies create this barrier by designing unique operating systems (e.g., IBM computers versus Macintosh computers) so that switching will require users to be retrained. In addition to learning costs, there are always perceived risks for customers when they try new products. Thus, customers try to remain loyal to the product brands they are used to using unless switching costs can be eliminated or reduced substantially.

Employ Major Distribution Channels to Distribute Your Products

The availability of distribution channels is a critical factor in market entry decisions unless the market entrant has its own distribution outlets. Market pioneers and early followers are likely to employ the largest and most successful distributors. Thus, late entrants face disadvantages and may choose not to enter markets unless they can overcome this barrier. Some market pioneers and early entrants negotiate contracts with their distributors so that they can limit the number of distributors available to potential competitors. However, the type of product (i.e., industrial versus consumer, including convenience, shopping, emergency, and unsought goods) plays an important role in the distribution strategy employed.

Introduce Technological Breakthrough Products

Introducing new products that are truly technological breakthroughs provide the innovative firm with a dominant market position until competitors catch up. Of course, technological breakthrough products are difficult to copy, and competitors may take quite some time to develop them. However, in order for companies to introduce such products and occupy leadership positions, they may need to have proprietary product technology, a good R&D department, trade secrets, or superior production processes.

Do Not Disclose Profit or Sales Information If Possible

When demand is uncertain, potential entrants do not wish to take risks. A potential entrant prefers to remain out of the market until it is convinced that there is room for another competitor in the market. Nondisclosure of profit and sales information is likely to keep potential entrants wondering about the demand. Empirical research shows that demand uncertainty can act as a barrier to entry (Perrakis and Warskett 1986). However, this is possible only in the introduction stage of the product life cycle. Furthermore, only privately held companies do not have to disclose profit and sales information. Thus, this barrier is a very short lived one.

Create Excess Capacity When Possible

Excess capacity enables incumbents to expand output and cut prices following the entry of new competition (Lieberman 1987). This condition makes market entry unattractive for potential entrants. Of course, excess capacity should be created only if it is profitable because it costs money to create excess capacity. The rules of economies of scale and price/demand factors have to be considered carefully before creating excess capacity.

HOW TO OVERCOME BARRIERS TO ENTRY

Entry barriers are likely to increase the cost of entry for potential entrants if they choose to follow the same strategies employed by firms already in the market. Matching the incumbent firms' products, prices, and promotional activities is an invitation for retaliation, with the outcome depending on who has more resources, commitment, and determination to succeed (Day 1984). Therefore, rather than entering a market with a strategy that requires head-on competition with incumbent firms, it may be more beneficial to identify the barriers and avoid them, if possible. Nevertheless, the great majority of firms try to follow the market leaders, competing with them head-on, even though they are in a poor position to do so (Yip 1982). Interestingly, in the study conducted by Yip (1982), none of the followers was able to capture the market share held by the leader incumbent firms.

Many successful followers and late entrants try to avoid competition from the firms already in the market by introducing improved versions of products, by offering similar products at lower prices, or by attempting to serve a well-defined unserved market segment. In other words, they attempt to differentiate their products. The success of Jolt Cola in a highly competitive soda market is an example of overcoming entry barriers. Jolt Cola, which contains a lot of sugar and caffeine, appeals to those consumers who are not so health conscious and who would like sugar or caffeine to be alert. Another product called Vivarin followed Jolt Cola's strategy, but differentiated itself as a *tablet* that keeps consumers alert.

Although barriers to entry in the airline industry are quite high, many new firms have entered this market during the last two decades. In fact, some incumbent airlines that had been in the market for a long time have been forced out of the market. According to *Fortune* (1991), since deregulation in 1978, 232 new U.S. airlines, including many commuter airlines, have entered the market; of these, 171 have either merged or declared bankruptcy. In addition, 23 older airlines that had been in the market for quite some time also went out of business. Pan American and Eastern airlines are the most recent ones to go out of business.

Promotion can help even the follower firms in overcoming barriers to entry. Urban and Star (1991) claim that second market entrants can buy market share through heavy promotion and surpass the pioneer in cumulative volume of production, becoming the low-cost producer. This situation also can be true for the third and the other subsequent entrants during the early phase of the market (i.e., during market introduction and the early part of the market growth stages of the product life cycle).

Conduct Market Research

Market research is essential to the success of most businesses. It is necessary to determine customer demand and customer needs, identify present and potential competitors, and examine company strengths and weaknesses before attempting to enter any market. Through marketing research, it is always possible to identify a particular need that is not being completely satisfied by the firms already in the market or to identify distinct market segments that may be responsive to the offerings of potential market entrants. Many late entrants become successful because they create some kind of "niche." These late entrants usually create niches by conducting appropriate market research studies.

Market research should identify the possible barriers and their heights. In addition, potential entrants should investigate the opportunities for creating barriers themselves. Market entry decisions may need to be postponed or abandoned, depending on the barriers. Some barriers are difficult to overcome, and it may be more profitable to decide not to enter markets or find other markets where barriers do not exist or where they are weak.

Identification of opinion leaders through market research is also important in directing promotional activities to the right target. Opinion leaders are people who influence the decisions of others because of their knowledge or expertise in a product category. For example, pharmacists are often consulted by consumers when purchasing some over-the-counter medications. Computer programmers or people with computer expertise are consulted by consumers when purchasing computers. Auto mechanics are consulted when buying automobiles. Identifying the opinion leaders will enable companies to target their promotional efforts to these leaders in a cost-efficient manner.

Promote Your Products Heavily through Advertising and Other Promotional Methods

Companies can effectively enter markets and face very little or no competition despite the fact that market pioneers are already in these markets. Empirical evidence suggests that if a pioneer does not have a disproportionate competitive advantage, later entrants may effectively battle the incumbent firms with heavy advertising (Carpenter and Nakamoto 1990).

Advertising or other promotional expenditures, however, may become sunk costs. Thus, some firms choose to enter markets that require little or no promotion. Industries with high advertising-to-sales ratios are usually regarded as posing significant market entry barriers to later entrants.   This is because the advertising efforts of later entrants have to be designed to create brand awareness as well as to change the established buying patterns of consumers (i.e., to induce brand switching) (Kerin, Varadarajan, and Peterson 1990). However, firms willing to invest money in promotion to battle the competition may overcome some barriers.

Use of this strategy is especially effective when the access to distribution channels barrier is high. Through promotion directed at final users of products, new market entrants are likely to create selective demand for their products (i.e., demand for a specific brand of product). A-1 Steak Sauce used this strategy very effectively by persuading consumers to ask for A-1 Steak Sauce when they dine at restaurants. This forced many restaurants to place A-1 on restaurant tables, just like ketchup or mustard. Kodak and Hallmark Cards have also used this strategy effectively by promoting directly to consumers. Kodak film processing has been promoted as superior to other brands, while Hallmark has promoted its cards as the ones to buy "when you care enough to send the very best."

Avoid Competition

Although it is extremely difficult to avoid competition in profitable markets, there have been cases where companies have successfully avoided competition. They have accomplished this by finding a market segment that is not being satisfied or by developing products that are substantially better than or different from the ones in the market. For example, Kao, a Japanese toiletry company, avoided competition by creating a new product that duplicates the effects of a hot spring. This product has changed the bath gel business in Japan (Ohmae 1984). However, one should note that a firm like Kao can avoid competition only temporarily until others enter the market with similar products.

To avoid barriers, several automobile telephone manufacturers have begun selling their products directly to car makers so that they can be factory-installed (Sheth and Ram 1987). As this example shows, sometimes new entrants can market their products to original equipment manufacturers. Of course, this situation does not apply to every product. Usually, products that can be components of other products fall into this category. Some small firms sell their new product ideas and designs to major industry leaders because these small companies choose to avoid barriers and competition, even when successful entry is possible.

It is also important to investigate the incumbent firms' profit positions because incumbent firms with high profits are likely to react to the threat of new entrants. Research has shown that incumbents that have profits to protect and that can cover transitory losses are more likely to react aggressively to drive out the new market entrants (Kessides 1986).

Reduce Customer Switching Costs

Yao (1988) suggests that new entrants and firms with low market shares should try to reduce switching costs by designing their systems (products) to be compatible with existing high-market-share systems. For example, many computer companies reduced customer switching costs by introducing IBM-compatible computers. Companies can also reduce switching costs by providing training and other incentives to potential customers.

Another method of reducing switching costs is to reduce production and operation costs so that lower prices can be offered to customers who face switching costs. However, this is easier said than done. In order to achieve cost savings, firms usually have to experience economies of scale in production and other business-related activities (e.g., advertising), benefit from learning curve effects, or utilize superior production processes that provide substantial cost savings.

In order for customers to switch from their current brands or products that they use, the products offered by new market entrants must provide significant performance value. For example, cassette players provided significant benefits over record players, even though customers faced switching costs. The fact that customers could record on cassette players/recorders was an important benefit to them. The introduction of compact disc players into the market is also an excellent example of overcoming customer switching costs. Despite the fact that recording cannot be done on compact disc players, they have made major inroads into the audio equipment market. The quality of sound provided by compact disc players surpasses the quality of sound in both cassette players and record players. Thus, customer switching costs, though still there, have not been as effective as some may think.

Enter the Market through Acquisition

This entry strategy is especially effective when entering firms face late market entry situations and when they lack knowledge and expertise in production, distribution, and marketing in the interested markets. Organizations wishing to avoid having their eggs in a single basket attempt to enter new markets. This diversification strategy can be risky, but firms can reduce risk by benefiting from the knowledge and expertise of the acquired companies in the interested markets. By using this strategy, companies eliminate some barriers and reduce others.

Enter the Market through Joint Ventures or Licensing Agreements

When market entry requires large investments for research and development and for other business activities, companies may find it beneficial to pool resources with other companies and share the expenses as well as the risks.

Also, licensing agreements can reduce many of the barriers to entry by limiting the amount of investment and by not committing company resources to a particular project.

Use Vertical Integration as a Market Entry Strategy

Some companies integrate vertically to create competitive advantages for themselves. They integrate their operations as a way of raising the stakes and discouraging potential new entrants (Buzzell and Gale 1987). Vertical integration often reduces the costs and provides control of many essential operations. This strategy is especially effective when incumbent firms possess cost advantages and easy access to raw materials, and when access to distribution channels is limited. Oil companies have used this strategy for many years. In addition to drilling and refining oil, most of them also own or franchise retail outlets.

QUESTIONS TO ASK BEFORE ENTERING A MARKET

Although many of the questions that should be asked are the same before making early or late market entry, some may apply only to early market entry decisions and others only to late market entry decisions. Thus, the following questions are divided into two categories. One should note that many of the questions are repeated for late market entry conditions.

Questions to Ask Before Early Market Entry

1. How much capital is required to enter the interested market?
2. Do you have the financial resources required required to
   a. purchase the necessary production or other equipment, if necessary?
   b. invest in research and development, if necessary?
   c. set up new distribution channels or motivate the existing ones so that they will distribute your product(s.?
   d. promote your product(s), in order to educate potential buyers and create primary demand?
   e. battle with potential competitors?
   f. update production or other equipment to improve your product(s) or keep up with the technology in your industry?
3. Will you be able to produce and sell at a volume that will achieve economies of scale?
4. Will you be able to benefit from learning curve effects?
5. Does your firm have the competencies needed to become and remain competitive once it has entered the market?
6. Is there a demand for your product?

7. Are there established channels of distribution, or will you have to create new distribution channels?
8. Are there any customer switching costs? If so, how high are these costs?
9. Are you among the first few entrants into the market? If not, who are the incumbents, and what are their strengths and weaknesses?
10. Who are the likely potential competitors? What are their strengths and weaknesses?
11. Do you have any experience in the market you wish to enter?
12. Are your present customers likely to purchase the product you are about to introduce?
13. Is the demand high enough to warrant market entry? What is the market potential?
14. Are any substitute products with lower costs available in the market? If not, is it possible for other firms to introduce substitute products?
15. Does the product require patenting? If so, how long will it take to get a patent?
16. Can your product be easily copied by competitors?
17. Is it likely that customers will develop brand loyalty to your product?
18. Will you be able to achieve cost advantages over potential entrants?
19. Will you be able to battle potential entrants through either price cuts or other promotional techniques?
20. If you have any trade secrets, will you be able to keep them proprietary?
21. How high will the marketing expenses be for your product?
22. Is the market you wish to enter capital intensive?
23. How many potential competitors do you expect will follow your entry into market, and how soon?
24. Is there a possibility of obtaining any government subsidy?
25. Is there any government licensing requirement?
26. How soon do you expect the technology to change in the interested market or industry?
27. How much are the sunk costs?
28. Will the supplier of raw materials be able to meet your demand?
29. How many potential suppliers are there?
30. Can you have any control over your suppliers?
31. Will the power held by suppliers have an impact on your production and pricing strategies?
32. Do you possess any strategic raw materials? If so, can you prevent the competitors from gaining access to your strategic raw materials?
33. Is there any threat to successful production, distribution, and marketing other than competitors?
34. Is is easy to exit from the market if an exit decision is necessary?

Questions to Ask Before Late Market Entry

1. How much capital is required to enter the interested market?

2. Does your firm have the financial resources and competencies needed to become competitive in the interested market?
3. How much are the sunk costs?
4. Have you had any experience in the interested market?
5. Is the market you wish to enter capital intensive?
6. Is there a possibility of obtaining any government subsidy?
7. Is there any government licensing requirement?
8. Are your present customers likely to purchase the product you are about to introduce?
9. Does your firm have a good reputation (i.e., brand recognition or brand preference)?
10. Is the market large enough to warrant market entry? Is there room for your firm and other potential market entrants?
11. What is the market growth rate?
12. Who are the present and potential competitors? What are their strengths and weaknesses?
13. How many incumbent firms are present in the interested market?
14. How will the incumbent firms react to your market entry?
15. How will the other potential market entrants react to your market entry?
16. Will you be able to battle potential entrants through either price cuts or other promotional techniques?
17. Do only a few companies hold the majority of the market (i.e., do a few firms have very large market shares, while many other firms have small shares)?
18. Will the present distribution channels carry your product?
19. Will you have to create your own distribution channels? Is it more profitable to create your own distribution channels?
20. Do the incumbent firms have a brand loyalty advantage?
21. Should you patent your product? Can you obtain a patent?
22. Do the incumbent firms have patents for their products?
23. Do the incumbents have significant economies of scale?
24. Can you produce and sell at a volume that will achieve economies of scale?
25. Can your firm achieve cost advantages (i.e., in material costs, distribution costs, etc.) over the incumbent firms ? Or can your firm match the competitors' prices or undercut them, if necessary ?
26. Can you enter the market with a better-quality product than the ones available in the market?
27. How many suppliers are there? Are they willing to supply your firm with adequate supplies?
28. Will the power held by suppliers have an impact on your production and pricing strategies?
29. Can you have any control over your suppliers?
30. How high are the marketing expenses for your product?
31. Are there any customer switching costs in the interested market?
32. Is there any threat to successful production, distribution, and marketing other than competitors?

33. Is it easy to exit from the market if an exit decision is necessary?

REFERENCES

Buzzell, Robert D., and Bradley T. Gale. 1987. *The PIMS Principles: Linking Strategy to Performance.* New York: Free Press.

Carpenter, Gregory S., and Kent Nakamoto. 1990. "Consumer Preference Formation and Pioneering Advantage." *Journal of Marketing Research* 26 August: 285-98.

Day, George S. 1984. *Strategic Market Planning: The Pursuit of Competitive Advantage.* St. Paul: West.

Fortune. 1991. "U.S. Carriers: More will Vanish." 123 (2): 13 (January 28).

Hall, William K. 1980. "Survival Strategies in a Hostile Environment." *Harvard Business Review* (September-October): 75-85.

Hitt, Michael A., and R. Duane Ireland. 1985. "Corporate Distinctive Competence, Strategy, Industry and Performance." *Strategic Management Journal* 6: 273-93.

Kerin, Roger A. P., Rajan Varadarajan, and Robert A. Peterson. 1990. *First Mover Advantages: A Synthesis and Critique.* Working Paper. Dallas: Southern Methodist University, 1-47.

Kessides, Ionnis N. 1986. "Advertising, Sunk Costs, and Barriers to Entry." *Review of Economics and Statistics* (Netherlands) 68 (February): 85-95.

Lieberman, Marvin B. 1987. "The Learning Curve, Diffusion, and Competitive Strategy." *Strategic Management Journal* 8 (September-October): 441-52.

Ohmae, Kenichi. 1984. "Getting Back to Strategy." *Harvard Business Review* (November-December): ES44.

Perrakis, Stylianos, and George Warskett. 1986. "Uncertainty, Economies of Scale, and Barriers to Entry." *Oxford Economic Papers (UK)* 38 (November): 58-74.

Sheth, Jagdish N., and S. Ram. 1987. *Bringing Competition to Market.* New York: John Wiley.

Urban, Glen, and Steven Star. 1991. *Advanced Marketing Strategy: Phenomena, Analysis and Decisions.* Englewood Cliffs, N.J.: Prentice-Hall.

Webster, Frederick, Jr. 1979. *Industrial Marketing Strategy.* New York: John Wiley.

Wiggins, Steven N., and W. J. Lane. 1983. "Quality Uncertainty, Search, and Advertising." *American Economic Review* 73 (5): 881-94.

Yao, Dennis A. 1988. "Beyond the Reach of the Invisible Hand: Impediments to Economic Activity, Market Failures, and Profitability." *Strategic Management Journal* 9 (Summer): 59-71.

Yip, George S. 1982. "Gateways to Entry." *Harvard Business Review* 60 (September- October): 85-92.

Chapter 9

Conclusions

Nearly all firms face some sort of barriers to entry when they attempt to introduce new products into an existing market or enter a market with products that are similar to those already in the market. Although the sources of barriers to entry and their heights differ from market to market, the objective of all barriers is the same: to deter the entry of competitors into a market so that the firms already in that market maximize their profits. Companies attempt to avoid or bypass these barriers by entering markets through acquisition or by developing their own niches. A large number of studies that have examined market entry barriers from various perspectives delineate the importance of barriers to entry for both consumer and industrial goods markets.

TYPES OF BARRIERS AND THEIR IMPORTANCE

Some barriers are easy to overcome, while others are almost impossible. In Chapter 1, a large number of barriers to entry were presented and divided into two categories: (1) competitor-activated or controllable barriers and (2) environmental or uncontrollable barriers. The first group of barriers is created by pioneer and early follower firms; these barriers usually can be overcome if potential entrants have the financial resources required to battle the incumbent firms. However, the second group of barriers is more difficult to overcome. The most important of these barriers include capital requirements and capital intensity of the market, sunk costs, government policy, number of firms present in a market, technology and technological change, magnitude of market shares held by incumbents, incumbents' expected reaction to market entry, and possession of or easy access to strategic raw materials.

The importance of barriers in terms of deterring market entry of competitors differs. Based on empirical evidence, product differentiation, customer loyalty, capital requirements to enter markets, and incumbents' cost advantages are the most important barriers in both consumer and industrial markets. Another barrier, customer switching costs, also emerges as a powerful barrier in industrial markets.

In order for firms to create the above barriers, certain conditions must be met. To achieve product differentiation, a firm must have a product that is better than its competitors' products. However, sometimes a company's brand name alone may create product differentiation due to favorable customer experiences with the same brand in the past. This is the same as the customer loyalty barrier and is more prevalent in industrial markets than in consumer markets because most industrial product purchases pose higher financial risks to buyers. It is also possible to achieve product differentiation through heavy advertising. Heavy advertising by incumbent firms acts as a barrier to entry unless potential market entrants can match or surpass the advertising expenditures of the incumbents.

The cost advantages barrier has its roots in incumbent firms' production capacities, learning curves, and other advantages, such as delivery costs, and the like. Producing at the level of scale economies appears to be a must for firms to have cost advantages. Superior production processes, trade secrets, and proprietary product technology also result in cost advantages. Potential market entrants will be at a disadvantage unless they also have similar sources of cost advantages.

The capital requirements barrier, which is basically a financial resource requirement barrier, is present in almost every new market. Firms can reduce this barrier if they can produce the new product by modifying their present production equipment and production systems. Usually, this barrier is higher in industrial markets since many industrial products are technical in nature and may require large capital outlays.

In order for incumbent firms to create the above barriers, they must be financially sound and enter the interested markets first. Once market entry is successfully accomplished, they can start creating barriers to entry for potential competitors. Needless to say, this requires strategic planning and commitment of financial resources in the interested markets.

The importance of barriers in deterring the market entry of competitors is different in consumer and industrial markets. These differences are largely due to the differences in marketing strategy development and planning. Customers, products, distribution channels, promotional techniques, and pricing strategies may also be different in consumer and industrial markets. In addition, the importance of barriers varies for early and late entry into consumer and industrial markets.

BARRIERS IN EARLY AND LATE MARKET ENTRY

Based on empirical evidence, incumbents' cost advantages, capital requirements for market entry, and product differentiation advantages are more important than the other barriers in both early and late entry into consumer markets. Although the importance of these barriers varies among themselves for early entry into industrial markets, the order of barriers in importance is the same as in consumer markets. For late entry into industrial markets, however, cost advantages, capital requirements, and customer switching costs are the three most important barriers. Interestingly, the government policy barrier is rated as one of the least important barriers in deterring market entry in the two studies performed.

In terms of early and late entry decisions in consumer and industrial markets, only a handful of the barriers differ in importance. For early and late entry into consumer and industrial markets, customer switching costs is the only barrier that differs in importance for deterring market entry by competitors. This barrier appears to be more important in late market entry conditions.

BARRIERS IN CONSUMER MARKETS VERSUS INDUSTRIAL MARKETS

When the importance of barriers is compared for consumer and industrial markets, five of the six barriers tested are significantly different. This shows that there is a clear difference in the importance of barriers in deterring market entry between consumer and industrial markets. The cost advantages, customer switching costs, and government policy barriers are more important for market decisions in industrial markets. However, the product differentiation and access to distribution channels barriers are more important for early entry decisions in consumer markets.

For late entry decisions in consumer and industrial markets, only two barriers are different. The product differentiation barrier is more critical in consumer markets when companies make late entry decisions. The customer switching costs barrier appears to be more important for late entry decisions in industrial markets than in consumer markets. No other barriers are found to be different in terms of deterring market entry. When this situation is compared with early market entry, it is clear that more barriers are different in terms of deterring market entry in early periods of the product life cycle.

MARKET ENTRY BARRIERS IN INTERNATIONAL MARKETS

Barriers to entry change form and strength in international markets. In addition, some new barriers are added to the list of barriers when marketing executives make market entry decisions in international markets. Some barriers will change further as the single European market emerges in 1992. Although foreign government policy has been cited as a barrier to entry in the literature for many years, other barriers have gained ground during the last decade. In addition to the foreign government policy barrier, four other barriers have been effective in deterring entry-cultural differences, product adaptation, access to distribution channels, and political uncertainty. Interestingly, the access to distribution channels barrier in international markets appears to be the most important in both early and late market entry decisions. Distribution channels and means of transportation in other countries are quite different from those in the United States. The government policy barrier follows the distribution channels barrier in terms of importance. The power of this barrier lies mainly in the government licensing requirements and the government subsidies given to domestic companies in foreign countries. For early and late market entry decisions into international markets, the political uncertainty, product adaptation, and cultural differences barriers follow the government policy barrier in that order.

It is clear that the 1992 unification of the European Economic Community (EEC) will have an impact on the barriers to entry for U. S. firms into the EEC market. However, this impact appears to be positive. The important issue seems to be the ability of U.S. firms to comply with the rules imposed by the EEC. The success of U.S. firms will depend on the timing of market entry, if they are not already in the European market, and on their skills in modifying their production and marketing to conform to EEC policies, if they are already in the market.

The strength of barriers in deterring market entry of foreign firms also depends on the country's stage of economic development. The barriers are not the same in Third World countries, or in developing countries, as they are in industrialized nations. The barriers that are most important in developing countries are cultural differences, language, access to distribution channels, government policy, product adaptation, stability of the currency exchange rate, changes in promotional programs, nationalism, political environment, corruption, and local competition. Although the same barriers are also important in Third World markets, the market opportunities in these countries are different; they are usually limited to food, medicine, agricultural production, transportation, and defense equipment. Although these markets are not very attractive, the competition is weak or nonexistent.

Barriers also differ between the Eastern Bloc nations and the Western world. The recent changes in the Eastern bloc nations are likely to influence the height of the barriers in these countries. It appears that the major barrier to entry, foreign government policy, has been weakened in the Eastern bloc nations, but some other barriers (e.g., economic environment) will take a long time to shrink.

In overcoming barriers to entry in international markets, market research is essential. However, it is important to note that market research in international markets is different. Some of the market research techniques used in U.S. markets cannot be implemented in many international markets due to respondent reactions or the availability of respondents for primary data- gathering techniques (e.g., illiteracy precludes self-administered surveys). In gathering secondary data, firms also face a lot of red tape. Furthermore, the secondary data gathered are not always accurate. Therefore, firms with interests in international markets must plan their marketing activities very carefully to avoid disaster.

PRODUCT LIFE CYCLE AND BARRIERS TO ENTRY

Barriers to entry vary in different stages of the product life cycle. While many of the barriers are high in the introduction stage and the early part of the growth stage, many also remain high in the later part of the growth stage and the maturity stage. Since the market introduction stage and the early phase of the growth stage represent early market entry, the barriers in these stages are the same as in early market entry situations. Similarly, the later part of the growth stage and the maturity stage symbolize late market entry conditions. Therefore, the discussion of barriers in late market entry situations applies here as well. The cost advantages and access to distribution channels barriers are crucial in the market introduction stage and the early part of the growth stage, while the capital requirements, customer switching costs, and government policy barriers remain important in the later part of the growth stage and the maturity stage.

Another form of barrier to entry that has not been mentioned as a barrier to entry is the barrier to exit. When barriers to exit are high, firms hesitate to enter markets. The barriers to exit prevail mainly because of the investments made and the operating and marketing fit present between the divestment candidate and the other units in the firm. In addition, psychological costs of market exit exist. Oftentimes, management personnel are committed to serving certain markets and perceive it as a challenge even if the business is not profitable. Furthermore, a market exit decision would mean failure for management personnel, and this is a factor that many companies try to avoid unless it is necessary.

In the study performed (see Chapter 5), forward vertical integration is considered the most important exit barrier in a declining industry, followed by backward integration, cost of divestment, and operating fit. In a mature industry, forward integration is again the most important exit barrier, followed by backward integration, cost of divestment, operating fit, marketing fit, and the number of years the unit has been with the firm. The results of the study also show that the stages of the product life cycle determine, at least in part, corporate strategies.

MANAGERIAL CONSENSUS ON BARRIERS TO ENTRY

The relationship between consensus on the significance of market entry barriers and firm performance was examined in Chapter 6. The rationale for such an analysis can be found in the strategy formulation and implementation literature. Is it better for marketing executives to agree or disagree on market entry decisions? If they agree on the importance of the barriers, of course, they are likely to agree on market entry decisions. Previous research shows that when there is consensus on the implementation of strategy, firms are more profitable. In terms of barriers to market entry, it is important to discover which barriers lead to success when there is consensus. This situation becomes more important when there is only a single barrier or group of barriers present in markets.

When executives face more than a single barrier (e.g., the six barriers presented in Chapter 6), consensus on the capital requirements and incumbents' cost advantages barriers is related to company performance in consumer markets. Similarly, for late market entry decisions, consensus on the customer switching costs, cost advantages, and capital requirements to enter markets barriers is associated with firm performance in consumer markets. For early entry into industrial markets, consensus on the access to distribution channels and capital requirements barriers is related to company performance. For late entry into industrial markets, in addition to consensus on the access to distribution channels and capital requirements barriers, consensus on the customer switching costs barrier is related to company success.

When executives consider barriers independently in the early entry into consumer markets decision, the cost advantages and the capital requirements barriers are related to company performance. For the late entry into consumer markets decision, in addition to the two preceding barriers, consensus on the customer switching costs barrier is associated with performance. In the early and late entry into industrial markets decisions, however, the situation is somewhat different. For early entry conditions, consensus on the capital requirements and access to distribution channels barriers is related to performance. For late entry, in addition to the two preceding barriers, consensus on the customer switching costs barrier is related to company performance.

PROFITABILITY AND BARRIERS TO ENTRY

In markets where barriers are high, incumbent firms enjoy large profits. This is largely due to the small number of firms present in such markets. Because of the high barriers, only strong firms are able to enter these markets and remain successful. Of course, when only a small number of firms are present in such markets, each firm has a larger market share or a bigger piece of the pie. Large market shares require large production volumes which often yield economies of scale and the benefits of learning curve effects. This situation gives cost advantages to the firms already in the market. As incumbent firms make profits, these profits raise another form of barrier to entry. Potential market entrants anticipate fierce competition from the incumbent firms, which are not willing to give up their highly profitable positions so easily. However, potential market entrants can become successful if they calculate the magnitude of the barriers present before market entry. In fact, the followers can even become more profitable than the incumbent firms when they enter markets with carefully designed marketing strategies.

The highest barriers are the ones that help incumbent firms profit the most. As already mentioned, cost advantages resulting from economies of scale and the learning curve, as well as other cost advantages such as delivery and raw material costs, are related to firm profitability. However, such barriers as product differentiation and customer loyalty allow the incumbent firms to charge premium prices for their products which, of course, is associated with profitability.

The customer switching costs barrier, although more important in industrial markets, gives incumbent firms a competitive advantage in some consumer markets as well. When this barrier is high, customers tend to be loyal unless competition can minimize or eliminate the costs of switching. However, having created customer switching costs, most incumbent firms have large market shares and often monopolize markets.

Access to distribution channels, capital requirements, government policy, and the other barriers work in the same way as the above barriers to keep potential competitors out of markets. By keeping the number of firms to a minimum, the incumbent firms usually maximize their profits. It is also important to note that some markets have a very large number of firms; yet only a few of them are profitable. In most cases, these profitable firms are the market leaders, with large market shares and much interest in their markets. It is also possible to find some small companies that are highly lucrative because they have successfully created some sort of marketing niche.

CREATING OR OVERCOMING BARRIERS TO ENTRY

Depending on the industry type, some barriers to entry originate from research and development (R&D). The costs of R&D serve as an independent barrier to entry because they are mainly sunk costs. Although operating an R&D department is costly, it pays off in the long run to have one. Since the R&D department's major function is to develop new products and improve the existing ones, R&D expenditures can be minimal when the competitive advantages that originate from these departments are considered. The first advantage that an R&D department can provide is product quality. This advantage easily leads to product differentiation and customer loyalty advantages that last for many decades. In addition, R&D departments also work on new and more cost efficient methods of production. The R&D work transforms into cost advantages that create crucial barriers to market entry. Product innovation is the key to success for most businesses, which, of course, requires investment in R&D.

In addition to obtaining cost advantages, product differentiation, and customer loyalty, there are other ways of creating barriers to entry: using a market penetration pricing strategy, developing or identifying distinctive competence, investing large sums of money in promotional activities, developing proprietary product knowledge, making arrangements with major distribution channels for exclusive rights, keeping sales and profit information proprietary, and engaging in activities that are likely to create customer switching costs.

Although barriers exist in almost all markets, they do not always seem to stop the entry of new competitors. In fact, new competitors are seen in new markets almost every day. The new market entrants are able to overcome the barriers to entry and sometimes create their own barriers once they enter market. Of course, overcoming the barrier to entry depends on the height of the barriers.

Some barriers are so high that it is almost impossible to overcome them, while others are rather low.

The first step in overcoming entry barriers is conducting market research. Through market research, it is possible to identify the barriers and their strengths so that appropriate actions can be taken. The decision not to enter a market is always an alternative and can sometimes be the best choice. Through market research, however, it is also possible to discover a niche and avoid competition. Although some companies see market research as an added burden, its payoff is much higher than that of advertising and several other marketing activities. Some firms may choose to use advertising and other promotional techniques instead of market research. It is really necessary to use both to successfully tackle barriers.

Other methods of overcoming barriers to entry include entering a market through acquisition of a company that is already in the market, entering a market through a joint venture, making licensing agreements that reduce or eliminate customer switching costs, and using vertical integration as a market entry strategy. Licensing agreements might be the best market entry strategy in international markets because they minimize risk.

Finally, initial market entrants (i.e., pioneers and early followers) and late entrants must ask themselves the important strategic questions before making any commitment to market entry. Although Chapter 8 gives long lists of questions to ask for both early and late market entry decisions, the most important questions include the following: Which barriers to entry exist? Can they be overcome? If so, how can they be overcome? What is the market potential? Who are the competitors? What product life cycle stage will the entering company be in? If it is late entry, what is the life of the product? Does the product provide something more beneficial than do the products already in the market? Are there any substitute products? Answering these and other questions requires situation analysis, which is normally conducted as part of marketing strategy planning. However, analysts must ask the right questions so that the answers obtained can be used as input for market entry decisions.

Appendix A: Market Entry Simulation Exercise

INTRODUCTION

This is an exercise that deals with market entry barriers and how you would decide to enter a market under certain market entry conditions. Please try to place yourself in the position of an executive who is about to make a market entry decision. The market entry barriers and the entry decisions are described below.

MARKET ENTRY BARRIERS

Cost Advantages of Incumbents: The cost advantages include the decline in unit cost of a product since the absolute value of production is large (i.e., due to economies of scale) as well as the reduction in cost per unit due to product know-how, design characteristics (i.e, through patents or secrecy), the learning or experience curve, (i.e., unit cost decline as the firm gains more experience in producing a product), and other cost advantages.

High Cost Advantages of Incumbents mean that the firms already in the market, the incumbents, have achieved substantial cost advantages over you, the new entrant. Low Cost Advantages of Incumbents imply that the incumbents have some cost advantages over you, but these advantages are not substantial.

Product Differentiation: Established firms have brand identification and customer loyalties which stem from past advertising, customer service, product differences, or simply being first into the industry.

High Product Differentiation of incumbents means the firms already in the market have achieved a product differentiation advantage over you, the new entrant. Low Product Differentiation means the incumbents do not have a strong advantage over you.

Capital Requirements: The need to invest financial resources to enter a market and compete in that market.

High Capital Requirements refer to conditions where firms already in the market have invested large financial resources into manufacturing and marketing a product, and entering such a market requires you, the new entrant, to invest heavily. Low Capital Requirements mean the opposite of the preceding.

Customer Switching Costs: One-time costs facing the buyer due to switching from one supplier's product to another's (i.e., employee retraining costs, cost of new ancillary equipment, cost and time in testing or qualifying a new source, need for new technical help, product redesign, etc.).

High Customer Switching Costs are the high costs associated with potential buyers' switching from one supplier to another. Firms already in the market try to create high Customer Switching Costs so that their customers do not switch to other suppliers. Low Customer Switching Costs mean the opposite.

Access to Distribution Channels: The extent that logical distribution channels for a product have already been served by the established firms already in the market.

High barriers in Access to Distribution Channels mean that firms already in the market have control over most of the available distribution channels. Therefore, the incumbents have advantages over you. Low barriers in Access to Distribution Channels mean the opposite.

Government Policy: The extent that government limits or forecloses entry into industries with such controls as licensing requirements and limits access to raw materials (i.e., regulated industries and environmental protection agency laws).

High Government Policy entry barriers imply that government limits entry into industries through some requirements. Thus, firms already in the market have advantages over you, the new entrant. Low Government Policy entry barriers mean the opposite.

MARKET ENTRY DECISIONS

Early Market Entry: Entering a market after the first firm has entered with a new product (i.e., early market entry may take place just on the heels of the first entrant) (Jain 1981).

Late Market Entry: Entering the market toward the tail end of the growth phase of the market or in the maturity phase of the market (Jain 1981).

Industrial Goods Markets: Includes markets where firms produce goods or services to be used in the production of other goods and services.

Consumer Goods Markets: Includes markets where firms produce goods or services for the public.

The following market conditions differ only in regard to the information presented to you about six market entry barriers. In each market condition, please consider the information presented to you and then arrive at your recommendation. Circle the number under decision A which indicates the percent chance that you would recommend early market entry into consumer goods markets. Repeat the same process for decisions B, C, and D. Again, *the percentages indicate the likelihood that you would recommend early or late market entry into consumer and industrial goods markets individually, given certain entry barrier conditions.*

Please note that each decision is independent and that the percentages do not have to add up to 100.

An example is provided below for you before you start.

EXAMPLE:

```
                    MARKET CONDITION # 1:
            . Cost Advantages of Incumbents.................High
            . Product Differentiation of Incumbents.........Low
            . Capital Requirements to Enter Market.........Low
            . Customer Switching Costs........................Low
            . Access to Distribution Channels.................Low
            . Government Policy...................................Low
```

With the level of these 6 market entry barriers in mind, indicate the chance you would recommend market entry (please circle percentages).

....*Decision A:* If the above represents an early market entry opportunity into Consumer Goods Market.

No Chance 0% 10% 20% 30% 40% 50% 60% 70% 80% 90% 100% Definite

....*Decision B:* If the above represents a late market entry opportunity into Consumer Goods Market.

No Chance 0% 10% 20% 30% 40% 50% 60% 70% 80% 90% 100% Definite

....*Decision C:* If the above represents an early market entry opportunity into Industrial Goods Market.

No Chance 0% 10% 20% 30% 40% 50% 60% 70% 80% 90% 100% Definite

....*Decision D:* If the above represents a late market entry opportunity into Industrial Goods Market.

No Chance 0% 10% 20% 30% 40% 50% 60% 70% 80% 90% 100% Definite

The decision maker in the above situation does not consider product differentiation that the incumbents have achieved very important when making early or late entry into consumer goods markets. Therefore, he perceives that there is an 80 percent chance he would recommend early or late market entry into consumer goods markets.

In contrast, the above decision maker feels that product differentiation is a little more important in industrial goods markets than in consumer goods markets. Thus he suggests early market entry 60 percent of the time. Similarly, he thinks that product differentiation of the incumbents is not that important when making late market entry into industrial goods markets, but he feels he would favor late entry a little more. Thus he suggests late market entry 70 percent of the time. Please note that the above situation is hypothetical and should not influence your decisions in this exercise.

PLEASE COMPLETE THE FOLLOWING 32 MARKET ENTRY CONDITIONS SINCE EACH IS DIFFERENT.

MARKET CONDITION # 1:

. Cost Advantages of Incumbents..................High
. Product Differentiation of Incumbents.........Low
. Capital Requirements to Enter Market.........Low
. Customer Switching Costs........................Low
. Access to Distribution Channels.................Low
. Government Policy..................................Low

With the level of these 6 market entry barriers in mind, indicate the chance you would recommend market entry (please circle percentages).

....*Decision A:* If the above represents an early market entry opportunity into Consumer Goods Market.

No Chance   0% 10% 20% 30% 40% 50% 60% 70% 80% 90% 100%   Definite

....*Decision B:* If the above represents a late market entry opportunity into Consumer Goods Market.

No Chance   0% 10% 20% 30% 40% 50% 60% 70% 80% 90% 100%   Definite

....*Decision C:* If the above represents an early market entry opportunity into Industrial Goods Market.

No Chance   0% 10% 20% 30% 40% 50% 60% 70% 80% 90% 100%   Definite

....*Decision D:* If the above represents a late market entry opportunity into Industrial Goods Market.

No Chance   0% 10% 20% 30% 40% 50% 60% 70% 80% 90% 100%   Definite

MARKET CONDITION # 2:

. Cost Advantages of Incumbents..................High
. Product Differentiation of Incumbents.........Low
. Capital Requirements to Enter Market.........Low
. Customer Switching Costs........................Low
. Access to Distribution Channels.................Low
. Government Policy..................................Low

With the level of these 6 market entry barriers in mind, indicate the chance you would recommend market entry (please circle percentages).

....*Decision A:* If the above represents an early market entry opportunity into Consumer Goods Market.

No Chance   0% 10% 20% 30% 40% 50% 60% 70% 80% 90% 100%   Definite

....*Decision B:* If the above represents a late market entry opportunity into Consumer Goods Market.

No Chance   0% 10% 20% 30% 40% 50% 60% 70% 80% 90% 100%   Definite

....*Decision C:* If the above represents an early market entry opportunity into Industrial Goods Market.

No Chance   0% 10% 20% 30% 40% 50% 60% 70% 80% 90% 100%   Definite

....*Decision D:* If the above represents a late market entry opportunity into Industrial Goods Market.

No Chance   0% 10% 20% 30% 40% 50% 60% 70% 80% 90% 100%   Definite

MARKET CONDITION # 3:

. Cost Advantages of Incumbents.................High
. Product Differentiation of Incumbents.........Low
. Capital Requirements to Enter Market.........Low
. Customer Switching Costs........................Low
. Access to Distribution Channels.................Low
. Government Policy..................................Low

With the level of these 6 market entry barriers in mind, indicate the chance you would recommend market entry (please circle percentages).

....*Decision A:* If the above represents an early market entry opportunity into Consumer Goods Market.

No Chance   0% 10% 20% 30% 40% 50% 60% 70% 80% 90% 100%   Definite

....*Decision B:* If the above represents a late market entry opportunity into Consumer Goods Market.

No Chance   0% 10% 20% 30% 40% 50% 60% 70% 80% 90% 100%   Definite

....*Decision C:* If the above represents an early market entry opportunity into Industrial Goods Market.

No Chance   0% 10% 20% 30% 40% 50% 60% 70% 80% 90% 100%   Definite

....*Decision D:* If the above represents a late market entry opportunity into Industrial Goods Market.

No Chance   0% 10% 20% 30% 40% 50% 60% 70% 80% 90% 100%   Definite

MARKET CONDITION # 4:

. Cost Advantages of Incumbents.................High
. Product Differentiation of Incumbents.........Low
. Capital Requirements to Enter Market.........Low
. Customer Switching Costs........................Low
. Access to Distribution Channels.................Low
. Government Policy..................................Low

With the level of these 6 market entry barriers in mind, indicate the chance you would recommend market entry (please circle percentages).

....*Decision A:* If the above represents an early market entry opportunity into Consumer Goods Market.

No Chance   0% 10% 20% 30% 40% 50% 60% 70% 80% 90% 100%   Definite

....*Decision B:* If the above represents a late market entry opportunity into Consumer Goods Market.

No Chance   0% 10% 20% 30% 40% 50% 60% 70% 80% 90% 100%   Definite

....*Decision C:* If the above represents an early market entry opportunity into Industrial Goods Market.

No Chance   0% 10% 20% 30% 40% 50% 60% 70% 80% 90% 100%   Definite

....*Decision D:* If the above represents a late market entry opportunity into Industrial Goods Market.

No Chance   0% 10% 20% 30% 40% 50% 60% 70% 80% 90% 100%   Definite

MARKET CONDITION # 5:

. Cost Advantages of Incumbents.................High
. Product Differentiation of Incumbents.........Low
. Capital Requirements to Enter Market.........Low
. Customer Switching Costs........................Low
. Access to Distribution Channels.................Low
. Government Policy...................................Low

With the level of these 6 market entry barriers in mind, indicate the chance you would recommend market entry (please circle percentages).

....*Decision A:* If the above represents an early market entry opportunity into Consumer Goods Market.

No Chance 0% 10% 20% 30% 40% 50% 60% 70% 80% 90% 100% Definite

....*Decision B:* If the above represents a late market entry opportunity into Consumer Goods Market.

No Chance 0% 10% 20% 30% 40% 50% 60% 70% 80% 90% 100% Definite

....*Decision C:* If the above represents an early market entry opportunity into Industrial Goods Market.

No Chance 0% 10% 20% 30% 40% 50% 60% 70% 80% 90% 100% Definite

....*Decision D:* If the above represents a late market entry opportunity into Industrial Goods Market.

No Chance 0% 10% 20% 30% 40% 50% 60% 70% 80% 90% 100% Definite

MARKET CONDITION # 6:

. Cost Advantages of Incumbents.................High
. Product Differentiation of Incumbents.........Low
. Capital Requirements to Enter Market.........Low
. Customer Switching Costs........................Low
. Access to Distribution Channels.................Low
. Government Policy...................................Low

With the level of these 6 market entry barriers in mind, indicate the chance you would recommend market entry (please circle percentages).

....*Decision A:* If the above represents an early market entry opportunity into Consumer Goods Market.

No Chance 0% 10% 20% 30% 40% 50% 60% 70% 80% 90% 100% Definite

....*Decision B:* If the above represents a late market entry opportunity into Consumer Goods Market.

No Chance 0% 10% 20% 30% 40% 50% 60% 70% 80% 90% 100% Definite

....*Decision C:* If the above represents an early market entry opportunity into Industrial Goods Market.

No Chance 0% 10% 20% 30% 40% 50% 60% 70% 80% 90% 100% Definite

....*Decision D:* If the above represents a late market entry opportunity into Industrial Goods Market.

No Chance 0% 10% 20% 30% 40% 50% 60% 70% 80% 90% 100% Definite

MARKET CONDITION # 7:

. Cost Advantages of Incumbents.................High
. Product Differentiation of Incumbents..........Low
. Capital Requirements to Enter Market.........Low
. Customer Switching Costs........................Low
. Access to Distribution Channels.................Low
. Government Policy..................................Low

With the level of these 6 market entry barriers in mind, indicate the chance you would recommend market entry (please circle percentages).

....*Decision A:* If the above represents an early market entry opportunity into Consumer Goods Market.

No Chance 0% 10% 20% 30% 40% 50% 60% 70% 80% 90% 100% Definite

....*Decision B:* If the above represents a late market entry opportunity into Consumer Goods Market.

No Chance 0% 10% 20% 30% 40% 50% 60% 70% 80% 90% 100% Definite

....*Decision C:* If the above represents an early market entry opportunity into Industrial Goods Market.

No Chance 0% 10% 20% 30% 40% 50% 60% 70% 80% 90% 100% Definite

....*Decision D:* If the above represents a late market entry opportunity into Industrial Goods Market.

No Chance 0% 10% 20% 30% 40% 50% 60% 70% 80% 90% 100% Definite

MARKET CONDITION # 8:

. Cost Advantages of Incumbents.................High
. Product Differentiation of Incumbents..........Low
. Capital Requirements to Enter Market.........Low
. Customer Switching Costs........................Low
. Access to Distribution Channels.................Low
. Government Policy..................................Low

With the level of these 6 market entry barriers in mind, indicate the chance you would recommend market entry (please circle percentages).

....*Decision A:* If the above represents an early market entry opportunity into Consumer Goods Market.

No Chance 0% 10% 20% 30% 40% 50% 60% 70% 80% 90% 100% Definite

....*Decision B:* If the above represents a late market entry opportunity into Consumer Goods Market.

No Chance 0% 10% 20% 30% 40% 50% 60% 70% 80% 90% 100% Definite

....*Decision C:* If the above represents an early market entry opportunity into Industrial Goods Market.

No Chance 0% 10% 20% 30% 40% 50% 60% 70% 80% 90% 100% Definite

....*Decision D:* If the above represents a late market entry opportunity into Industrial Goods Market.

No Chance 0% 10% 20% 30% 40% 50% 60% 70% 80% 90% 100% Definite

MARKET CONDITION # 9:

. Cost Advantages of Incumbents.................High
. Product Differentiation of Incumbents.........Low
. Capital Requirements to Enter Market.........Low
. Customer Switching Costs........................Low
. Access to Distribution Channels.................Low
. Government Policy..................................Low

With the level of these 6 market entry barriers in mind, indicate the chance you would recommend market entry (please circle percentages).

....*Decision A:* If the above represents an early market entry opportunity into Consumer Goods Market.

No Chance 0% 10% 20% 30% 40% 50% 60% 70% 80% 90% 100% Definite

....*Decision B:* If the above represents a late market entry opportunity into Consumer Goods Market.

No Chance 0% 10% 20% 30% 40% 50% 60% 70% 80% 90% 100% Definite

....*Decision C:* If the above represents an early market entry opportunity into Industrial Goods Market.

No Chance 0% 10% 20% 30% 40% 50% 60% 70% 80% 90% 100% Definite

....*Decision D:* If the above represents a late market entry opportunity into Industrial Goods Market.

No Chance 0% 10% 20% 30% 40% 50% 60% 70% 80% 90% 100% Definite

MARKET CONDITION # 10:

. Cost Advantages of Incumbents.................High
. Product Differentiation of Incumbents.........Low
. Capital Requirements to Enter Market.........Low
. Customer Switching Costs........................Low
. Access to Distribution Channels.................Low
. Government Policy..................................Low

With the level of these 6 market entry barriers in mind, indicate the chance you would recommend market entry (please circle percentages).

....*Decision A:* If the above represents an early market entry opportunity into Consumer Goods Market.

No Chance 0% 10% 20% 30% 40% 50% 60% 70% 80% 90% 100% Definite

....*Decision B:* If the above represents a late market entry opportunity into Consumer Goods Market.

No Chance 0% 10% 20% 30% 40% 50% 60% 70% 80% 90% 100% Definite

....*Decision C:* If the above represents an early market entry opportunity into Industrial Goods Market.

No Chance 0% 10% 20% 30% 40% 50% 60% 70% 80% 90% 100% Definite

....*Decision D:* If the above represents a late market entry opportunity into Industrial Goods Market.

No Chance 0% 10% 20% 30% 40% 50% 60% 70% 80% 90% 100% Definite

MARKET CONDITION # 11:

. Cost Advantages of Incumbents.................High
. Product Differentiation of Incumbents.........Low
. Capital Requirements to Enter Market.........Low
. Customer Switching Costs.........................Low
. Access to Distribution Channels.................Low
. Government Policy..................................Low

With the level of these 6 market entry barriers in mind, indicate the chance you would recommend market entry (please circle percentages).

....*Decision A:* If the above represents an early market entry opportunity into Consumer Goods Market.

No Chance 0% 10% 20% 30% 40% 50% 60% 70% 80% 90% 100% Definite

....*Decision B:* If the above represents a late market entry opportunity into Consumer Goods Market.

No Chance 0% 10% 20% 30% 40% 50% 60% 70% 80% 90% 100% Definite

....*Decision C:* If the above represents an early market entry opportunity into Industrial Goods Market.

No Chance 0% 10% 20% 30% 40% 50% 60% 70% 80% 90% 100% Definite

....*Decision D:* If the above represents a late market entry opportunity into Industrial Goods Market.

No Chance 0% 10% 20% 30% 40% 50% 60% 70% 80% 90% 100% Definite

MARKET CONDITION # 12:

. Cost Advantages of Incumbents.................High
. Product Differentiation of Incumbents.........Low
. Capital Requirements to Enter Market.........Low
. Customer Switching Costs.........................Low
. Access to Distribution Channels.................Low
. Government Policy..................................Low

With the level of these 6 market entry barriers in mind, indicate the chance you would recommend market entry (please circle percentages).

....*Decision A:* If the above represents an early market entry opportunity into Consumer Goods Market.

No Chance 0% 10% 20% 30% 40% 50% 60% 70% 80% 90% 100% Definite

....*Decision B:* If the above represents a late market entry opportunity into Consumer Goods Market.

No Chance 0% 10% 20% 30% 40% 50% 60% 70% 80% 90% 100% Definite

....*Decision C:* If the above represents an early market entry opportunity into Industrial Goods Market.

No Chance 0% 10% 20% 30% 40% 50% 60% 70% 80% 90% 100% Definite

....*Decision D:* If the above represents a late market entry opportunity into Industrial Goods Market.

No Chance 0% 10% 20% 30% 40% 50% 60% 70% 80% 90% 100% Definite

MARKET CONDITION # 13:

```
. Cost Advantages of Incumbents.................High
. Product Differentiation of Incumbents.........Low
. Capital Requirements to Enter Market.........Low
. Customer Switching Costs........................Low
. Access to Distribution Channels.................Low
. Government Policy..................................Low
```

With the level of these 6 market entry barriers in mind, indicate the chance you would recommend market entry (please circle percentages).

....*Decision A:* If the above represents an early market entry opportunity into Consumer Goods Market.

No Chance   0%   10%   20%   30%   40%   50%   60%   70%   80%   90%   100%   Definite

....*Decision B:* If the above represents a late market entry opportunity into Consumer Goods Market.

No Chance   0%   10%   20%   30%   40%   50%   60%   70%   80%   90%   100%   Definite

....*Decision C:* If the above represents an early market entry opportunity into Industrial Goods Market.

No Chance   0%   10%   20%   30%   40%   50%   60%   70%   80%   90%   100%   Definite

....*Decision D:* If the above represents a late market entry opportunity into Industrial Goods Market.

No Chance   0%   10%   20%   30%   40%   50%   60%   70%   80%   90%   100%   Definite

MARKET CONDITION # 14:

```
. Cost Advantages of Incumbents.................High
. Product Differentiation of Incumbents.........Low
. Capital Requirements to Enter Market.........Low
. Customer Switching Costs........................Low
. Access to Distribution Channels.................Low
. Government Policy..................................Low
```

With the level of these 6 market entry barriers in mind, indicate the chance you would recommend market entry (please circle percentages).

....*Decision A:* If the above represents an early market entry opportunity into Consumer Goods Market.

No Chance   0%   10%   20%   30%   40%   50%   60%   70%   80%   90%   100%   Definite

....*Decision B:* If the above represents a late market entry opportunity into Consumer Goods Market.

No Chance   0%   10%   20%   30%   40%   50%   60%   70%   80%   90%   100%   Definite

....*Decision C:* If the above represents an early market entry opportunity into Industrial Goods Market.

No Chance   0%   10%   20%   30%   40%   50%   60%   70%   80%   90%   100%   Definite

....*Decision D:* If the above represents a late market entry opportunity into Industrial Goods Market.

No Chance   0%   10%   20%   30%   40%   50%   60%   70%   80%   90%   100%   Definite

MARKET CONDITION # 15:

. Cost Advantages of Incumbents.................High
. Product Differentiation of Incumbents.........Low
. Capital Requirements to Enter Market..........Low
. Customer Switching Costs........................Low
. Access to Distribution Channels.................Low
. Government Policy..................................Low

With the level of these 6 market entry barriers in mind, indicate the chance you would recommend
market entry (please circle percentages).

....*Decision A:* If the above represents an early market entry opportunity into Consumer Goods Market.

No Chance   0% 10% 20% 30% 40% 50% 60% 70% 80% 90% 100%   Definite

....*Decision B:* If the above represents a late market entry opportunity into Consumer Goods Market.

No Chance   0% 10% 20% 30% 40% 50% 60% 70% 80% 90% 100%   Definite

....*Decision C:* If the above represents an early market entry opportunity into Industrial Goods Market.

No Chance   0% 10% 20% 30% 40% 50% 60% 70% 80% 90% 100%   Definite

....*Decision D:* If the above represents a late market entry opportunity into Industrial Goods Market.

No Chance   0% 10% 20% 30% 40% 50% 60% 70% 80% 90% 100%   Definite

MARKET CONDITION # 16:

. Cost Advantages of Incumbents.................High
. Product Differentiation of Incumbents.........Low
. Capital Requirements to Enter Market.........Low
. Customer Switching Costs........................Low
. Access to Distribution Channels.................Low
. Government Policy..................................Low

With the level of these 6 market entry barriers in mind, indicate the chance you would recommend
market entry (please circle percentages).

....*Decision A:* If the above represents an early market entry opportunity into Consumer Goods Market.

No Chance   0% 10% 20% 30% 40% 50% 60% 70% 80% 90% 100%   Definite

....*Decision B:* If the above represents a late market entry opportunity into Consumer Goods Market.

No Chance   0% 10% 20% 30% 40% 50% 60% 70% 80% 90% 100%   Definite

....*Decision C:* If the above represents an early market entry opportunity into Industrial Goods Market.

No Chance   0% 10% 20% 30% 40% 50% 60% 70% 80% 90% 100%   Definite

....*Decision D:* If the above represents a late market entry opportunity into Industrial Goods Market.

No Chance   0% 10% 20% 30% 40% 50% 60% 70% 80% 90% 100%   Definite

MARKET CONDITION # 17:

```
. Cost Advantages of Incumbents.................High
. Product Differentiation of Incumbents.........Low
. Capital Requirements to Enter Market.........Low
. Customer Switching Costs........................Low
. Access to Distribution Channels.................Low
. Government Policy...................................Low
```

With the level of these 6 market entry barriers in mind, indicate the chance you would recommend market entry (please circle percentages).

....*Decision A:* If the above represents an early market entry opportunity into Consumer Goods Market.

No Chance   0% 10% 20% 30% 40% 50% 60% 70% 80% 90% 100%   Definite

....*Decision B:* If the above represents a late market entry opportunity into Consumer Goods Market.

No Chance   0% 10% 20% 30% 40% 50% 60% 70% 80% 90% 100%   Definite

....*Decision C:* If the above represents an early market entry opportunity into Industrial Goods Market.

No Chance   0% 10% 20% 30% 40% 50% 60% 70% 80% 90% 100%   Definite

....*Decision D:* If the above represents a late market entry opportunity into Industrial Goods Market.

No Chance   0% 10% 20% 30% 40% 50% 60% 70% 80% 90% 100%   Definite

MARKET CONDITION # 18:

```
. Cost Advantages of Incumbents.................High
. Product Differentiation of Incumbents.........Low
. Capital Requirements to Enter Market.........Low
. Customer Switching Costs........................Low
. Access to Distribution Channels.................Low
. Government Policy...................................Low
```

With the level of these 6 market entry barriers in mind, indicate the chance you would recommend market entry (please circle percentages).

....*Decision A:* If the above represents an early market entry opportunity into Consumer Goods Market.

No Chance   0% 10% 20% 30% 40% 50% 60% 70% 80% 90% 100%   Definite

....*Decision B:* If the above represents a late market entry opportunity into Consumer Goods Market.

No Chance   0% 10% 20% 30% 40% 50% 60% 70% 80% 90% 100%   Definite

....*Decision C:* If the above represents an early market entry opportunity into Industrial Goods Market.

No Chance   0% 10% 20% 30% 40% 50% 60% 70% 80% 90% 100%   Definite

....*Decision D:* If the above represents a late market entry opportunity into Industrial Goods Market.

No Chance   0% 10% 20% 30% 40% 50% 60% 70% 80% 90% 100%   Definite

MARKET CONDITION # 19:

. Cost Advantages of Incumbents.................High
. Product Differentiation of Incumbents.........Low
. Capital Requirements to Enter Market..........Low
. Customer Switching Costs........................Low
. Access to Distribution Channels.................Low
. Government Policy...................................Low

With the level of these 6 market entry barriers in mind, indicate the chance you would recommend market entry (please circle percentages).

....*Decision A:* If the above represents an early market entry opportunity into Consumer Goods Market.

No Chance   0% 10% 20% 30% 40% 50% 60% 70% 80% 90% 100%   Definite

....*Decision B:* If the above represents a late market entry opportunity into Consumer Goods Market.

No Chance   0% 10% 20% 30% 40% 50% 60% 70% 80% 90% 100%   Definite

....*Decision C:* If the above represents an early market entry opportunity into Industrial Goods Market.

No Chance   0% 10% 20% 30% 40% 50% 60% 70% 80% 90% 100%   Definite

....*Decision D:* If the above represents a late market entry opportunity into Industrial Goods Market.

No Chance   0% 10% 20% 30% 40% 50% 60% 70% 80% 90% 100%   Definite

MARKET CONDITION # 20:

. Cost Advantages of Incumbents.................High
. Product Differentiation of Incumbents.........Low
. Capital Requirements to Enter Market.........Low
. Customer Switching Costs........................Low
. Access to Distribution Channels.................Low
. Government Policy...................................Low

With the level of these 6 market entry barriers in mind, indicate the chance you would recommend market entry (please circle percentages).

....*Decision A:* If the above represents an early market entry opportunity into Consumer Goods Market.

No Chance   0% 10% 20% 30% 40% 50% 60% 70% 80% 90% 100%   Definite

....*Decision B:* If the above represents a late market entry opportunity into Consumer Goods Market.

No Chance   0% 10% 20% 30% 40% 50% 60% 70% 80% 90% 100%   Definite

....*Decision C:* If the above represents an early market entry opportunity into Industrial Goods Market.

No Chance   0% 10% 20% 30% 40% 50% 60% 70% 80% 90% 100%   Definite

....*Decision D:* If the above represents a late market entry opportunity into Industrial Goods Market.

No Chance   0% 10% 20% 30% 40% 50% 60% 70% 80% 90% 100%   Definite

MARKET CONDITION # 21:

. Cost Advantages of Incumbents.................High
. Product Differentiation of Incumbents.........Low
. Capital Requirements to Enter Market.........Low
. Customer Switching Costs.........................Low
. Access to Distribution Channels.................Low
. Government Policy....................................Low

With the level of these 6 market entry barriers in mind, indicate the chance you would recommend market entry (please circle percentages).

....*Decision A:* If the above represents an early market entry opportunity into Consumer Goods Market.

No Chance 0% 10% 20% 30% 40% 50% 60% 70% 80% 90% 100% Definite

....*Decision B:* If the above represents a late market entry opportunity into Consumer Goods Market.

No Chance 0% 10% 20% 30% 40% 50% 60% 70% 80% 90% 100% Definite

....*Decision C:* If the above represents an early market entry opportunity into Industrial Goods Market.

No Chance 0% 10% 20% 30% 40% 50% 60% 70% 80% 90% 100% Definite

....*Decision D:* If the above represents a late market entry opportunity into Industrial Goods Market.

No Chance 0% 10% 20% 30% 40% 50% 60% 70% 80% 90% 100% Definite

MARKET CONDITION # 22:

. Cost Advantages of Incumbents.................High
. Product Differentiation of Incumbents.........Low
. Capital Requirements to Enter Market.........Low
. Customer Switching Costs.........................Low
. Access to Distribution Channels.................Low
. Government Policy....................................Low

With the level of these 6 market entry barriers in mind, indicate the chance you would recommend market entry (please circle percentages).

....*Decision A:* If the above represents an early market entry opportunity into Consumer Goods Market.

No Chance 0% 10% 20% 30% 40% 50% 60% 70% 80% 90% 100% Definite

....*Decision B:* If the above represents a late market entry opportunity into Consumer Goods Market.

No Chance 0% 10% 20% 30% 40% 50% 60% 70% 80% 90% 100% Definite

....*Decision C:* If the above represents an early market entry opportunity into Industrial Goods Market.

No Chance 0% 10% 20% 30% 40% 50% 60% 70% 80% 90% 100% Definite

....*Decision D:* If the above represents a late market entry opportunity into Industrial Goods Market.

No Chance 0% 10% 20% 30% 40% 50% 60% 70% 80% 90% 100% Definite

---

MARKET CONDITION # 23:

. Cost Advantages of Incumbents.................High
. Product Differentiation of Incumbents..........Low
. Capital Requirements to Enter Market.........Low
. Customer Switching Costs........................Low
. Access to Distribution Channels.................Low
. Government Policy..............................,......Low

With the level of these 6 market entry barriers in mind, indicate the chance you would recommend market entry (please circle percentages).

....*Decision A:* If the above represents an early market entry opportunity into Consumer Goods Market.

No Chance 0% 10% 20% 30% 40% 50% 60% 70% 80% 90% 100% Definite

....*Decision B:* If the above represents a late market entry opportunity into Consumer Goods Market.

No Chance 0% 10% 20% 30% 40% 50% 60% 70% 80% 90% 100% Definite

....*Decision C:* If the above represents an early market entry opportunity into Industrial Goods Market.

No Chance 0% 10% 20% 30% 40% 50% 60% 70% 80% 90% 100% Definite

....*Decision D:* If the above represents a late market entry opportunity into Industrial Goods Market.

No Chance 0% 10% 20% 30% 40% 50% 60% 70% 80% 90% 100% Definite

MARKET CONDITION # 24:

. Cost Advantages of Incumbents.................High
. Product Differentiation of Incumbents.........Low
. Capital Requirements to Enter Market.........Low
. Customer Switching Costs........................Low
. Access to Distribution Channels.................Low
. Government Policy..............................Low

With the level of these 6 market entry barriers in mind, indicate the chance you would recommend market entry (please circle percentages).

....*Decision A:* If the above represents an early market entry opportunity into Consumer Goods Market.

No Chance 0% 10% 20% 30% 40% 50% 60% 70% 80% 90% 100% Definite

....*Decision B:* If the above represents a late market entry opportunity into Consumer Goods Market.

No Chance 0% 10% 20% 30% 40% 50% 60% 70% 80% 90% 100% Definite

....*Decision C:* If the above represents an early market entry opportunity into Industrial Goods Market.

No Chance 0% 10% 20% 30% 40% 50% 60% 70% 80% 90% 100% Definite

....*Decision D:* If the above represents a late market entry opportunity into Industrial Goods Market.

No Chance 0% 10% 20% 30% 40% 50% 60% 70% 80% 90% 100% Definite

MARKET CONDITION # 25:

. Cost Advantages of Incumbents.................High
. Product Differentiation of Incumbents.........Low
. Capital Requirements to Enter Market..........Low
. Customer Switching Costs........................Low
. Access to Distribution Channels.................Low
. Government Policy...................................Low

With the level of these 6 market entry barriers in mind, indicate the chance you would recommend market entry (please circle percentages).

....*Decision A:* If the above represents an early market entry opportunity into Consumer Goods Market.

No Chance   0% 10% 20% 30% 40% 50% 60% 70% 80% 90% 100%   Definite

....*Decision B:* If the above represents a late market entry opportunity into Consumer Goods Market.

No Chance   0% 10% 20% 30% 40% 50% 60% 70% 80% 90% 100%   Definite

....*Decision C:* If the above represents an early market entry opportunity into Industrial Goods Market.

No Chance   0% 10% 20% 30% 40% 50% 60% 70% 80% 90% 100%   Definite

....*Decision D:* If the above represents a late market entry opportunity into Industrial Goods Market.

No Chance   0% 10% 20% 30% 40% 50% 60% 70% 80% 90% 100%   Definite

MARKET CONDITION # 26:

. Cost Advantages of Incumbents.................High
. Product Differentiation of Incumbents.........Low
. Capital Requirements to Enter Market.........Low
. Customer Switching Costs........................Low
. Access to Distribution Channels.................Low
. Government Policy...................................Low

With the level of these 6 market entry barriers in mind, indicate the chance you would recommend market entry (please circle percentages).

....*Decision A:* If the above represents an early market entry opportunity into Consumer Goods Market.

No Chance   0% 10% 20% 30% 40% 50% 60% 70% 80% 90% 100%   Definite

....*Decision B:* If the above represents a late market entry opportunity into Consumer Goods Market.

No Chance   0% 10% 20% 30% 40% 50% 60% 70% 80% 90% 100%   Definite

....*Decision C:* If the above represents an early market entry opportunity into Industrial Goods Market.

No Chance   0% 10% 20% 30% 40% 50% 60% 70% 80% 90% 100%   Definite

....*Decision D:* If the above represents a late market entry opportunity into Industrial Goods Market.

No Chance   0% 10% 20% 30% 40% 50% 60% 70% 80% 90% 100%   Definite

---

MARKET CONDITION # 27:

```
. Cost Advantages of Incumbents.................High
. Product Differentiation of Incumbents.........Low
. Capital Requirements to Enter Market.........Low
. Customer Switching Costs........................Low
. Access to Distribution Channels.................Low
. Government Policy..................................Low
```

With the level of these 6 market entry barriers in mind, indicate the chance you would recommend market entry (please circle percentages).

....*Decision A:* If the above represents an early market entry opportunity into Consumer Goods Market.

No Chance 0% 10% 20% 30% 40% 50% 60% 70% 80% 90% 100% Definite

....*Decision B:* If the above represents a late market entry opportunity into Consumer Goods Market.

No Chance 0% 10% 20% 30% 40% 50% 60% 70% 80% 90% 100% Definite

....*Decision C:* If the above represents an early market entry opportunity into Industrial Goods Market.

No Chance 0% 10% 20% 30% 40% 50% 60% 70% 80% 90% 100% Definite

....*Decision D:* If the above represents a late market entry opportunity into Industrial Goods Market.

No Chance 0% 10% 20% 30% 40% 50% 60% 70% 80% 90% 100% Definite

---

MARKET CONDITION # 28:

```
. Cost Advantages of Incumbents.................High
. Product Differentiation of Incumbents.........Low
. Capital Requirements to Enter Market.........Low
. Customer Switching Costs........................Low
. Access to Distribution Channels.................Low
. Government Policy..................................Low
```

With the level of these 6 market entry barriers in mind, indicate the chance you would recommend market entry (please circle percentages).

....*Decision A:* If the above represents an early market entry opportunity into Consumer Goods Market.

No Chance 0% 10% 20% 30% 40% 50% 60% 70% 80% 90% 100% Definite

....*Decision B:* If the above represents a late market entry opportunity into Consumer Goods Market.

No Chance 0% 10% 20% 30% 40% 50% 60% 70% 80% 90% 100% Definite

....*Decision C:* If the above represents an early market entry opportunity into Industrial Goods Market.

No Chance 0% 10% 20% 30% 40% 50% 60% 70% 80% 90% 100% Definite

....*Decision D:* If the above represents a late market entry opportunity into Industrial Goods Market.

No Chance 0% 10% 20% 30% 40% 50% 60% 70% 80% 90% 100% Definite

MARKET CONDITION # 29:

```
. Cost Advantages of Incumbents.................High
. Product Differentiation of Incumbents.........Low
. Capital Requirements to Enter Market.........Low
. Customer Switching Costs.........................Low
. Access to Distribution Channels.................Low
. Government Policy..................................Low
```

With the level of these 6 market entry barriers in mind, indicate the chance you would recommend market entry (please circle percentages).

....*Decision A:* If the above represents an early market entry opportunity into Consumer Goods Market.

No Chance 0% 10% 20% 30% 40% 50% 60% 70% 80% 90% 100% Definite

....*Decision B:* If the above represents a late market entry opportunity into Consumer Goods Market.

No Chance 0% 10% 20% 30% 40% 50% 60% 70% 80% 90% 100% Definite

....*Decision C:* If the above represents an early market entry opportunity into Industrial Goods Market.

No Chance 0% 10% 20% 30% 40% 50% 60% 70% 80% 90% 100% Definite

....*Decision D:* If the above represents a late market entry opportunity into Industrial Goods Market.

No Chance 0% 10% 20% 30% 40% 50% 60% 70% 80% 90% 100% Definite

MARKET CONDITION # 30:

```
. Cost Advantages of Incumbents.................High
. Product Differentiation of Incumbents.........Low
. Capital Requirements to Enter Market.........Low
. Customer Switching Costs.........................Low
. Access to Distribution Channels.................Low
. Government Policy..................................Low
```

With the level of these 6 market entry barriers in mind, indicate the chance you would recommend market entry (please circle percentages).

....*Decision A:* If the above represents an early market entry opportunity into Consumer Goods Market.

No Chance 0% 10% 20% 30% 40% 50% 60% 70% 80% 90% 100% Definite

....*Decision B:* If the above represents a late market entry opportunity into Consumer Goods Market.

No Chance 0% 10% 20% 30% 40% 50% 60% 70% 80% 90% 100% Definite

....*Decision C:* If the above represents an early market entry opportunity into Industrial Goods Market.

No Chance 0% 10% 20% 30% 40% 50% 60% 70% 80% 90% 100% Definite

....*Decision D:* If the above represents a late market entry opportunity into Industrial Goods Market.

No Chance 0% 10% 20% 30% 40% 50% 60% 70% 80% 90% 100% Definite

MARKET CONDITION # 31:

```
. Cost Advantages of Incumbents.................High
. Product Differentiation of Incumbents.........Low
. Capital Requirements to Enter Market.........Low
. Customer Switching Costs........................Low
. Access to Distribution Channels.................Low
. Government Policy...................................Low
```

With the level of these 6 market entry barriers in mind, indicate the chance you would recommend market entry (please circle percentages).

....*Decision A:* If the above represents an early market entry opportunity into Consumer Goods Market.

No Chance   0% 10% 20% 30% 40% 50% 60% 70% 80% 90% 100%   Definite

....*Decision B:* If the above represents a late market entry opportunity into Consumer Goods Market.

No Chance   0% 10% 20% 30% 40% 50% 60% 70% 80% 90% 100%   Definite

....*Decision C:* If the above represents an early market entry opportunity into Industrial Goods Market.

No Chance   0% 10% 20% 30% 40% 50% 60% 70% 80% 90% 100%   Definite

....*Decision D:* If the above represents a late market entry opportunity into Industrial Goods Market.

No Chance   0% 10% 20% 30% 40% 50% 60% 70% 80% 90% 100%   Definite

MARKET CONDITION # 32:

```
. Cost Advantages of Incumbents.................High
. Product Differentiation of Incumbents.........Low
. Capital Requirements to Enter Market.........Low
. Customer Switching Costs........................Low
. Access to Distribution Channels.................Low
. Government Policy...................................Low
```

With the level of these 6 market entry barriers in mind, indicate the chance you would recommend market entry (please circle percentages).

....*Decision A:* If the above represents an early market entry opportunity into Consumer Goods Market.

No Chance   0% 10% 20% 30% 40% 50% 60% 70% 80% 90% 100%   Definite

....*Decision B:* If the above represents a late market entry opportunity into Consumer Goods Market.

No Chance   0% 10% 20% 30% 40% 50% 60% 70% 80% 90% 100%   Definite

....*Decision C:* If the above represents an early market entry opportunity into Industrial Goods Market.

No Chance   0% 10% 20% 30% 40% 50% 60% 70% 80% 90% 100%   Definite

....*Decision D:* If the above represents a late market entry opportunity into Industrial Goods Market.

No Chance   0% 10% 20% 30% 40% 50% 60% 70% 80% 90% 100%   Definite

Appendix B: Market Entry Simulation Exercise for Entry into International Markets

INTRODUCTION

This is an exercise that deals with market entry barriers and how you would decide to enter an international market under certain market entry conditions. Please try to place yourself in the position of an executive who is about to make a market entry decision into an international consumer market. The international market entry barriers and market entry conditions are described below.

A **barrier** is anything that decreases the likelihood, scope, or speed of the potential competitors' entering the international market.

Cultural Differences: Differences in values, customs, norm of behavior, and business practices between the culture of the market entrant and that of the target market, which influence market entry decisions.

Product Adaptation: Whether and what product modifications are necessary in order to enter an international market (e.g., changes in product specifications, packaging, etc.).

Access to Distribution Channels: Availability of distribution channels in international markets.

Stability of Currency Exchange Rate: The degree and frequency of changes in the value of the currencies used, which influence the financial risk factor.

Foreign Government Policy: The extent that government limits entry into markets by imposing licensing requirements, tariffs, taxes, etc., and limiting access to raw materials.

Early Market Entry: Entering a market after the first firm has entered with a new product (i.e. early entry may take place just on the heels of the first entrant).

Late Market Entry: Entering the market toward the tail end of the growth phase of the market or in the maturity phase of the market.

Consumer Goods Markets: Includes markets where firms produce goods or services for the public.

MARKET ENTRY CONDITION # 1:

. Cultural Barriers ....High
. Product Adaptation Barrier ....Low
. Access to Distribution Channels Barrier ....Low
. Currency Exch. Rate Stability Barrier ....Low
. Foreign Government Policy Barrier ....Low

With the level of these 5 market entry barriers in mind, indicate the chance you would recommend market entry (please circle the percentages).

...**Decision A:** If the above represents an early market entry opportunity into a foreign market.

No Chance   0%   10%   20%   30%   40%   50%   60%   70%   80%   90%   100%   Definite

...**Decision B:** If the above represents a late market entry opportunity into a foreign market.

No Chance   0%   10%   20%   30%   40%   50%   60%   70%   80%   90%   100%   Definite

MARKET ENTRY CONDITION # 2:

. Cultural Barriers ....Low
. Product Adaptation Barrier ....High
. Access to Distribution Channels Barrier ....Low
. Currency Exch. Rate Stability Barrier ....Low
. Foreign Government Policy Barrier ....Low

With the level of these 5 market entry barriers in mind, indicate the chance you would recommend market entry (please circle the percentages).

...**Decision A:** If the above represents an early market entry opportunity into a foreign market.

No Chance   0%   10%   20%   30%   40%   50%   60%   70%   80%   90%   100%   Definite

...**Decision B:** If the above represents a late market entry opportunity into a foreign market.

No Chance   0%   10%   20%   30%   40%   50%   60%   70%   80%   90%   100%   Definite

MARKET ENTRY CONDITION # 3:

```
. Cultural Barriers ......................................Low
. Product Adaptation Barrier .........................Low
. Access to Distribution Channels Barrier .......High
. Currency Exch. Rate Stability Barrier ..........Low
. Foreign Government Policy Barrier .............Low
```

With the level of these 5 market entry barriers in mind, indicate the chance you would recommend market entry (please circle the percentages).

...Decision A: If the above represents an early market entry opportunity into a foreign market.

No Chance 0% 10% 20% 30% 40% 50% 60% 70% 80% 90% 100% Definite

...Decision B: If the above represents a late market entry opportunity into a foreign market.

No Chance 0% 10% 20% 30% 40% 50% 60% 70% 80% 90% 100% Definite

MARKET ENTRY CONDITION # 4:

```
. Cultural Barriers ......................................High
. Product Adaptation Barrier .........................High
. Access to Distribution Channels Barrier .......High
. Currency Exch. Rate Stability Barrier ..........Low
. Foreign Government Policy Barrier .............Low
```

With the level of these 5 market entry barriers in mind, indicate the chance you would recommend market entry (please circle the percentages).

...Decision A: If the above represents an early market entry opportunity into a foreign market.

No Chance 0% 10% 20% 30% 40% 50% 60% 70% 80% 90% 100% Definite

...Decision B: If the above represents a late market entry opportunity into a foreign market.

No Chance 0% 10% 20% 30% 40% 50% 60% 70% 80% 90% 100% Definite

MARKET ENTRY CONDITION # 5:

. Cultural Barriers ....Low
. Product Adaptation Barrier ....Low
. Access to Distribution Channels Barrier ....Low
. Currency Exch. Rate Stability Barrier ....High
. Foreign Government Policy Barrier ....Low

With the level of these 5 market entry barriers in mind, indicate the chance you would recommend market entry (please circle the percentages).

...**Decision A**: If the above represents an early market entry opportunity into a foreign market.

No Chance   0%   10%   20%   30%   40%   50%   60%   70%   80%   90%   100%   Definite

...**Decision B**: If the above represents a late market entry opportunity into a foreign market.

No Chance   0%   10%   20%   30%   40%   50%   60%   70%   80%   90%   100%   Definite

MARKET ENTRY CONDITION # 6:

. Cultural Barriers ....High
. Product Adaptation Barrier ....High
. Access to Distribution Channels Barrier ....Low
. Currency Exch. Rate Stability Barrier ....High
. Foreign Government Policy Barrier ....Low

With the level of these 5 market entry barriers in mind, indicate the chance you would recommend market entry (please circle the percentages).

...**Decision A**: If the above represents an early market entry opportunity into a foreign market.

No Chance   0%   10%   20%   30%   40%   50%   60%   70%   80%   90%   100%   Definite

...**Decision B**: If the above represents a late market entry opportunity into a foreign market.

No Chance   0%   10%   20%   30%   40%   50%   60%   70%   80%   90%   100%   Definite

MARKET ENTRY CONDITION # 7:

. Cultural Barriers ....High
. Product Adaptation Barrier ....Low
. Access to Distribution Channels Barrier ....High
. Currency Exch. Rate Stability Barrier ....High
. Foreign Government Policy Barrier ....Low

With the level of these 5 market entry barriers in mind, indicate the chance you would recommend market entry (please circle the percentages).

...**Decision A:** If the above represents an early market entry opportunity into a foreign market.

No Chance 0% 10% 20% 30% 40% 50% 60% 70% 80% 90% 100% Definite

...**Decision B:** If the above represents a late market entry opportunity into a foreign market.

No Chance 0% 10% 20% 30% 40% 50% 60% 70% 80% 90% 100% Definite

MARKET ENTRY CONDITION # 8:

. Cultural Barriers ....Low
. Product Adaptation Barrier ....High
. Access to Distribution Channels Barrier ....High
. Currency Exch. Rate Stability Barrier ....High
. Foreign Government Policy Barrier ....Low

With the level of these 5 market entry barriers in mind, indicate the chance you would recommend market entry (please circle the percentages).

...**Decision A:** If the above represents an early market entry opportunity into a foreign market.

No Chance 0% 10% 20% 30% 40% 50% 60% 70% 80% 90% 100% Definite

...**Decision B:** If the above represents a late market entry opportunity into a foreign market.

No Chance 0% 10% 20% 30% 40% 50% 60% 70% 80% 90% 100% Definite

MARKET ENTRY CONDITION # 9:

. Cultural Barriers ....Low
. Product Adaptation Barrier ....Low
. Access to Distribution Channels Barrier ....Low
. Currency Exch. Rate Stability Barrier ....Low
. Foreign Government Policy Barrier ....High

With the level of these 5 market entry barriers in mind, indicate the chance you would recommend market entry (please circle the percentages).

...**Decision A:** If the above represents an early market entry opportunity into a foreign market.

No Chance   0%   10%   20%   30%   40%   50%   60%   70%   80%   90%   100%   Definite

...**Decision B:** If the above represents a late market entry opportunity into a foreign market.

No Chance   0%   10%   20%   30%   40%   50%   60%   70%   80%   90%   100%   Definite

MARKET ENTRY CONDITION # 10:

. Cultural Barriers ....High
. Product Adaptation Barrier ....High
. Access to Distribution Channels Barrier ....Low
. Currency Exch. Rate Stability Barrier ....Low
. Foreign Government Policy Barrier ....High

With the level of these 5 market entry barriers in mind, indicate the chance you would recommend market entry (please circle the percentages).

...**Decision A:** If the above represents an early market entry opportunity into a foreign market.

No Chance   0%   10%   20%   30%   40%   50%   60%   70%   80%   90%   100%   Definite

...**Decision B:** If the above represents a late market entry opportunity into a foreign market.

No Chance   0%   10%   20%   30%   40%   50%   60%   70%   80%   90%   100%   Definite

MARKET ENTRY CONDITION # 11:

. Cultural Barriers ....High
. Product Adaptation Barrier ....Low
. Access to Distribution Channels Barrier ....High
. Currency Exch. Rate Stability Barrier ....Low
. Foreign Government Policy Barrier ....High

With the level of these 5 market entry barriers in mind, indicate the chance you would recommend market entry (please circle the percentages).

...**Decision A:** If the above represents an early market entry opportunity into a foreign market.

No Chance 0% 10% 20% 30% 40% 50% 60% 70% 80% 90% 100% Definite

...**Decision B:** If the above represents a late market entry opportunity into a foreign market.

No Chance 0% 10% 20% 30% 40% 50% 60% 70% 80% 90% 100% Definite

MARKET ENTRY CONDITION # 12:

. Cultural Barriers ....Low
. Product Adaptation Barrier ....High
. Access to Distribution Channels Barrier ....High
. Currency Exch. Rate Stability Barrier ....Low
. Foreign Government Policy Barrier ....High

With the level of these 5 market entry barriers in mind, indicate the chance you would recommend market entry (please circle the percentages).

...**Decision A:** If the above represents an early market entry opportunity into a foreign market.

No Chance 0% 10% 20% 30% 40% 50% 60% 70% 80% 90% 100% Definite

...**Decision B:** If the above represents a late market entry opportunity into a foreign market.

No Chance 0% 10% 20% 30% 40% 50% 60% 70% 80% 90% 100% Definite

MARKET ENTRY CONDITION # 13:

. Cultural Barriers ....High
. Product Adaptation Barrier ....Low
. Access to Distribution Channels Barrier ....Low
. Currency Exch. Rate Stability Barrier ....High
. Foreign Government Policy Barrier ....High

With the level of these 5 market entry barriers in mind, indicate the chance you would recommend market entry (please circle the percentages).

...**Decision A:** If the above represents an early market entry opportunity into a foreign market.

No Chance 0%   10%   20%   30%   40%   50%   60%   70%   80%   90% 100%   Definite

...**Decision B:** If the above represents a late market entry opportunity into a foreign market.

No Chance 0%   10%   20%   30%   40%   50%   60%   70%   80%   90% 100%   Definite

MARKET ENTRY CONDITION # 14:

. Cultural Barriers ....Low
. Product Adaptation Barrier ....High
. Access to Distribution Channels Barrier ....Low
. Currency Exch. Rate Stability Barrier ....High
. Foreign Government Policy Barrier ....High

With the level of these 5 market entry barriers in mind, indicate the chance you would recommend market entry (please circle the percentages).

...**Decision A:** If the above represents an early market entry opportunity into a foreign market.

No Chance 0%   10%   20%   30%   40%   50%   60%   70%   80%   90% 100%   Definite

...**Decision B:** If the above represents a late market entry opportunity into a foreign market.

No Chance 0%   10%   20%   30%   40%   50%   60%   70%   80%   90% 100%   Definite

MARKET ENTRY CONDITION # 15:

. Cultural Barriers ....Low
. Product Adaptation Barrier ....Low
. Access to Distribution Channels Barrier ....High
. Currency Exch. Rate Stability Barrier ....High
. Foreign Government Policy Barrier ....High

With the level of these 5 market entry barriers in mind, indicate the chance you would recommend market entry (please circle the percentages).

...**Decision A:** If the above represents an early market entry opportunity into a foreign market.

No Chance 0% 10% 20% 30% 40% 50% 60% 70% 80% 90% 100% Definite

...**Decision B:** If the above represents a late market entry opportunity into a foreign market.

No Chance 0% 10% 20% 30% 40% 50% 60% 70% 80% 90% 100% Definite

MARKET ENTRY CONDITION # 16:

. Cultural Barriers ....High
. Product Adaptation Barrier ....High
. Access to Distribution Channels Barrier ....High
. Currency Exch. Rate Stability Barrier ....High
. Foreign Government Policy Barrier ....High

With the level of these 5 market entry barriers in mind, indicate the chance you would recommend market entry (please circle the percentages).

...**Decision A:** If the above represents an early market entry opportunity into a foreign market.

No Chance 0% 10% 20% 30% 40% 50% 60% 70% 80% 90% 100% Definite

...**Decision B:** If the above represents a late market entry opportunity into a foreign market.

No Chance 0% 10% 20% 30% 40% 50% 60% 70% 80% 90% 100% Definite

Selected Bibliography

Alden, Vernon R. 1987. "Who Says You Can't Crack Japanese Markets?" *Harvard Business Review* (January - February): 52-56.

Anderson, Carl R., and Carl P. Zeithaml. 1984. "Stage of the Product Life Cycle, Business Strategy, and Business Performance." *Academy of Management Journal* 27 (1): 5-24 (March).

Bain, J. S. 1968. *Industrial Organization*. 2d ed. New York: John Wiley.

Barrett, M. 1988. "A New Chapter for Europe." *Euromoney* (UK) (September): 2-5.

Baumol, William. J., and Robert D. Willig. 1981. "Fixed Costs, Sunk Costs, Entry Barriers and Sustainability of Monopoly." *Quarterly Journal of Economics* 96 (August): 405-31.

Beaty, Randolf P., John F. Reim, and Robert Schapperle. 1985. "The Effect of Entry on Bank Shareholder Wealth: Implications for Interstate Banking." *Journal of Banking Research* 16 (Spring): 8-15.

Berlew, Kingston F. 1984. "The Joint Venture - A Way into Foreign Markets." *Harvard Business Review* 62 (July-August): 48-51.

Biggadike, Ralph E. 1976. "Entry Strategy and Performance." Ph.D. diss., Harvard Business School.

Blake, R. R., and J. S. Mouton. 1967. "Reactions to Intergroup Competition Under Win-Lose Conditions." *Management Science* 7: 420-35.

Bourgeois, L. 1980. "Performance and Consensus." *Strategic Management Journal* 1 (July-September): 227-48.

____. 1985. "Strategic Goals, Perceived Uncertainty, and Economic Performance in Volatile Environments." *Academy of Management Journal* 28: 548-73.

Brozen, Yale. 1971. "Bain's Concentration and Rates of Return Revisited." *Journal of Law and Economics* 14 (October): 351-69.

Buzzell, Robert D., and P. W. Farris. 1976. *Marketing Costs in Consumer Goods Industries*. Report no. 76-111. Cambridge, Mass.: Marketing

Science Institute.

Buzzell, Robert, and Badley T. Gale. 1987. *The PIMS Principles: Linking Strategy to Performance.* New York: Free Press.

Buzzell, Robert D., and B. T. Gale, and R. G. M. Sultan. 1975. "Market Share: A Key to Profitability." *Harvard Business Review* 5 (January-February): 97-106.

Buzzell, Robert D., and Frederick D. Wiersema. 1981. "Successful Share Building Strategy." *Harvard Business Review* 59 (January-February): 135-44.

Carpenter, Gregory S., and Kent Nakamoto. 1990. "Consumer Preference Formation and Pioneering Advantage." *Journal of Marketing Research* 26 (August): 285-98.

Caves R. E., and Michael E. Porter. 1977. "From Entry Barriers to Mobility Barriers." *Quarterly Journal of Economics* (May): 241-69.

Chen, A. H., and L. J. Merville. 1986. "An Analysis of Divestiture Effects Resulting from Deregulation." *Journal of Finance* 39 (December): 997-1010.

Comanor, William S., and Thomas S. Wilson. 1979. "The Effect of Advertising on Competition: A Survey." *Journal of Economic Literature* 17 (July): 453-76.

Cooper, R. G. 1979. "The Dimensions of New Product Success and Failure." *Journal of Marketing* 43 (Summer): 93-103.

Crawford, Jean. 1975. "Seller Concentration, Entry Barriers, and Profit Margins: A Comment." *Industrial Organization Review* 3 (Fall): 176-78.

Day, George S. 1975. "A Strategic Perspective in Product Planning." *Journal of Contemporary Business* 4 (Spring): 1-34.

_____. 1984. *Strategic Market Planning: The Pursuit of Competitive Advantage.* St. Paul: West.

_____. 1986. *Analysis for Strategic Marketing Decisions.* St. Paul: West.

Demsetz, Harold. 1982. "Barriers to Entry." *American Economic Review* 72 (March): 47-57.

Dess, G. G. 1987. "Consensus on Strategy Formulation and Organizational Performance: Competition in a Fragmented Industry. *Strategic Management Journal* 8: 259-77.

Dess, G. G., and N. K. Origer. 1987. "Environment, Structure, and Consensus in Strategy Formulation: A Conceptual Integration." *Academy of Management Review* 12: 313-30.

Dixit, Avinash. 1980. "The Role of Investment in Entry Deterrence." *Economic Journal* 90: 95-106.

Dixit, Avinash, and Albert S. Kyle. 1985. "The Use of Protection and Subsidies for Entry Promotion and Deterrence." *American Economic Review* 75 (March): 139-52.

Duhaime, I. M., and I. S. Baird. 1987. "Divestment Decision-Making: The Role of Business Unit Size."*Journal of Management* 13: 483-98.

Duhaime, I. M., and J. H. Grant. 1984. "Factors Influencing Divestment Decision-Making: Evidence from a Field Study." *Strategic Management Journal* 5: 301-18.

Fornell, Cleas, William T. Robinson, and Birger Wernerfelt. 1985. "Consumption Experience and Sales Promotion Expenditures." *Management Science* 31 (September): 1084-1105.

Gale, B. T. 1972. "Market Share and Return on Investment." *Review of Economics and Statistics* 54 (November): 412-23.

Gatignon, Hubert, Erin Anderson, and Kristiaan Helsen. 1989. "Competitive Reactions to Market Entry: Explaining Interfirm Differences." *Journal of Marketing Research* 26 (February): 44-55.

Glazer, A. 1985. "The Advantages of Being First." *American Economic Review* 75 (June): 473-80.

Grabowski, Henry, and John Vernon. 1986. "Longer Patents for Lower Imitation Barriers: The 1984 Drug Act." *American Economic Review* 76 (May): 195-98.

Grinyer, P., and D. Norburn. 1977-1978. "Planning for Existing Markets: An Empirical Study."*International Studies in Management and Organization* 7: 99-122.

Hall, William K. 1980. "Survival Strategies in a Hostile Environment." *Harvard Business Review* (September-October): 75-85.

Harrigan, Kathryn Rudie. 1980. *Strategies for Declining Businesses*. Lexington, Mass.: Lexington Books.

_____. 1981. "Barriers to Entry and Competitive Strategies." *Strategic Management Journal* 2 (4): 395-412.

_____. 1981. "The Effect of Exit Barriers upon Strategic Flexibility." *Strategic Management Journal* 2 (2): 165-76.

Hax, Arnold C., and Nicholas S. Majluf. 1982. "Competitive Cost Dynamics: The Experience Curve." *Interfaces* 12 (5): 25-34 (October).

Hitt, Michael A., and R. Duane Ireland. 1985. "Corporate Distinctive Competence, Strategy, Industry and Performance." *Strategic Management Journal* 6: 273-93.

Hrebiniak, L. G., and C. C. Snow. 1982. "Top Management Agreement and Organizational Performance." *Human Relations* 35: 1139-58.

Jain, Subhash C. 1981. *Marketing Planning and Strategy*. Cincinati, Ohio: South-Western.

Kessides, Ionnis N. 1986. "Advertising, Sunk Costs, and Barriers to Entry." *Review of Economics and Statistics* (Netherlands) 68 (February): 85-95.

Kim, Chan W., and R. A. Mauborgne. 1988. "Becoming an Effective Global Competitor." *Journal of Business Strategy* 9 (January-February): 33-37.

King, Ronald H., and Arthur A. Thompson, Jr. 1982. "Entry and Market Share Success of New Brands in Concentrated Markets." *Journal of Business Research* 10: 371-83.

Klemperer, Paul. 1987. "Markets with Consumer Switching Costs." *Quarterly Journal of Economics* (May): 375-94.

Kotler, Philip. 1986. "Megamarketing." *Harvard Business Review* (March-April): 117-24.

Krouse, Clement G. 1984. "Brand Name as a Barrier to Entry: The ReaLemon Case." *Southern Economics Journal* 51 (October): 495-502.

Lambkin, Mary. 1988. "Order of Entry and Performance in New Markets." *Strategic Management Journal* 9 (Summer): 127-40.

Lieberman, Marvin B. 1987. "Excess Capacity as a Barrier to Entry." *Journal of Industrial Economics* 35 (June): 607-27.

_____. 1987. "The Learning Curve, Diffusion, and Competitive Strategy." *Strategic Management Journal* 8 (September-October): 441-52.

McFarlan, Warren F. 1984. "Info. Technology Changes the Way You Compete." *Harvard Business Review* 62 (May-June): 98-103.

MacMillan, I. C., D. C. Hambrick, and D. L. Day. 1982."The Product Portfolio and Profitability - A PIMS-Based Analysis of Industrial Product Businesses." *Academy of Management Journal* 25 (December): 733-55.

May, Thornton. 1987. "When Barriers Are Irrelevant or Undefended: Non-Bank Banks Cash-In." *Business Horizons* 30 (July - August): 51-55.

Miller, Alex, William Gartner, and Robert Wilson. 1989. "Entry Order, Market Share and Competitive Advantage: A Study of Their Relationships in New Corporate Ventures." *Journal of Business Venturing* 4 (May): 197-209.

Netter, Jeffrey M. 1983. "Political Competition and Advertising as a Barrier to Entry." *Southern Economic Journal* 50 (October): 510-20.

Perrakis, Stylianos, and George Warskett. 1986. "Uncertainty, Economies of Scale, and Barriers to Entry." *Oxford Economic Papers* (UK) 38 (November): 58-74.

Porter, Michael. 1979. "How Competitive Forces Shape Strategy." *Harvard Business Review* 57 (March-April): 137-45.

_____. 1980. *Competitive Strategy: Techniques for Analyzing Industries and Competitors.* New York: Free Press.

_____. 1985. *Competitive Advantage.* New York: Free Press.

_____. 1985. "Technology and Competitive Advantage." *Journal of Business Strategy* 5 (3): 60-78 (Winter).

Quelch, John A., and Robert D. Buzzell. 1990. *The Marketing Challenge of 1992.* Reading, Mass.: Addison-Wesley.

Ricks, D. 1983. *Big Business Blunders: Mistakes in Multinational Marketing.* Homewood, Ill.: Dow Jones-Irwin.

Robinson, William T. 1988. "Sources of Market Pioneer Advantages: The Case of Industrial Goods Industries." *Journal of Marketing Research* 25 (February): 87-94.

Robinson, William T., and Cleas Fornell. 1985. "Sources of Market Pioneering Advantages in Consumer Goods Industries." *Journal of Marketing Research* 22 (August): 305-17.

Schmalensee, Richard. 1981. "Economies of Scale and Barriers to Entry." *Journal of Political Economy* 89 (6): 1228-38.

_____. 1982. "Product Differentiation Advantages of Pioneering Brands." *American Economic Review* 72 (3): 350-71.

_____. 1983. "Advertising and Entry Deterrence: An Exploratory Model." *Journal of Political Economics* 90 (August): 636-53.

Schnaars, Stephen P. 1986. "When Entering Growth Markets, Are Pioneers Better than Poachers?" *Business Horizons* (March-April): 27-36.

Shepherd, W. G. 1979. *The Economics of Industrial Organization*. Englewood Cliffs, N.J.: Prentice-Hall.

Sheth, Jagdish N., John Wiley, and S. Ram. 1987. *Bringing Competition to Market*. New York.

Shimaguchi, Mitsuaki, and William Lazer. 1979. "Japanese Distribution Channels: Invisible Barriers to Market Entry." *MSU Business Topics* 27 (Winter): 49-62.

Smiley, Robert H. 1988. "Empirical Evidence on Strategic Entry Deterrence." *International Journal of Industrial Organizations* 6 (June): 167-80.

Smiley, Robert H., and S. Abraham Ravid. 1983. "The Importance of Being First: Learning Price and Strategy." *Quarterly Journal of Economics* (May): 353-62.

Spence, Michael A. 1980. "Notes on Advertising, Economies of Scale, and Entry Barriers." *Quarterly Journal of Economics* 95 (November): 493-507.

Srinivasan, Kannan. 1988. "Pioneering Versus Early Following in New Product Markets." Ph. D. diss., University of California, Los Angeles.

Thietart, R. A., and R. Vivas. 1984. "An Empirical Investigation of Success Strategies for Businesses Along the Product Life Cycle." *Management Science* 30 (December): 1405-23.

Thorelli, Hans B., and Stephen C. Burnett. 1981. "The Nature of Product Life Cycles for Industrial Goods Businesses." *Journal of Marketing* 45 (Fall): 97-108.

Urban, Glen L., Theresa Carter, Steven Gaskin, and Zofia Mucha 1986. "Market Share Rewards to Pioneering Brands: An Empirical Analysis and Strategic Implications." *Management Science* 32 (6): 645-59 (June).

Urban, Glen, and Steven Star. 1991. *Advanced Marketing Strategy: Phenomena, Analysis and Decisions*. Englewood Cliffs, N.J.: Prentice-Hall.

Walters, Kenneth D., and R. Joseph Monsen. 1979. "State-Owned Business Abroad: New Competitive Threat." *Harvard Business Review* (March - April): 160-67.

Wasson, Chester R. 1978. *Dynamic Competitive Strategy and Product Life Cycles*. Austin, Tex.: Austin Press.

Whitney, J. C., and R. A. Smith. 1983. "Effects of Group Cohesiveness on Attitude Polarization and the Acquisition of Knowledge in a Strategic Planning Context." *Journal of Marketing Research* 20: 167-76.

Wightman, David W. L. 1987. "Competitive Advantage Through Information Technology." *Journal of General Management* 12 (Summer): 37-45.

Williamson, O. E. 1963. "Selling Expense as a Barrier to Entry." *Quarterly Journal of Economics* 77 (February): 112-28.

Yao, Dennis A. 1988. "Beyond the Reach of the Invisible Hand: Impediments to Economic Activity, Market Failures, and Profitability." *Strategic Management Journal* 9 (Summer): 59-71.

Yelle, Louis E. 1980. "Industrial Life Cycles and Learning Curves: Interaction of Marketing and Production." *Industrial Marketing Management* 9: 311-18.

Yip, G. S. 1982. *Barriers to Entry: A Corporate Strategy Perspective.* Lexington, Mass.: D. C. Heath.

_____. 1982. "Gateways to Entry." *Harvard Business Review* 60 (September-October): 85-92.

Index

Access to distribution
  channels, 5, 16, 58, 63, 140,
  167
Access to raw materials, 7, 22,
  50, 146
Advertising, 5, 16, 48, 141, 143

Brand identification, 8-9
Buying center, 30

Canada and U.S. trade treaty,
  66-67
Capital intensity, 6, 19
Capital requirements, 6, 19,
  86, 144, 162
Competition, 60, 99
Competitor-activated barriers, 2-3,
  11, 161
Competitors (number of), 6,
  49, 141, 145
Consensus, 125-32, 165-66
Consumer market, barriers
  in, 8, 45, 47, 87, 89, 163
Corruption, 62
Cost advantages, 4, 11, 14, 37,
  62, 86, 162
Creating barriers, 149-53, 167
Cultural barriers, 56, 62
Currency exchange rate, 60

Customer switching costs, 5,
  15, 58, 140, 142, 151, 156, 166

Demand uncertainty, 36
Distinctive competence, 150
Divestiture, 99, 102

Economic barriers, 104
Economic environment, 62
Environmental barriers, 2, 3,
  161
European Economic
  Community (EEC), 65-66
Exit barriers, 104, 110-18

Global competition, 61
Government licensing
  requirements, 6, 20, 139
Government policy, 59, 63, 86,
  145
Government subsidies, 6, 20,
  141

Incumbents' reaction, 3, 7, 9,
  139, 145
Industrial markets, 29, 45, 47,
  130, 163, 166
International markets, 53,
  163-64; direct exporting 54;

direct investment, 54; indirect exporting 54; joint ventures, 54-55; licensing, 54

Language barrier, 57
Learning curve, 12, 140

Managerial barriers, 104-8
Market decline, 97-102
Market entry: into developed countries, 67-68; into developing countries, 68-69; into eastern bloc countries, 69; into underdeveloped countries, 70
Market entry: early entry:, 32-37, 63, 87, 89, 128, 131, 137-38, 140, 157-58, 162-63, 168; incumbents' reaction to; 7, 22; late entry, 36, 40-43, 63, 87 - 88, 129-31, 138-39, 158-59, 162-63
Market exit, 7, 21, 141-42
Market share, 7, 21, 141-42

Nationalism, 61

Overcoming barriers, 70-71, 149, 153-57, 167-68

PIMS, 33-35, 78, 109
Pioneering, 32-36
Political environment, 62-63
Price, 5, 18, 31, 48, 141, 143
Product adaptation, 60, 63
Product differentiation, 4, 10, 15, 36, 86, 140, 144, 166
Product life cycle, 75, 164-65; decline stage, 84; growth stage, 81-82, 87; introduction stage, 78-81; maturity stage, 82-84, 87
Production process, 4, 14, 47, 140
Promotion, 61
Proprietary product technology, 6, 19, 49, 139
Research and development, 5, 17, 37, 48, 143
Selling expense, 6, 18, 49, 139

Strategic barriers, 104, 106-7
Strategic raw materials, 8, 23, 50, 139, 146
Sunk cost, 7, 22, 50, 139

Technology and technological change, 7, 21, 50, 139, 145
Trade secrets, 5, 18, 49

About the Authors

FAHRI KARAKAYA is Associate Professor of Marketing and Director of the MBA program at University of Massachusetts, Dartmouth. He has published in the *Journal of Marketing* and other journals and presented scholarly papers at numerous national conferences. Prior to joining academia, he held several marketing management positions.

MICHAEL J. STAHL is Associate Dean for Research and External Affairs in the College of Business Administration at the University of Tennessee in Knoxville. In the early 1970s, he was the program manager on the design and development of a communications satellite. He has published over thirty journal articles and several management books, including the Quorum book *Competing Globally Through Customer Value* (1991).